PSYCHOLOGY;

OR,

THE SCIENCE OF MIND.

BY

REV. OLIVER S. MUNSELL, D. D.,
PRESIDENT OF ILLINOIS WESLEYAN UNIVERSITY.

NEW YORK:
D. APPLETON AND COMPANY,
549 & 551 BROADWAY.
1871.

PREFACE.

To the practical teacher of Psychology, who has spent years in the recitation-room, no apology is needed for presenting a new text-book in that much-contested field; for every true teacher realizes that, however much has been accomplished in the past, very much more remains to be done before Psychology as a science can take rank, in perfection of form and in completeness of evolution, with some of its more advanced congeners in the hierarchy of science. The writer of this new candidate for popular favor does not flatter himself that, in this work, he has accomplished the long-sought desideratum of a true positive science of mind, adequate to the wants of humanity in the afternoon of the nineteenth century; but he ventures to indulge the hope that, while he has added something to the logical evolution and classification of the *mental faculties, processes, and products*, he has at the same time, as the result of sixteen years of labor in the recitation-room, been enabled to present the recognized facts and principles of Psychology in a form which will commend itself to the unbiassed judgment of the practical teacher, and tend, in some degree, to popularize this important but much-neglected science. It is useless to consume time in pointing out the novelties that appear in this book; the teacher will readily detect them, and to his candid judgment they are unreservedly committed, with the hope that, if they do not always find acceptance, they may at least provoke to a reëxamination of the contested points, and thus lead to more perfect results in the future.

In the years of study during which the author has been preparing for this special work, which has been, and is, to him a labor of love, he has used freely all the works that have been within his reach that treated directly or indirectly of his theme, but it is impracticable for him to attempt even to specify his obligations to particular authors, as he has not, in fact, used any in the immediate work of preparing this manuscript for the press. In conclusion, it only remains for him, unreservedly, to commit his work to the candid criticism of a generous public.

THE AUTHOR.

ILLINOIS WESLEYAN UNIVERSITY,
BLOOMINGTON, ILL., *February*, 1871.

GENERAL ANALYSIS AND INDEX.

INTRODUCTION.

PAGE

SEC. V.—GENERAL ANALYSIS AND CLASSIFICATION.

BOOK I.—THE INTELLECT

PRELIMINARY DISCUSSION.

CHAPTER I.—CONSCIOUSNESS: ITS NATURE AND LIMITATIONS.

SECTION I.—NATURE OF CONSCIOUSNESS.

SEC. II.—LIMITATIONS OF CONSCIOUSNESS.

SEC. III.—VALIDITY OF CONSCIOUSNESS.

CHAPTER II.—CONSCIOUSNESS: ITS PRODUCTS.

Preliminary Analysis.

EVOLUTION OF THE PRODUCTS OF CONSCIOUSNESS.

SECTION I.—PERCEPTS: THEIR NATURE, CONDITIONS, AND LIMITATIONS.

PAGE

Sec. III.—The Category of Relation.

Sec. IV.—Coördination and Correlation of the Categories of Being, Limitation, and Relation.—Evolution of the Concept of God.

Sec. V.—Resultant Conceptions.

THE INTELLECT.—ITS SECOND MOVEMENT.

CONCEPTION.

CONCEPTION: ITS FIRST ELEMENT.

MEMORY.

THE INTELLECT.—SUPPLEMENTARY TOPICS.

DIVISION FIRST—SLEEP.

Preliminary Analysis.

EVOLUTION OF THE FORMS OF SLEEP.

CLASS I.—NATURAL SLEEP

Preliminary Analysis.

PAGE

DIVISION SECOND—INSANITY.

Preliminary Discussion.

BOOK II.—THE SENSIBILITIES.

PRELIMINARY DISCUSSION.

THE SENSIBILITIES: DIVISION FIRST.

THE EMOTIONS.

Preliminary Discussion.

THE SENSIBILITIES: DIVISION SECOND.

THE DESIRES.

Preliminary Analysis.

PAGE

CHAPTER I.—THE SELFISH PROPENSIONS.

SECTION I.—SELF-LOVE.

SEC. II.—CURIOSITY, ACQUISITIVENESS, AND AMBITION.

CHAPTER II.—THE SOCIAL PROPENSIONS.

SECTION I.—SOCIALITY, OR THE DESIRE OF SOCIETY.

SEC. II.—IMITATIVENESS, APPROBATIVENESS, EMULATION, AND VERACITY.

PAGE

SUPPLEMENTARY TOPICS.

HOPE AND FEAR.

THE DESIRES: CLASS THIRD.

PSYCHICAL: THE AFFECTIONS AND MORAL IMPULSES.

Preliminary Discussion.

DIVISION I.—THE AFFECTIONS.

Preliminary Discussion.

SECTION I.—PSYCHOLOGICAL BASIS OF THE AFFECTIONS.

SEC. II.—CLASSIFICATION OF THE AFFECTIONS.

PAGE

CHAPTER I.—THE MALEVOLENT AFFECTIONS.

Preliminary Discussion.

Section I.—Malevolence toward Animals.

Sec. II.—Malevolence toward Men.

CHAPTER II.—THE BENEVOLENT AFFECTIONS.

Preliminary Discussion.

Analysis of the Benevolent Affections.

Section I.—Love of Home and Country.

Sec. II.—Benevolence to Animals.

BOOK III.—THE WILL.

PRELIMINARY ANALYSIS.

PSYCHOLOGY.

INTRODUCTION.

SECTION I.—NATURE AND DESIGN OF THE WORK.

PSYCHOLOGY, or the Science of Mind, from its intrinsic interest and importance, has engaged the attention of thoughtful men from a very early period of human development; and, despite its inherent difficulties, still maintains its prominence in the hierarchy of science. The special characteristics which determined its early and persistent study indicate, *a priori*, its inherent difficulties, and suggest the probability that it will be one of the last, if not actually the last, of the positive sciences to reach perfection.

¶ I. **Nature of Science in General.**—Science is simply systematized knowledge, using the latter term in its true generic sense; it must, therefore, be contradistinguished, alike, from crude collections of mere facts, and from unverified hypotheses. Much that passes under the name of science, has no claim to the title. It may be valuable in its own proper sphere, or it may be a preparative for science; but it is not science.

¶ II. **Methods of Science.**—The methods of modern science are so well ascertained and so familiar, that it were idle to stop to enunciate them here. They have been defined with an accuracy and precision that practically leave nothing to be desired. Sir William Hamilton has, perhaps, stated them in their ultimate form, as applied to the study of psychology, as follows:

1. "*The Law of Parcimony:* That no fact be assumed as a fact of consciousness, but what is ultimate and simple.

2. "*The Law of Integrity:* That the whole facts of consciousness be taken without reserve or hesitation, whether given as constituent or as regulative data.

3. "*The Law of Harmony:* That nothing but the facts of consciousness be taken; or, if inferences of reasoning be admitted, that these, at least, be recognized as legitimate, only as deduced from, and in subordination to, the immediate data of consciousness, and every position rejected as illegitimate which is contradictory of these."

¶ **III. Application of the Methods of Science to the Study of the Phenomena of Mind.**—The application of these laws to the study of psychology, simple and direct, as the problem would seem to be, results, as all experience proves, in the evolution of problems complex and difficult, in direct proportion to their intrinsic importance. It is proposed here—

1. To ascertain the actual phenomena of mind.

2. To determine their real significance; and

3. To coördinate them in accordance with their normal relations of succession and interdependence, guarding carefully against the introduction of any *imaginary* element, on the one hand, and against the omission or suppression of any real element on the other.

Sec. II.—Definition of Mind.

Antecedently there would seem to be but little necessity for any definition of a term so familiar; but there are, in fact, few terms which more imperiously demand accurate determination, since it is not infrequently used in wholly variant senses. It may be defined—

¶ I. **Negatively; i. e., by Isolation.**—It may thus be distinguished:

1. *From matter and its phenomena.*—Here, the decisive test is the *disparity of attributes*. *Mind* is characterized by thoughts, feelings, and volitions; *matter*, by extension, resistance, etc., etc. Until, therefore, these attributes can be iden-

tified or harmonized with each other, it is unphilosophical and absurd to refer them to a common entity or substance.

2. *From force and its phenomena.*—From these it is discriminated by its relations. Force is an *attribute* of mind; but *it is not* mind. We are conscious that mind exerts force, but we find it impossible even to conceive that *simple force* can, by any possibility, be transformed into thoughts, feelings, and volitions.

3. *From spirit*, conceived apart from physical organization.—From this it is discriminated by its relations and conditions. Mind, as we know it, is *embodied* spirit.

¶ II. **Positively, by Determination.**—1. Of the conditions under which alone we actually detect its presence and existence; i. e., as inhering in a vital organism, too familiar to us to need description here.

2. *Of its attributes.*—These have already been declared, incidentally, to be *thought, feeling, and volition*, phenomena which need no definition, since they are vitally present to the consciousness of every one who seeks to know mind.

¶ III. **Supplementary Problem.**—Is physical organization a *necessary* or an *accidental* attribute of mind?

This question, from its intrinsic importance, claims at least a passing notice. The question of the actual existence of mind, or spirit, apart from physical organization, belongs elsewhere, and cannot be discussed here. Limiting, therefore, the discussion to the minor question, we remark:

1. That the actual developments of the mind and the body maintain no necessary or uniform proportion to each *other*. As facts of experience, physical strength and mental imbecility, and mental power and physical disability, are found to be entirely compatible with each other; thus showing that there is no necessary interdependence between them.

2. The phenomena of dreams, somnambulism, and of the dying hour, demonstrate that they are capable of independent action, and indicate, not obscurely, that physical organization is an *accidental*, and *not an essential*, condition of the existence and functions of mind.

SEC. III.—NATURE AND LIMITATIONS OF THE SCIENCE OF MIND.

¶ I. **It is the Science of Organized or Embodied Mind, and not of Pure Spirit.**—Psychology, as we conceive it, is the science of embodied mind, and not of pure spirit. However it may be with man in some other state of existence, here on earth we know and can know mind, or spirit, only as it is manifested in and through physical organization. Any attempt therefore to determine, *a priori*, its nature and attributes would be purely hypothetical, as well as foreign to our purpose. Moreover, for all the uses of psychology, a science of pure spirit, were it possible to man, would be wholly of speculative value.

¶ II. **It is a Science of Phenomena, and not of Noumena.**—That is to say, it has to do with *the attributes*, and not with *the essence* of mind. It must not, therefore, be confounded with pure metaphysics. The two have their necessary and legitimate points of contact; but their spheres are not identical, nor are the terms psychology and metaphysics synonymes.

SEC. IV.—METHODS OF INVESTIGATION.

There have been bitter and protracted controversies in reference to the true method of investigating the phenomena of mind, and three schools have emerged, viz.:

¶ I. **Of Cerebral Physiologists and Phrenologists.**—This energetic class of modern thinkers insists that the only rational and scientific method of studying mind is by and through the study of the physical organism. This school subdivides into the phrenologists, who lay special stress upon the study of the cranial developments; and the physiologists, who insist upon a thorough comprehension, not merely of the physiology of the brain, but also of the whole man.

This is neither the time nor place to enter into any discussion of either phrenological or physiological psychology. Should we grant the substantial truth of either or of both systems, it is not apparent how either of them or both combined could relieve us from the necessity of studying mind and its phenomena from the stand-point of the personal consciousness. The assumption that either the exclusive phrenological or the physiological study of mind is adequate to the wants of science, would be fairly paralleled only by the assertion that a person totally ignorant of the properties of steam could adequately study and comprehend the steam-engine, either by a careful external examination of a disused locomotive on a side-track, or by an equally-careful decomposition and examination of the same engine piece by piece, conjoined to a close external observation of a similar engine as it moves majestically by, on the main track. The steam-engine, to the man who is ignorant of the nature and properties of steam, is an unsolved and an insoluble mystery. No less mysterious must the phenomena of mind ever be to him who ignores the light of consciousness, and seeks, by the most approved methods of phrenology and physiology alone, to penetrate the mysteries of this science. It is freely admitted that both phrenologists and physiologists have made important contributions to the science of psychology, but the question is not, how much they have accomplished, but what could they have accomplished unaided by the *prior* researches of psychologists into the facts of consciousness for the last three thousand years. How much knowledge of perception, for example, can be gained by the study of the mechanism of the eye and the laws of optics, apart from the facts of consciousness? It is true the physiologist can trace the ray of light from the external object to the retina of the eye, may *hypothesize* (to *theorize* is beyond his power) upon the transmission of nervous impressions from the affected retina to the brain; but no stretch of physiological ingenuity can reveal how that nervous impression is transformed into *a thought*. Nor can phrenology aid us in this dilemma, by contributing its much-vaunted fact that men of large perceptive powers have certain parts of the cranium specially developed; for that is only telling us that large mechanical operations require large workshops. After the physiologists and the phrenologists have exhausted all their science, and all their hypotheses as well, we are just as far from comprehending the real phenomena of perception proper as we were before. Phrenology and physiology have a wide scope for evolution, and a fruitful field of effort, but the pretensions so ostentatiously made, that either one or both of them together can supersede the ordinary methods of psychologic investigation, are absurdly false.

¶ II. **Of Transcendental Metaphysicians.**—This school, passing to exactly the opposite extreme, seeks to evolve a complete *a priori* science of psychology from a few observed or assumed facts; shutting its eyes, in happy unconsciousness, to the fact that, ordinarily, the conclusions reached are so foreign to actual human experience, that *it* may utterly fail to furnish reliable data either to confirm or confute these magnificent hypotheses. But this whole process is so alien to the spirit of genuine modern science, that it may safely be discounted without further notice.

¶ III. **Of Modern Psychologists.**—This school bases all its processes upon a scientific examination of the actual facts of consciousness, availing itself, at the same time, of the labors of the physiologist and phrenologist, so far as they cast any real light upon the problem; and it seeks, by a true induction from all the observed facts, to evolve a genuine and comprehensive science of mind. The facts of consciousness are, it is obvious, open to examination by a twofold process, namely:

1. *To a direct analysis of the phenomena of the personal consciousness.*—This is a process, *sui generis*, peculiar to the science of psychology, and of inestimable value. No one who has studied astronomy can have overlooked the difficulties that have beset astronomers, in all ages, growing out of the fact that our earth, from whose surface they attempt to determine the movements and relations of the heavenly bodies, is not in the centre of motion. The psychologist, in the field of the personal consciousness, possesses precisely

the advantages for the study of mind that the astronomer would possess for the study of the solar system, could he transfer his observatory to the surface of the sun; for he can place himself in the very centre of the grand intellectual forces of the human soul, and study them at his pleasure from the centre of their common orbits.

2. *To an indirect analysis; by observing other men, personally or historically.*—This second source of knowledge enables us to verify the conclusions reached through the first, and to detect any thing *casual* or *individual* in the personal consciousness. We are thus enabled to eliminate false elements, which might otherwise enter into and vitiate our inductions. The psychologist possesses no slight advantage in the fact that all *genuine* human history is nothing else than a grand treasury of psychological facts stored up by impartial minds, regardless of psychological theories. Any induction, therefore, professedly based upon facts of consciousness, which contains elements, or data, of which no trace can be found in the evolutions of human history, may, so far forth at least, be safely condemned. So, on the other hand, any analysis of the facts of consciousness which ignores or discards elements of thought whose presence and influence in human history are unmistakable, must, for like cause, be rejected as radically imperfect.

Sec. V.—General Analysis and Classification.

A primary analysis of the facts of consciousness reveals decisively *three*, and *but three*, elements, namely, *thought*, *feeling*, and *volition*.

¶ **I. Evolution of the Phenomena of Thought originating the Concept of the Intellect.**—The first and basal fact of all mental phenomena is obviously *thought*, in its manifold forms and relations. Remove that, and man sinks at once in the scale of being, below the animal, with its delicate instincts and semi-reason. The term itself is indefinable, save to the consciousness of a being capable of thought, and to him it needs no definition. Thought presupposes a power, function, or faculty of thought, and suggests, or in fact necessitates, the conception of a department of mind termed the intellect, whose specific function is the generation and evolution of thought.

¶ II. **Evolution of the Phenomena of Feeling originating the Concept of the Sensibilities.**—Coördinate with the functions of thought, or the intellect, are the phenomena of feeling and the functions of the sensibilities. Feelings, emotions, desires, affections, moral impulses, are things "familiar as household words." Differing as they do, decisively, from thought and its phenomena, they are yet almost inseparably connected with it in human experience, and their relations of mutual interdependence constitute one of the most difficult problems of psychology.

¶ III. **Evolution of the Phenomena of Volition originating the Concept of the Will.**—The phenomena of volition and the functions of *the will* complete and close the circle. Nature's order is, usually, *I think—I feel—I will;* or, I approve—I love—I resolve to possess; or, yet again, I disapprove—I loathe—I resolve to reject. Volition, like feeling and thought, is primitive and indefinable, and is known only in consciousness.

¶ IV. **Relations and Coördination of the Three Departments of Mind.**—Generically, *thought, feeling, and volition,* include all the phenomena of mind. Any system of psychology, therefore, which includes them, is potentially complete, and any which exscinds either is fatally incomplete. Here, curiously, the radical impotence, alike of phrenology and physiology, as *exclusive* methods for the study of mind, emerges; for neither the one nor the other, unaided by a psychological examination of the facts of consciousness, could attain to this radical classification of the faculties of mind. Corresponding to this general conception, mind will be considered under three grand divisions, viz.:

Book I.—The Intellect.

Book II.—The Sensibilities.

Book III.—The Will.

BOOK I.—THE INTELLECT.

PRELIMINARY DISCUSSION.

CHAPTER I.—CONSCIOUSNESS: ITS NATURE AND LIMITATIONS.

Section I.—Its Nature.

Underlying every form of mental action, but specially prominent in the sphere of the intellect, are the phenomena of *consciousness*, or, as it is sometimes called, distinctively, *self-consciousness.* This has been variously defined to be a *special* faculty—an *accompaniment* of all the special faculties, and *the common ground, or basis*, of all the faculties. It is, therefore, indispensable, in the outset, to investigate its nature and relations.

¶ I. **Definition of Consciousness.**—Like all other primitive mental processes, it is necessarily simple and indefinable, save by a process of isolation in thought, by which it may be separated from its accidental adjuncts, and be made to stand out, clearly and discretely, in its own proper individuality.

1. *Negatively: consciousness is not a special faculty.*—It cannot be reduced to the same rank or category as memory, imagination, etc., without absurdity. Men do not say, "Through the faculty of consciousness, I know that I remember or imagine this or that thing." A memory and my consciousness of it are not two distinct acts of two distinct faculties, but a single indivisible act of mind. Nor yet is it, as some have affirmed, a special accompaniment of all the

special faculties when in action, for like reason; this is only a variant form of the preceding theory, and stands or falls with it.

2. *Positively: consciousness is simply mind in action.*—Mental action, and consciousness of mental action, are not diverse but identical processes. They can be separated neither logically nor chronologically, and the attempt to do so perplexes rather than simplifies our analysis of the mental powers. It is idle to spend time in the discussion of a problem like this, which must be decided at last, if at all, by an appeal to the common consciousness of mankind, whose decision the thoughtful student will readily detect in the ordinary forms of human speech. For example, men do not say, "I am conscious that I imagine, or that I recollect, this or that;" but, simply, "I recollect, I imagine." In other words, they intuitively identify the consciousness of the act with the act itself, and regard them as being one and indivisible. Again, if the act and the consciousness of the act be resultants of different powers or faculties of mind, they may exist apart, and we may have consciousness apart from any act of mind whatsoever; and, on the other hand, acts of memory, imagination, etc., without any corresponding act of consciousness—a theory so utterly at variance with all human experience that to state it is to refute it. *Consciousness is simply mind in action, under its natural or normal conditions.*

¶ II. **Conditions of Consciousness.**—Consciousness postulates, as its conditions of normal action:

1. *A healthy organism*, or, in the trite words of the old adage, "*Mens sana in corpore sano;*" not indeed that it, or we, would assert that *perfect* bodily health or organization is essential to valid mental action. The latter may, and often does, coexist with shattered health and a diseased organism; but it is, nevertheless, impaired by the physical lesion. The phenomena of temporary and permanent insanity resulting from injury to or disorganization of the brain and nervous systems, attest but too sadly the intimate connection between consciousness and a healthy physical organism.

2. *Suitable external conditions.*—Intelligence, like simple vitality, demands suitable external conditions for its evolution. Could a human being be conceived as coming into the world and maintaining an existence for an indefinite period without the use of any of its senses, it could never, under these supposed conditions, arrive at *any* degree of intelligent self-consciousness whatsoever, but must simply remain dormant, because all the necessary *external* conditions of intelligence would be wanting.

3. *Attention.*—The question has sometimes been raised, "Can there be consciousness without *any* degree of attention whatsoever?" This problem is confessedly a difficult one, since its final decision must rest upon the testimony of consciousness itself; and it were a truism to say that we cannot follow that, step by step, to its vanishing point, as we must do, to decide this point decisively. So far as the requisite process is practicable, the indications all are that there must be *some* degree of attention as an essential condition of intelligent consciousness. Those holding the contrary hypothesis ordinarily appeal for proof to facts like those in which the skilful artisan successfully performs the most delicate operations of his peculiar craft and yet all the while seems to be intent upon something else. A slight analysis will, however, show that the argument is more plausible than real. No fact is better ascertained than that he *could not* have done so in the outset of his apprenticeship. Then each separate physical act required a separate act of attention, but, with practice, the degree of attention required diminished, until, at last, the act became *seemingly*, but *not* really, *automatic.* The conclusion, therefore, is practically decisive, that attention is an indispensable condition of consciousness.

Of attention itself, it is needless to discourse at length; its nature and conditions are familiar to every thoughtful student. Nor is it more to the purpose to discuss the many familiar fanciful theories concerning it that are sometimes propounded. One perhaps deserves notice, viz.: can a man attend to more than one thing at a time?—To this the answer must be, decidedly, yes! The laws of harmony, in music, here furnish a decisive *experimentum crucis*, for *discord* and *concord* are alike possible only on condition that we are able to attend to two or more absolutely simultaneous sounds at the same time.

Sec. II.—Limitations of Consciousness.

Having thus determined, proximately, the nature and conditions of consciousness, it becomes necessary, in like manner, to ascertain its normal limitations.

¶ I. **Consciousness, in Time, is limited to the Now.**—I am not conscious of a *past* state or modification of mind, however vividly I may recall or reproduce it in memory; nor yet am I conscious of a mental state that is future, i. e., that has not yet come into being, however nearly the mind approximates toward it. Consciousness of an act, and the act itself, are strictly simultaneous, and can be discriminated from each other neither logically nor chronologically. It may, therefore, be postulated decisively, that consciousness, *in time, is limited to the now.*

¶ II. **Consciousness, in Space, is limited to the Here.**—I am conscious of that, and that only, which is present, i. e., face to face with me, and within the proper sphere of the personality. The question how far and in what sense I am conscious of a remote object, for example, of a bird singing in a tree, will be considered hereafter in connection with the phenomena of sensation. In the stricter sense of the term, in which it is here considered, the consciousness can neither act, nor be conceived as acting, where it is not. Without, therefore, attempting to define the precise limits of *the conscious personality*, it is obvious that consciousness must be limited to its sphere.

¶ III. **Consciousness, in Fact, is limited to the Actual.**—I am conscious *of that which is*, and *not* of that *which may be.* Under the category of existence, however, as thus conceived, much that is intangible to sense-perception must be recognized. It includes, obviously, all acts or states of the soul, the most intangible and evanescent as well as the most obtrusive and permanent. Consciousness seizes upon the subtle play of the fancy, and daguerreotypes *that* upon memory as readily as it grasps the content of the most obtrusive sense-perception, or the most ponderous conclusion of the discursive judgment.

¶ IV. **In Essence, Consciousness is limited to the Phenomenal.**—I am conscious of mind in action, in and through its attributes or phenomena; but not of mind in repose, i. e., of mind, *per se*, in its essence. The question is sometimes raised, "Does consciousness grasp simply the act or its content, or does it take cognizance of the mind as acting?" The problem is curiously important, and it is much as if one by-stander should ask another, as a locomotive-engine flits by, "Did you perceive *the locomotive*, or *the motion*, or *the locomotive in motion?*" It is obvious the reply must be, "I perceived all three." Under the conditions of the problem, the perception of either, without the others, is a simple impossibility. So of mind, no man is or can be conscious of mind in a state of repose, i. e., of mind *in essence*, *for consciousness is itself activity*, and the conception is, therefore, self-contradictory; but the hypothesis that we are conscious only of the results or products of mental activity is not less absurd, for it contradicts every intelligible conception or definition of consciousness, which, as an integral element or condition of every mental state or act, must needs accompany and take cognizance of the act, at every stage of its existence or evolution, and must, therefore, take cognizance of the mind as acting, as well as of the resultant or product of its activity. While, therefore, consciousness does not, and cannot, give us knowledge of mind *in its essence*, it does, and must, take cognizance of mind *in action*, and *not* merely *of the products* of mental activity. Our knowledge of mind, therefore, is *real* and *immediate*, and *not* wholly *secondary* and *inferential.*

SEC. III.—VALIDITY OF CONSCIOUSNESS.

¶ I. **Its Testimony cannot be verified.**—No fact, psychologically, is better ascertained than that the testimony of consciousness cannot, in any way whatsoever, be verified by man. It must be accepted unhesitatingly and absolutely, or not at all; there is no middle ground. The moment the possibility of doubt is admitted, consciousness is incapacitated to prosecute the inquiries necessary either decisively to establish, or to destroy its own validity; and there is no faculty of mind independent of consciousness which can conduct the investigation. To doubt the testimony of consciousness is, therefore, *de facto*, to destroy it. Were testimony, *pro* or *con.*, as to the validity of consciousness possible, which it is not, there is no tribunal, save that of consciousness, to which it can be addressed, and to appeal to a *discredited* judge to decide upon his own credibility is to the last degree absurd.

¶ II. **Its Testimony cannot, rationally, be challenged.**—This proposition is the necessary counterpart of the preceding one. He who would challenge the truth of consciousness must do it by and through the agency or testimony of consciousness itself, i. e., practically, he must accept its testimony *as true*, only, when it testifies to its own deceitfulness and falsehood—a procedure so self-contradictory that to state it is to condemn it. Nor does it avail the objector to reply that it is competent to cross-examine a witness and destroy his testimony by exposing his inconsistencies and self-contradictions. This is true only on condition that there are certain recognized laws of thought, or logic, by which the harmony or contradictions of his testimony can be determined; but, when the testimony of consciousness is impeached, that impeachment invalidates *every process* of thought, and *every canon* of logic as well, and renders any rational determination of the problem morally impossible.

¶ III. **Faith in Consciousness is at once necessary and rational.**—No man actually does or can doubt the clear, well-ascertained, decisive testimony of his own consciousness. To do so, were to abjure reason, and to accept insanity as the highest result of human thought—the *Ultima Thule* of human progress. The most absolute of skeptics, and the most credulous of believers, are practically one in their unhesitating (*actual*, not *theoretical*) reliance upon the testimony of consciousness. They may differ widely as the poles in reference to that testimony—the one may postulate it as the all-sufficient witness of the wildest vagaries of his faith, while the other limits it to the strictest assertion of his doubts, or skepticism; but both alike, consciously or unconsciously, postulate its validity and build their faiths and doubts upon it.

CHAPTER II.—CONSCIOUSNESS, ITS PRODUCTS.

Preliminary Analysis.

Evolution of the Products of Consciousness.

¶ I. **Evolution of the Percept.**—The slightest and most casual analysis of the facts or contents of consciousness reveals the presence of a class of mental phenomena denominated, ordinarily, percepts or perceptions; expressed, usually in the familiar words, "I perceive thus and so." The phenomenon in question is so familiar and so radical, as an element of human thought, that its evolution requires no special metaphysical acumen. Perception through sensation is literally the door of the human soul, through which alone it holds communication with the external world, and obtains the necessary material for its multiform processes.

¶ II. **Evolution of the Concept.**—The materials of thought thus obtained in perception are grasped in memory, and reproduced in imagination, under the form of *concepts*, or *notions*, which, in this aspect of them, are simple mental pictures of the external object, where that is a material entity—or simple notions where the object conceived is a metaphysical entity or relation. A fact should be distinctly noted here, which will be discussed hereafter, namely, that under the general term *concept* must be included, not merely *mental* *pictures* more or less perfect of objects of sense, but also *our notions* of metaphysical entities and relations which are not, and cannot be, objects of sense.

¶ III. **Evolution of Judgments, Beliefs, or Faiths.**—Beyond and behind the percept and the concept, consciousness reveals to us the third and highest form of intellectual product, namely: judgments, beliefs, or faiths, founded upon a comparison of percept with percept, or of concept with concept, thus originating propositions, or judgments; and then, by a secondary comparison of judgment with judgment, originating syllogisms, or trains of reasoning—the primary and secondary processes alike resulting *in a judgment, belief, or faith.* In this process the intellect attains to its ultimate product, i. e., it attains to that form of development best calculated, as will be seen in the sequel, to react upon the sensibilities and the will, and so transform or transmute itself into voluntary action or vital power.

SEC. I.—PERCEPTS: THEIR NATURE, CONDITIONS, AND LIMITATIONS.

¶ I. **Nature of Perception.**—Perception, like all other primitive mental processes, is indefinable, save to the consciousness of a sentient being. It is nothing more nor less than the cognition, or knowledge, which mind takes of actual existence in and through its organs of sense and the phenomena of sensation, using those terms generically rather than specifically. Perception, cognition, or knowledge (for here the terms are used interchangeably), cannot therefore legitimately be limited, as sensationalists demand, to the simple products of sense-perception, but must be held to include knowledge of the world of mind made known or perceived in consciousness, which sustains in some respects the same relation to the sphere of mind that the senses do to the world of matter.

Men do not say of an object of sense distinctly perceived and recognized, "I *think* that book lies upon the table," or that "this watch is ticking in my hand." Their uniform

expression, under such circumstances, is, "I *perceive* (or *know*) that the book lies upon the table;" or that "the watch is ticking in my hand." Men do not easily consent to use the terms "*think* or *believe*," in such connections. They realize, instinctively, that if this be not knowledge there is no knowledge possible to man. So, also, men do not say, "I think or believe that *I think*, or *I feel*, or I *will*, thus and so:" but, "I am *conscious* (or *know*) that I think, feel, or will, thus and so." Here, again, they intuitively challenge for themselves *knowledge of*, and not simple *belief in*, the existence of the mental states affirmed. It is obvious that, in both cases, *knowledge*, or *perception*, is limited to the *now* and the *here;* or, in other words, to that which is present in space and time. I do not and cannot *know* that which *was yesterday* or *is yonder*.

¶ II. **The Conditions of Perception.**—A slight analysis of any act of perception reveals obtrusively the external or material element usually denominated a sensation. This element is so familiar that to name it is to bring it at once, fully and fairly, before the consciousness of every thoughtful reader. It is not strange, therefore, that many thinkers, engrossed by its beauty and importance, have lost sight of the fact that it does not and cannot account for the *actual* phenomena of perception. A rigorous analysis of any single percept whatsoever reveals elements which simple sensation, however modified or transformed, does not and cannot give. For example, take the simple affirmation, "I perceive this stone is heavy." In this proposition, among other things, we discriminate the following elements, viz.: first, *I, or self*, the percipient subject; second, *not-self*, the stone, or perceived object; third, *space*, or the common locality of subject and object; fourth, *time*, as common to both; fifth, *the attributes* of the stone, etc. Now, a very slight analysis of the simple sensation of touch, by which I determine or perceive the stone to be heavy, reveals the fact decisively that it does not and cannot, *in and of itself*, give all these elements. It assuredly does not and cannot originate or reveal the concepts of self, space, and time, however it may be affirmed to make known to me the stone and its attributes or qualities. This single example of sensation may fairly be taken as a normal type of the whole class; it follows, therefore, decisively, that simple sensation does not and cannot account for all the elements of human thought.

We are forced, therefore, to seek in mind itself *for a second and coördinate source of knowledge*, or intelligence; and we find it in that power or faculty of the soul which has been appropriately termed *intuition, or the intuitive faculty*, and which subordinates to itself a special manifestation of the personal consciousness whereby it takes cognizance of the phenomena of the internal world; i. e., of the phenomena of mind, just as, by the medium of the senses, it takes cognizance of the phenomena of the external world. This process, however, although it unquestionably enters into intuition as an integrant element, must not be mistaken for the process of intuition properly so called. *That*, in its proper sense, must be restricted to the evolution of the resultant perception, cognition, or knowledge, from the data given in sensation and consciousness, the former giving the *external*, and the latter the *internal* factors of the complex problem. Grasping the elements thus furnished (whose nature will be ascertained in the sequel), intuition, in virtue of its own necessary laws, affirms, "I perceive this stone to be heavy;" and, in this affirmation, it postulates at least the existence of *self—the I; of not-self—the stone; of space; of time, and of causation*, besides other residual corollaries which will be considered hereafter. We thus attain at once, potentially at least, to the integral elements of all thought.

¶ III. **Limitations of Perception, or Knowledge.**—Perception is, in view of the preceding discussions, obviously limited to the *actual, known now and here*, and *not yesterday, nor yonder*. This is the resultant of the fact that the senses, on the one hand, and consciousness, on the other, only take cognizance of that which comes within their respective spheres of action, and that they are, therefore, limited, as before noted, to *the now* in time, and *the here* in space. The validity and extent of the knowledge we actually obtain through perception will be discretely considered hereafter.

SEC. II.—CONCEPTS: THEIR NATURE, CONDITIONS, AND LIMITATIONS.

¶ I. **Their Nature: the Representation of the Ideal.**—Passing from the sphere of perception, we meet with a second and derivative class of mental products based upon our *percepts;* namely, *concepts*, or *notions*. These represent, in general, the matter or substance of our percepts, and are, so far as all material objects or relations are concerned, the mental pictures which we form of those objects and relations. It must be remembered, however, that the concept, or notion, is not limited in its office to the representation of *sensible* objects merely; it no less truly, though more vaguely, represents *supersensible* objects also. As representing the latter, however, the concept cannot be defined to be a mental picture; such an expression, even figuratively applied, is calculated to mislead, and has, unquestionably, been the source of much misconception and many errors. In reference to all supersensible objects, the term *notion*, perhaps, better expresses the real thought involved than the term *concept*, as it has not, like the latter, become identified with the idea of a mental picture. It is too obvious to require discussion, in the light of the distinction here made, that we do form concepts, or notions, of a multitude of supersensible objects, of which, in the very nature of things, it is utterly impossible that we should form any mental picture whatsoever. Decisive examples of this psychological principle may be found in the facts that the man born blind cannot, in the first sense noted, conceive color, nor the man born deaf conceive sound, yet both do unquestionably, in the second sense noted, form concepts, or notions, of color and sound.

Concepts are, therefore, taken in their broader generic sense as including concepts proper and notions proper, and serve to express the ideas which the mind forms of all possible objects of thought, whether *sensible* or *supersensible*, *real* or *ideal.* As compared with the percept, which represents *the actual*, the concept becomes the representative of *the ideal*, *the possible.* The one represents the world *of Nature*, the other, the world *of thought;* the one is *known*, the other *conceived.*

¶ II. **Their Conditions: Memory, Imagination, and the Synthetic Judgment.**—The concept, as we have seen, is based upon the percept, but differs from it essentially in this, that the lattter represents that which is present, *now* and *here*, while the former always represents *the absent*, *the then*, and *the yonder.* In fact, the percept itself, as well as the object of perception, must disappear in order to the formation of the concept. It is obvious, therefore, that the first condition precedent of the formation of the concept is an act of memory, whereby the contents of the percept can be held firmly in the grasp of consciousness until the latter can, in accordance with its own laws, evolve from them the derivative concept. This evolution necessarily involves an act of comparison, and here, perhaps as well as anywhere, the fact may be distinctly announced that, in *a general* but *real* sense, all intellectual acts whatsoever involve an act of comparison either explicitly or implicitly, though, ordinarily, we correctly identify comparison, as a special act, with the functions of judgment. In the evolution of the concept, using the term in its generic sense, there must, therefore, be the synthesis of an act of memory, an act of the imagination, and an act of the synthetic judgment. Technically, however, it has been customary to separate the latter from the others, and to consider it in connection with the analytic judgment; but viewing psychology, as we do, in the light of the *processes* and *products* of mind rather than of its *so-called* faculties, it seems best to group it here as an essential element of conception.

In the formation of concepts of objects of perception *having a material existence*, both imagination and the synthetic judgment enter as essential elements; but in the formation of concepts of *supersensible* objects the imagination, practically, does not enter as a factor, and the process is solely that of a synthetic comparison. It results necessarily from this, as will appear in the sequel, that the spheres of conception and imagination are not, as has been affirmed, identical with each other.

¶ III. **Their Limitation: the Canon of Non-contradiction.**—Concepts, as the representatives, not of *reality* but of *possibility*, are limited only by the logical canon of non-contradiction; that is, they must not evolve self-contradictory attributes. No other rational limitation, it would seem, can be fixed to them, *a priori;* nor is any other necessary, so long as the true relation of the concept to the percept, on the one hand, and to judgment or belief on the other, is kept steadily in view. Grave errors, however, manifest themselves at once, when conception and imagination are strictly identified with each other, and then are made, either separately or conjointly, conditions of *the knowable* or *cognizable:* yet precisely this mistake is apparent in the writings of some distinguished thinkers who should have discriminated sharply what they have, in fact, confounded. It is obvious that such a mistake could only originate in an entire misapprehension of the true relations of the concept to the normal processes of thought. The fact should, therefore, be distinctly remembered, that the concept is the representative of the *ideal* and the *possible*, and *not* of the *actual* or the *true.*

SEC. III.—JUDGMENTS OR BELIEFS: THEIR NATURE, CONDITIONS, AND LIMITATIONS.

¶ I. **Their Nature: the Determination of the True.**—The third grand step in the process of thought brings us to the final or ultimate form of intellectual activity; namely, to a judgment, belief, or faith. The poverty of our metaphysical vocabulary here compels us to use terms illy adapted to the purpose to which they are applied. The term judgment, best meets the conditions of the problem, but it is ambiguous, from the fact that it is used indifferently to express *the mental faculty*, *the process*, and *the product*. It is liable, therefore, in any given case, to a threefold ambiguity; but nothing better offers itself as a substitute, and the terms here used as synonymes, namely, belief and faith, are scarcely, if at all, less ambiguous.

A judgment is nothing more nor less than the decision of the agreement or disagreement of two concepts when brought into relation with each other as the subject and predicate of a proposition; or, otherwise, it may be declared to be the determination of a *truth*, either subjective or objective. Mind seeks, by a comparison of concept with concept, as representatives of the *ideal*, or *possible*, to determine the several and contradictory spheres of the *true* and the *false*. In other words, *truth* is the ultimate end, or aim, of all normal intellectual activity, and, in pursuit of it, mind passes from the comparatively narrow sphere of *the actual*, given in perception, through the boundless realms of *the ideal*, to its goal in the sunny realms *of truth*.

¶ II. **Their Conditions: Inference, immediate and mediate.**—Judgments, or beliefs, as a product of mental action, result from a process of analytical comparison. In their first movement, they involve a simple comparison of concept with concept, in the proposition; in the second, a comparison of proposition with proposition, as in the syllogism. In the one case, we have the copula linking concept to concept; in the other, proposition linked to proposition, in a chain of reasoning. These several processes will be discretely analyzed hereafter; it suffices at present simply to indicate their nature and relations to judgments, or beliefs, as ultimate mental products.

¶ III. **Their Limitations: the Canons of Thought.**—The limitations of the reasoning faculty, in the formation of *normal* judgments, or *rational* beliefs, must be sought in the canons of thought, viz.:

1. The law of identity, which compels us to recognize the

equality of a thing with itself—of a whole and the sum of all its parts. Its mathematical expression is the identical equation, A=A.

2. The law of contradiction, which declares that that which is contradictory (i. e., self-contradictory) is unthinkable. Its mathematical formula is A <> not-A.

3. The law of excluded middle, which compels us, of two contradictory notions, to affirm one and deny the other, refusing any middle term whatsoever. Its mathematical formula is either A=B or A=not-B.

4. The law of sufficient reason, which compels us to believe that nothing exists save for, or in virtue of, a sufficient reason.

Thought cannot transcend its own essential conditions, and hence cannot transcend these intuitive axiomatic canons, which are, in fact, universally recognized in *the actual thought* of myriads, who have never heard so much of them as their names, yet none the less yield spontaneous allegiance to their rightful authority.

A subsidiary question of the *objective* validity of these laws, i. e., of their legitimate application as criteria of objective existence, emerges here, but cannot be intelligently considered; it suffices to note the fact of their *subjective* validity *as laws of thought*, and that is undeniable. In them, therefore, we have the clearly-defined limitations of the judging or reasoning faculty.

Sec. IV.—Coördination of the Products of Consciousness.—Modes of Knowledge.

¶ I. Intuitive, Necessary, or Presentative Knowledge.—Using the term knowledge in its popular, unscientific sense, it presents itself in a threefold form, corresponding, in general, to our percepts, our concepts, and our judgments. The first of these, knowledge through perception, is the only form entitled, in true scientific usage, to the name; and it may be decisively discriminated from the other forms by the fact that it is *immediate*, *necessary*, or *presentative*. In a real sense, it may be said that the soul, *in perception*, is face to face with the actual existences or entities which it *perceives*, *cognizes*, or *knows*. Perception *proper* is never based upon *mediate* or *remote* inference, but, as will appear more clearly in the sequel—

1. *Upon actual intuition; or*,
2. *Upon immediate and necessary inference.*

It is obvious that the sphere of human knowledge, as thus conceived, though real and important, is narrow, and is but a shadow, or penumbra, as compared with divine omniscience. Man knows in part—sees through a glass darkly: God knows absolutely and without limitation.

¶ II. **Conceptual or Ideal Knowledge.**—In the popular sense, we recognize a second form or mode of knowledge, answering to our concepts, giving us knowledge of the *ideal* world. This is knowledge, not of what is, but of what conceivably may be. Man, starting from the actual known in perception, seeks to grasp the possible in all its ideal forms, seeking in thought a higher unity than perception realizes; and, in the lofty conceptions of the ideal hopes, to find the true, in which alone the actual and the ideal find that unity which the soul demands.

¶ III. **Probable or Mediate Knowledge.**—The third form or mode of knowledge corresponds to our judgments, or beliefs, and is *probable* or *mediate* in its character. It is both technically and essentially derivative, known not intuitively or presentatively in itself, but mediately or representatively, in and through other truths known immediately. It is needless to add, however, that the chain may be lengthened indefinitely, and may be traced back through many successive links before a foundation of *intuitive* or *presentative* truth is reached, and that, with the introduction of each new link in the chain, new possibilities of error and mistake arise, demanding the most jealous watchfulness on the part of the inquirer after truth. In our inquiry into presentative knowledge, the fact was noted that man knows in part only, while God knows absolutely; here, the complementary remark is strictly pertinent, that man reasons, i. e., he knows one truth in and through other truths previously known; but God *never* reasons, that is, never knows, one truth in and through another. Man doubts, mistakes, errs; God never doubts, never mistakes, never errs.

CHAPTER III.—CONSCIOUSNESS: ITS PROCESSES.

Preliminary Discussion.

Origin of Thought.

¶ I. **The Actual Processes of the First Evolution of Thought are hidden by the Veil of Childhood.**—In attempting to ascertain the origin of human thought, we are met at once by the supreme difficulty that its first evolution is hopelessly hidden from us by the impenetrable veil of childhood. The soul learns to think, to feel, and to will, before it is capable of observing or registering its thoughts, feelings, and volitions. Nowhere else is the impotency of the exclusive physiological and phrenological modes of studying mental phenomena more apparent than at this point, where we most need aid; but here they are hopelessly silent, or else content themselves, at best, with talking learnedly of the gradual hardening of the substance of the brain, and the enlargement of the cranium, preparing them for their proper functions. It is safe, however, to say that they do not now, and never can, cast one single ray of light upon the problem, *How does mind think?*

¶ II. **The Potential Process discoverable.**—Though we cannot follow, psychologically, the actual processes of the first evolution of thought in the mind of the child, we can, nevertheless, approximate satisfactorily to the potential process, by a rigid analysis of the actual elements of thought, and of their several relations to the *thinking subject* and to the *object of thought.*

SEC. I.—EVOLUTION OF THE MATERIALS OF THOUGHT.—CONTENT OF THE PERCEPT.

¶ I. **Special Conditions of the Problem.**—It is obvious that the normal conditions of the problem could only be fully met on the hypothesis that we could realize the actual experience of Adam as he came in the vigor of a complete manhood by an immediate act of *creation* (*not generation*) from the hand of God. As thus conceived, his mind must have been awakened at once into conscious activity, without any of the gradual developments or obscuring veils of childhood. If, therefore, we can seize upon him, *in thought*, at the instant he became "a living soul," we may approximate, potentially at least, to the method in which his slumbering soul was awakened to conscious activity. In order to do this, it is only necessary to conceive any one of his senses to be acted upon by a normal excitant; as his eye by a ray of light, his ear by the song of a bird, his touch by contact with an external object, and at once all the complex machinery of thought is wakened to vital action, and the man comes to the consciousness of a *perception* involving at once a recognition of his own existence and that of the external world, as represented by the immediate object of perception. In that *typical percept*, as our subsequent analysis will reveal, the soul comes, potentially at least, into possession of all the elements of thought.

¶ II. **Analysis of a Typical Percept.**—If, then, this typical percept be rigidly analyzed, it will be found to contain:

1. *Actually*, the dual percepts of self and not-self. The soul, in other words, comes at once to a consciousness of self, or the ego—the thinking subject, and of not-self, the non-ego—the perceived object; i. e., representatively considered, man and the universe. It is obvious that man, in the perceptive act, cannot come to the consciousness or knowledge of the one factor, *self*, without a corresponding consciousness or knowledge of the other factor, *not-self.* He cannot, in fact, know them apart from each other, for, by the laws of

thought, "the knowledge of *contradictories* is one." I cannot, for example, intelligently use the pronoun "*I*," save on the condition that I recognize a *not-self* from which I thus discriminate myself. This dual perception, therefore, gives us, actually, man and the universe; i. e., *the category of being.*

2. *Potentially*, but necessarily and immediately:

(*a*) The concepts or intuitions of the *space* where (here), the *time* when (now), and the *cause* why, the perceptive act occurred. The very terms of the proposition affirming the perceptive act involve these elements, necessarily and immediately. I cannot possibly affirm any distinct percept whatever, without affirming that I perceive it *now* and *here;* i. e., under the limitations of space and time. So, by a like necessity, I am compelled to recognize the law of causation, linking the external object to the subjective sensation. Space, time, and cause, therefore, as necessary, implicit conditions of *every* percept whatsoever, may conveniently be grouped under the category of limitation. As thus grouped, time appears as the representative of *protensive*, space of *extensive*, and cause of *intensive*, quantity. Time, therefore, may be represented by a mathematical line, space by an indefinite sphere, and cause by force. Again, each of these factors vindicates its right to a place in the category of limitation, by the fact that each is necessarily conceived under the contradictory concepts of the limited and unlimited; i. e., *the finite and infinite.*

(*b*) The concepts or intuitions of the *true*, the *beautiful*, and the *good.* These intuitions are less obtrusive in their character than space, time, and cause, but are not now, and never have been, wanting to the consciousness of man, and must be recognized as primitive intuitions of the soul. For obvious reasons, aside from mere convenience or logical symmetry, they may be grouped under the category of relation. Truth, beauty, and goodness, are obviously relative to some being or beings who recognize their existence and relations.

3. *Inferentially*, but *immediately*, the still more general concepts of the *finite*, the *infinite*, and *their relations*.

These concepts emerge at once in consciousness when the category of being is coördinated with that of limitation. Self, the universe, space, time, cause, alike suggest the dual concepts or attributes of limited and unlimited, i. e., of finite and infinite. On the one hand, thought grasps the concepts of self, and the universe, or not-self, as finite or limited in space, in time, and in causation, and, in that conception of *finite* being, it comes, by virtue of the canon of contradiction, to the conception, at the same instant, of *Infinite* Being, i. e., of God, filling alike space and time, the adequate, because infinite uncaused Cause of all things. We thus attain to the concepts of man, the universe, and God, the essential integers or factors of all thought. Stress is here laid upon the fact that the inferences by which these results are reached are *necessary* and *immediate*, and carry with them, so far as any human process can, *absolute certitude*.

¶ III. **Discrimination of the Subjective and Objective Elements in the Typical Percept.**—Distinctness requires, in addition to the preceding analysis, an investigation of the *relative number* and *value* of the subjective and objective elements in the typical percept, determining yet more definitely the origin of our actual knowledge. The preceding analysis, if it has not wholly failed to accomplish the ends sought, has indicated, not obscurely, the relative nature and importance of these elements, viz.:

1. *Sensation.*—This, as has been previously noted, furnishes at once the occasion and the stimulus of all mental activity. Apart from sensation, it is difficult, perhaps impossible, for us to conceive how mind could be called into action at all; or, if called into action, how it could ever come to the knowledge of the external world. In sensation, however, the soul comes at once to the dual and indivisible consciousness of self and not-self, of man and the universe. It is idle perhaps, to add formally, that this consciousness is *not*

a mere *transformed* sensation, whatever that may mean; and the advocates of this strange doctrine not only fail to tell us that, but, still more strangely, ignore the fact that it is logically incumbent upon them to do so. The hypothesis that thoughts are mere transformed sensations is only an unphilosophical attempt to escape from a legitimate necessity of thought, by substituting *words* for *ideas*, and must perish the moment its advocates attempt to define even to themselves what they mean by a *transformed sensation.* No ordinary use of the adjective *transformed* will meet the obvious necessities of the case; for example, when the hand comes in contact with a resisting body, there is nothing in that mere physical contact inducing vibrations or pulsations of the nervous fluids, which, *however transformed*, can reappear *in consciousness* as a *perception* of self and not-self as coexisting in space and time. In other words, mind is not *a mere dynamometer*, registering the force of impact acting upon the organs of sense; but a true *causal agent*, reacting upon and adding new and independent elements to the materials actually furnished in sensation. We are thus compelled to recognize in perception a second real coördinate element, viz.:

2. *Intuition.*—This, as has been previously noted, subserves a double function, viz.:

(*a*) That of a special consciousness, giving immediate knowledge of the states, affections, and activities of the soul. It thus sustains, to the internal world of mind, relations strictly analogous to those which the organs of sense sustain to the material world. The two thus exactly complement and supplement each other, and render possible that perfect synthesis of the subjective and objective elements indispensable to the typical percept.

(*b*) That of a conscious intelligence, of whose *essence* knowledge must be predicated as an *attribute.* As thus conceived it is distinctly the faculty of knowledge, *immediate* and *direct*, as contradistinguished from judgment, or the faculty of *mediate* knowledge. Its special function is to seize upon the content of consciousness, in the typical percept, and to evolve, actually or potentially, their several values and relations. One remark should perhaps be interposed at this juncture, namely: it is not affirmed, nor is it necessary to affirm, that, in the primal or typical act of perception, the mind distinctly evolves and brings into the sphere of actual consciousness all the elements, *actual*, *potential*, and *inferential*, inhering in *every* true percept. This, in fact, it does not do; that work is gradual, and may require years, or may never be completed in the life of the individual: just as a man may purchase a tract of land, and wait for years before he ascertains all its real elements of value; or he may in fact possess it during a long life, and yet *never* realize *all* its values, as conveyed in fee-simple in the original title-deed.

Another thought is pertinent here. It is sometimes objected that, if the percept be more than a transformed sensation, we have an effect resulting from *no adequate* cause, for there is nothing else from which mind can derive the superadded elements. The objection, it is hardly necessary to say, is a bare sophism, since it ignores, wilfully, the fact *that it is as much of the nature of mind to know, as it is of the fire to burn*, and it is no more mysterious that it should do so. The objection, moreover, ignores also the fact that, in every scientific analysis whatsoever, man must reach a point beyond which his researches cannot penetrate. Thus, for example, the chemist, when he discovers an irreducible or simple element, seeks to determine its actual properties and affinities, but never dreams of asking the question, *why it possesses such and such properties*. Why, then, should the positive psychologist ignore the fact *that to know* is as really an ultimate attribute of mind as combustibility is of carbon, no more strange and no more incomprehensible?

SEC. II. REPRESENTATION OF THE MATERIALS OF THOUGHT. —CONCEPTION.

¶ I. Retention and Reproduction: the Functions of Memory.—The office and functions of memory are familiar and easily comprehended as facts. This faculty is to mind what his treasure-house is to the miner, as well as what his forceps are to the artisan, dealing with and manipulating delicate objects too small to be grasped by his clumsy fingers. It seizes upon and stores away the precious materials of knowledge and thought obtained in perception, reproduces them at the pleasure of the will, and holds them, in whatsoever point of view may seem most advantageous for eliciting and exhausting their several values. Without memory all mental development and all real progress would be impossible, for each percept would utterly pass away in giving place to its successor, and would leave no sign to show that it had ever existed. Mind would be a blank, and existence less significant than even the fitful shadows of a half-forgotten dream.

¶ II. **Representation of the Materials of Thought: the Functions of Imagination.**—It does not satisfy the wants of the soul simply to retain and reproduce at pleasure the percepts which it has experienced. To stop there, were to forego a moiety at least of all the pleasures and values they are capable of offering to it. To realize these, it is indispensable that it should bring forth its rich stores of material from the treasury of memory, examine, and reëxamine them, singly, and in combination with each other; nay, more, that it should seek, by the power of a creative fancy, to evolve from them, in the boundless realms of the *ideal*, all the hitherto unconceived values that inhere in them, or in any wise pertain to them. Herein we have the office and functions of the imagination, which seeks, from the *actual* world known in perception, to evolve an *ideal* world of truth, beauty, and goodness, adequate to the limitless wants of an undying soul, that cannot and ought not to rest satisfied in its earth-home. The evolution of the ideal, in all its rich and varied forms, is therefore the peculiar work of the imagination.

¶ III. **Classification of the Materials of Thought: functions of the Synthetic Judgment.**—The sphere and functions of the imagination have already been shown to be less general than those of perception, since they are limited (as will appear more fully in the sequel) to *sensible* objects, i. e., to such as are capable of being reproduced in a true mental picture. But a moiety at least of the elements of thought given in perception must be classed as *supersensible*, and as not being susceptible of being so reproduced and represented; and hence, if subjected to any representative process whatsoever, must be amenable to one different from that of imagination.

Again, a second and independent mental necessity demands likewise a supplementary process. The multiplicity of individual objects and attributes given in perception is so great as to threaten to overwhelm memory and confuse consciousness, unless this boundless variety can be reduced to order and unity. To this result the processes of the synthetic judgment, viz., *abstraction*, *generalization*, and *classification*, directly tend. It thus evolves in conception a higher unity than the processes of imagination alone could give, and more thoroughly mediates and prepares the materials of thought for their final evolution under the necessary forms of the analytic judgment or reason.

SEC. III.—ELABORATION OF THE MATERIALS OF THOUGHT.

Our percepts and concepts are alike uniformly complex in their character as present to consciousness; and one of the first normal movements of mind is to reverse the processes of the synthetic judgment, and to analyze the complex percept or concept, by evolving the proximate, and (if possible) the ultimate elements contained therein; not, indeed, for the purpose of returning to the multiplicity of perception, but of evolving a principle of higher unity based upon a scientific analysis of the unity of conception. This analytic process presents itself as a twofold movement, or evolution, viz.:

1. *The inductive process*, whereby we discover new or hitherto unknown truths. And—

2. *The deductive process*, whereby we evolve *potentially* known, but *actually* unknown, truths, from premises obtained by perception or induction.

These two processes united give us the complete forms of the true analytic judgment, or, if the terms be preferred, of the *discursive reason*, in whose lofty and self-sustained flights the human intelligence culminates and achieves its ultimate end, or final cause; namely, a vital faith in truth and in God, which lifts us up from the plane of the earthly to that of the heavenly.

Sec. IV.—Summary of Results.

Our intellectual processes, in the light of the preceding discussions, may be grouped under the following distinct classes, viz.:

I.—*Perception, or cognition*, based upon: first, sensation; and second, intuition.

II.—*Conception*, based upon: first, memory; second, imagination; and third, the synthetic judgment.

III.—*Judgment, or belief*, based upon the processes of: first, induction; and second, deduction.

This analysis is, if we do not misconceive it, at once simple, logical, and exhaustive; albeit, the terms are, as will be noted more clearly in the sequel, used, outside of their ordinary loose significations, in a definite and determinate order.

THE INTELLECT: ITS FIRST MOVEMENT.

PERCEPTION.

Preliminary Discussion.

It will readily be observed that the classification adopted in this treatise varies from that proposed by Sir William Hamilton, by basing perception upon a complete synthesis of sensation and intuition; thus identifying it, strictly, with *cognition*, or *knowledge*, in the proper sense. The reasons for this variation have in part been given, and will appear more fully in the sequel; but it seemed proper to refer to them here. The separation of perception from intuition, in the first place, seemed to be illogical, precluding, as it unquestionably does, all natural grouping and classification of intellectual processes and products; and, in the second place, divorcing perception from intuition, it reduced the former to the status of a mere transformation or reproduction of sensation, destroying utterly the real significance of the *subjective* elements involved in it, which, if they exist at all, must be referred to intuition as their only possible source, or origin.

Perception will, therefore, in the present treatise, be considered under the following general heads, viz.:

I.—Sensation;

II.—Intuition; and,

III.—Cognition, or the synthesis of the elements of perception.

PERCEPTION: ITS FIRST ELEMENT.

SENSATION.

CHAPTER I.—ITS NATURE AND CONDITIONS.

Preliminary Remarks.

No subject is more familiar to human thought, and none, *a priori*, would seem to be more comprehensible than sensation and its phenomena, interwoven as they are with all the multiform experiences of our daily life, and familiar to us as household things. Men are, however, slow to learn that simplicity and familiarity of experience are not identical. Whether viewed in its physiological or psychical relations, sensations offer now, as in the days of Aristotle, some of the most difficult as well as most interesting problems known to man. Not, indeed, that progress has not been made, but that each new discovery, while it has thrown new and clearer light upon the problems of the hour, has, at the same time, revealed other and higher problems before unknown. But there is, nevertheless, in the history of the past, the guaranty of a brighter future, of which the labors of the past have been true John Baptists.

Sec. I.—Conditions of Sensation.

¶ I. **Its First Condition: a Sentient Soul.**—In order to attain to any accurate comprehension of the *nature* of sensation, it is necessary to determine precisely the conditions under which alone its phenomena occur. These conditions may be reduced to three, and but three.

Its first condition is obviously the existence of a sentient soul, or true ego, in the proper sense of the terms. The distinction is here broadly taken between the *material* and *spiritual* natures of man; and self, or the ego, in the highest sense of the terms, is predicated of the spiritual nature exclusively. No fact of consciousness is better ascertained than the presence in the soul of a consciousness of a spiritual self superior to the physical organism that enshrines it. Animals share with man in many of the phenomena of sensation, yet fail in the highest and characteristic elements which mark it in man as a phenomenon *sui generis*, because this higher spiritual nature, the basal condition of true sensation, is wanting.

¶ II. **Its Second Condition: a Sentient Organism.**—The second normal condition of sensation is obviously a sentient organism whose function is to mediate between the object of sense and the sentient soul. The question of the possible life of the sentient soul apart from its organs of sense, and of the nature and possibilities of consciousness, under those, to us, abnormal conditions, however interesting, belongs not to this discussion. The fact, however, may be noted, that men in all ages have realized a profound conviction that such a life exists, originating in part, perhaps, in the fact that in somnambulism the soul *sees* with closed eyes, and acts apparently independently of its physical organs of sense.

The sensorium itself is so familiar to us, that it need not

be described here; it suffices to mark its existence as the second condition precedent of sensation.

¶ III. **Its Third Condition.**—The third condition precedent of a normal sensation is obviously an external excitant, or object, acting upon the soul through the medium of the sensorium and the organs of sense. It is needless, at this point, to investigate the particular forms which the external object may from time to time assume; that will be done in the sequel. It is only necessary, here, distinctly to note the fact of the necessary presence of an external exciting cause, or object, in every normal act of sensation whatsoever.

In the synthesis of the *three* conditions precedent, noted above, i. e., of an external object acting upon the sentient soul, through the sensorium, we have a true typical sensation.

Sec. II.—Nature of Sensation.

¶ I. **Sensation is a Primitive Fact of Consciousness.**—Sensation is a primitive fact of consciousness, which cannot be resolved into any principle or process more simple than itself. We may analyze the conditions under which its phenomena manifest themselves, may ascertain some of the steps in the complex process, and may approximate to some of its more patent relations to the higher movements of mind, but, after all, much remains that is, and ever must be, mysterious. The point of contact, between the sentient soul and the physical organism which it inhabits and animates, is undiscovered and apparently undiscoverable. We may, for example, trace a ray of light from the sun to a material object, as a tree, a house, or a mountain, and from this to the pictured image of it on the retina of the eye; we may ascertain (perhaps comprehend) the laws of the emission, transmission, reflection, and refraction of light, but the most rigid analysis fails us in the attempt to pass from that image pictured on the retina to the sensation of color in the mind. All attempts to follow the process, through the functions of the optic nerve and of the brain, have utterly failed. The sensation of color may possibly be a *transformed vibration*, or *pulsation*, of the optic nerve and brain, but, if so, we do not know it, and, if we did, could not comprehend either the mode or the significance of the transformation. To account for *thought*, as Condillac has done, by asserting an idea to be nothing more than a transformed sensation, is to use words without meaning.

¶ **II. Sensation is a Psychical and not a Physiological Process.**—The discrimination here made is, in the highest degree, important; is, in fact, fundamental. The successive steps already sketched, in the process of sensation, clearly indicate the point of contact between *the psychical* and *the physiological* processes. The passage of the ray of light from the luminous body to the retina of the eye is purely mechanical, and in accordance with the well-ascertained laws of the emission, transmission, reflection, and refraction of light. Thus far, all is clear, philosophical, and comprehensible; but, beyond the image on the retina, all is obscure and incomprehensible. Physiologists tell us of vibrations and pulsations of the nerves and brain, and assure us that they are indispensable conditions precedent of sensation, but these facts cast no light whatever upon the nature of sensation, for that is *not* a vibration, or pulsation.

Every requirement of the laws of rational induction demands that we should discriminate accurately between the physiological conditions of sensation and the sensation itself, which, as a fact of consciousness, is purely *psychical*, or *spiritual*. *How the mind* takes cognizance of the affections, states, or conditions of the *physical organism* we know not, and probably shall never know. The *physiological* process will probably be more definitely ascertained hereafter, on the one hand, and the psychical evolution of sense, perception, be better comprehended, on the other; but there is no reason to hope that we shall ever be able to comprehend the connecting link between them. *That* lies beyond the reach of the scalpel of the anatomist, as well as the grasp of the personal consciousness.

CHAPTER II.—THE FORMS OR MODES OF SENSATION.

Preliminary Analysis.

Ordinarily men use the terms sense and sensation only in reference to what may be termed the special senses, as the smell, the taste, the sight, the hearing, and the touch, which are characterized by the common fact that each is based upon a special organ or organs adapted to the wants of its own peculiar functions. A slight analysis, however, will reveal the fact that we possess other forms or modes of sensation, which cannot scientifically be referred to either of the special senses, although, somewhat loosely, they have been included under the sense of touch. Such are the sensations of cold and heat, hunger and satiety, pain and pleasure, languor and weariness, etc. These are all characterized by the common fact or peculiarity that they have not, like the special senses, any peculiar organs upon which their functions depend, but seem to inhere in, or fasten upon, the whole, or else on the various parts of the complex organism, or body. They may, therefore, with propriety, be called the general senses.

Our senses, then, may fitly be considered under the following general divisions and subdivisions, viz.:

I.—*The General Senses.*—These may be subdivided into:

1. *Muscular sensations*, which seat themselves in the muscular system, as weariness, languor, etc.

2. *Organic sensations*, seating themselves in special organs, as hunger in the stomach.

II.—*The Special Senses*, viz.: 1. *Smell.* 2. *Taste.* 3. *Hearing.* 4. *Sight.* 5. *Touch.*

Sec. I.—The General Senses: Muscular Sensations.

¶ I. **Their Nature and Conditions.**—The muscular sensations, as such, inhere in and belong to what is termed the muscular system, and fasten upon no special part or portion of it. Wherever the muscular tissue is present with its accompanying nerves and blood-vessels, these sensations, such as muscular locality, languor, weariness, elasticity, vitality, manifest themselves.

¶ II. **Their Relations and Final Cause.**—The muscular sensations subserve two important purposes in the economy of humanity, namely:

1. They indicate muscular locality. Every person is conscious of the readiness with which, at any time, without the aid of any of his special senses, he determines the relative position of any member of his body, and this power is only lost by the paralysis, temporary or permanent, of the corresponding nerves. Of the importance of such knowledge it were idle to speak, its value is self-evident.

2. They indicate, decisively, the condition or wants of the muscular apparatus. Thus the sense of languor and weariness warns of the necessity of rest or repose; and so of the rest. They are Nature's sentinels to guard the body from harm.

SEC. II.—THE GENERAL SENSES: ORGANIC SENSATIONS.

¶ I. **Their Nature and Conditions.**—The organic sensations differ from the muscular, in the fact that they are, to a certain degree, localized in particular organs, and are, as it were, adjuncts or indices of the special functions of those organs. Among them may be classed palpitation of the heart, neuralgic pains in the head, face, or teeth, hunger and satiety in the stomach, etc., etc. The organic sensations are peculiar also, in the fact that, in general, they depend for their existence upon some abnormal condition of the particular organ in which they inhere. Thus hunger and satiety alike indicate tendencies away from the normal state of the stomach, justifying the remark of a distinguished writer, that "a perfectly healthy man hardly knows that he has a stomach; a dyspeptic scarcely realizes that he has any thing else."

¶ II. **Their Final Cause and Relations.**—The relations of these sensations to the welfare of the organism as a whole is obtrusively evident. Pain is an ever-watchful sentinel, guarding even the most careless against the approach of danger, by warning them of greater evils to come. Hunger is the faithful mentor that reminds us of the wants of our bodies; satiety, the guardian that tells us when those wants are satisfied. It were useless, in a treatise like the present, to attempt an exhaustive catalogue of these sensations; it suffices to indicate their general nature and relations to the organism.

Sec. III.—The Special Senses: the Smell.

¶ I. **Its Physiological Organs and Conditions.**—The physiological organs and conditions of this sensation are familiar —the nose, with its sensitive lining membrane, an expansion of the olfactory nerve, constituting the *subjective organ;* and the presence in the atmosphere of minute particles of matter thrown off from odoriferous bodies, and coming in contact with this olfactory membrane, constituting, *perhaps*, the *objective condition.* In reference to certain classes of odors, as camphor and musk, the presence of odoriferous particles is proved by the gradual waste of the parent body; in others, as cedar or sandal-wood, no such waste is apparent, but may be fairly assumed.

¶ II. **Its Physiological and Psychical Products.**—Of the process of smelling, beyond the synthesis of its subjective and objective conditions, we know nothing; of its physiological products, but little more. Physiologists do indeed, in all such cases of special sensation, either postulate or demonstrate a pulsation, or vibration, of the olfactory nerve in smelling, and of the optic nerve in seeing, etc., etc.; but here their science ends ingloriously, for they cannot, even by hypothesis, account for the fact that the pulsations, or vibrations, of the one nerve produce the phenomena or sensation of smell, while those of the other produce the sensation of sight. Nor can they distinguish any difference in the substance of the several nerves, or in the law or rhythm of their vibrations, and, if they could, the problem would still remain a mystery why the one produced the phenomena of smell, and the other those of vision. These facts prove conclusively, if proof were necessary, that the sensations themselves are *purely and exclusively psychical* products, known only in consciousness.

¶ III. **Its Relations to Externality.**—Our previous analysis postulates distinctly two well-marked mechanical or spatial relations, viz.:

1. An extended and localized sensorium; viz., the nose and its extended lining membrane; and,

2. Material particles, or a vibrating medium in space, coming in contact with the sensorium.

These spatial elements, as conditions precedent of the sensation, prove conclusively that this sensation alone would furnish, though obscurely, all the absolutely indispensable elements of a typical percept, and mediate for us, therefore, the essential elements of thought.

Sec. IV.—The Special Senses: the Taste.

¶ I. **Its Physiological Organs and Conditions.**—The organ of taste is the tongue, with its numerous papillæ and nervous filaments. It is at the same time an organ of touch proper, of a very delicate character, and this fact, if not distinctly marked, is liable to lead to confusion in the investigation of its phenomena. The nerves of touch predominate in and around the point of the tongue; the nerves of taste, near its base, or root. Every sensation of taste is, therefore, if strictly analyzed, twofold, involving at once *savor* and *resistance*.

The physiological conditions of taste are easily determined, and may be reduced to the simple contact of the external excitant, in a liquid or semi-liquid form, with the tongue. An insoluble body is tasteless, since in its solid form it cannot come into true normal contact with the gustatory nerve, while it may, and will, exert its full force upon the tactual nerves. The only sensations, therefore, returned by the contact of such a body with the tongue must be *mus-*

cular, *organic*, or *tactual*. Of such a body, we necessarily say that it is tasteless. It may be hot or cold, rough or smooth, hard or soft, heavy or light; but all these qualities are revealed through other than the true gustatory nerves; these respond only to the chemical, and not at all to the mechanical, qualities of bodies.

¶ II. **Its Physiological and Psychical Products.**—Here, as in the case of the smell, there is much of doubt and obscurity resting upon the whole problem. The physiological products can only be determined analogically, and must be, as in the previous case, resolved into some special form of nerve vibration, or pulsation, which we can in no wise identify or even connect with the true psychical sensation of savor. Much remains to be done, both chemically and physiologically, before the true relations of the excitant body to the gustatory nerves can be determined, and still more before we can comprehend the relations of either to the psychical sensation. The latter must remain to us, meantime, a primitive and indefinable phenomenon known only in consciousness.

¶ III. **Its Relations to Externality.**—The relations of taste to externality, may, practically, be identified with those of touch, in virtue of its secondary function as an organ of touch. How far space or externality is involved in the functions of the true gustatory nerves is a far more difficult problem. There is room to question whether, apart from its functions of touch, taste could give any thing else than purely subjective conditions; and, so far forth, facts seem to confirm the prevalent opinion that taste, as such, cannot originate the idea of externality. In fact, however, taste is never dissevered from touch, and the idea is consequently never wanting.

Sec. V.—The Special Senses: the Hearing.

¶ I. **Its Physiological Organs and Conditions.**—In passing from the taste to the hearing, we come as it were into a new world, presenting an entirely new order of phenomena.

The physiological organ of hearing, the ear, is a complex of nerves, membranes, bones, etc., etc., arranged in a singular congeries of openings, or canals, in the substance of the temporal bones, the obvious design of which is to take up and convey to the brain the vibrations, or pulsations, of the sonant body. The essential conditions of the sensation are the vibrations of the sonant body and the intervention, between it and the external ear, of a vibratory medium, as air, water, etc. The fact is well ascertained that in a perfect vacuum no sound could exist, and that, other things being equal, the denser the medium, the more perfect is the transmission of sound.

¶ II. **Its Physiological and Psychical Products.**—The physiological product, in this process, has already been declared to be vibrations, or pulsations, transmitted from the sonant body to the auditory nerve, through the complex apparatus of the external and internal ears. The psychical product is familiarly known to us, in consciousness, as sound, in its various modifications of loud and soft, articulate and inarticulate, musical and discordant, etc. Here, as in the senses previously noticed, the *unlikeness* of the physiological to the psychical product is obtrusively evident, fully justifying the seemingly paradoxical statement, that, "if there were no ears, there would be no sounds;" and, perhaps, equally justifying the beautiful fancy of the old Greek philosopher, in reference to the music of the spheres. Physiologically, the fact is well ascertained that no two men hear under precisely the same physical conditions. One will distinguish sound on a lower key than the other; while the other will, perhaps, follow sound to a higher key than his comrade can do. Thus, if a sonant body were made to vibrate in their presence, very slowly at first, the vibrations will be apparent to the eye before any sound is heard. Now, let the rate of vibration be gradually increased, and first one, and then the other, will detect sound, with ordinarily an appreciable interval between them. If the acceleration be still continued, a point will at length be reached when first one, and then the other, will cease to hear any sound, the vibrations still continuing. No sound is heard at either extreme, because the human ear is incapable of distinguishing such vibrations outside of a certain maximum and minimum of velocity.

¶ III. **Its Relations to Externality.**—Here, as in the previous cases noted, the external excitant may be decisively discriminated; namely, the sonant body. Here, also, the occasional presence of abnormal conditions must be noted, such as the roaring or singing in the ears that attends upon certain forms of disease, arising ordinarily from a congested state of the blood-vessels of the auditory apparatus, abnormally exciting or stimulating the auditory nerve, which, of necessity, responds in the only mode possible to it, by producing a sensation of sound. In some cases it is probable that the indefinite roaring or singing, actually perceived, results from a preternatural sensitiveness of the auditory nerve, rendering audible sounds produced by pulsations of the atmosphere, which the ear in its normal state is incapable of distinguishing.

In its spatial relations, hearing ranks above either smell or taste, the phenomena of sound offering readily to the intuitive consciousness all the data necessary for the affirmation alike of space and externality.

Sec. VI.—The Special Senses: the Sight.

¶ I. **Its Physiological Organs and Conditions.**—The physiological organs of sight, viz., the eyes, are distinctly marked, and their physiological and mechanical laws or conditions are well ascertained. The scientist readily and satisfactorily traces the ray of light in its passage through space, from the luminous body to the object of vision, and thence to the eye, and satisfactorily accounts for every step in the process, including the picture on the retina. Thus far the process is easy and satisfactory; the nature of the organs and the laws of the reflection, refraction, and transmission of light are definitely ascertained, but, beyond this, all is unsolved and perhaps insoluble mystery. The existence of an image of the external object on the retina of the eye in no wise helps us to comprehend the sensation of sight. That image existed on the retinas of men's eyes for thousands of years before its presence was even suspected, and even now we know of its existence only indirectly and inferentially; and the fact, when known, casts no light whatever upon the psychical problems of the sensation of sight.

¶ II. **Its Physiological and Psychical Products.**—The physiological products of the sense of sight are limited to the image on the retina and to the resulting vibrations, or pulsations, of the optic nerve. The functions of the image on the retina, in its relations to vision, we cannot even guess, much less determine scientifically; we know only that it is an indispensable condition precedent to it.

The psychical product, i. e., the sensation proper, is that of light and shade, or color with its necessary conditions. Fundamental among these must be reckoned surface, i. e., extension, inasmuch as an *unextended* color is a simple contradiction or nonentity. Here, again, the non-similarity between the external cause and the subjective phenomena of vision is, like the congeneric relations of hearing, obtrusively evident; so that it may safely be said that, were there no eyes in the universe, there would be no color or light in the proper sense of those terms.

¶ III. **Its Relations to Externality.**—Like every other special sense, the eye demands its own proper external excitant in order to its normal action; and this excitant is the ray of light falling upon the cornea and refracted to the retina, producing there an image corresponding to the luminous body from which it was emitted, or the non-luminous one by which it was reflected. An abnormal case must be noted, where the phenomena of imperfect vision are produced by pressure upon the eyeball of the closed eye, by a blow upon the head, or by congestion of the brain. The relations of these several cases to perception proper will be discussed hereafter; it suffices here to note the fact that each case presupposes a real external excitant, however delusive the sensation.

The relations of vision to space have already been decisively marked. Color, if perceived at all, must necessarily be perceived as extended; an *unextended* point is invisible. There is, however, much reason to doubt whether the third dimension of space is given by the eye, as our estimates of distance by the eye are obviously *acquired* perceptions; and the phenomena of perspective prove that distance, i. e., the third dimension of space, is a *judgment*, and not a *percept*.

Sec. VII.—The Special Senses: the Touch.

¶ I. **Its Physiological Organs and Conditions.**—In the sense of touch, we meet with a curious variation from the analogy of the other special senses, approximating it to the character of a general sense, and going far toward justifying the theory that touch is a general sense, constituting it the underlying condition or principle of all the special senses. This peculiarity is found in the fact that it is not dependent, like the taste, upon a single organ; or, like the sight or hearing, upon a pair of complementary organs; but is found to inhere with more or less perfection in all parts of the sentient organism. It is true it is developed or manifested in a higher degree in some parts of the body than in others, as in the lips, and in the tips of the fingers, insomuch that the hands are popularly regarded as the peculiar organs of touch.

The conditions of touch are few, and amount to little else than simple contact between the external object and the subjective organ. The resultant sensation of course varies with the nature, extent, and conditions of that contact, resulting in corresponding modifications in the sensation.

¶ II. **Its Physiological and Psychical Products.**—Any analysis of the physiological products of the sense of touch reveals the intimate relation between it and the muscular sense; hence, unquestionably originated the fact that the two were uniformly confounded with each other by the earlier psychologists. Touch ordinarily gives, in addition to its own proper products, muscular products likewise, such as heat or cold, pleasure or pain, pressure or weight, etc., etc. Touch proper involves, physiologically: 1. Resistance; 2. Surface, and its more obvious conditions; and 3. Form; i. e., body in its true sense. Its psychical products must, from the poverty of our metaphysical language, be characterized by the same terms. Perhaps, however, the error lies in recognizing resistance, surface, and form, as we actually *think* them, as physiological products, since that term, strictly used, only expresses the actual physiological resultants of the contact of the external body with the organs of touch, which are, as usual, vibrations, or pulsations, of the tactual nerves.

¶ III. **Its Relations to Externality.**—The fact has already been noted that touch is regarded by many acute thinkers as the only sense by and through which, *primarily*, we have real access to the external world, and that our knowledge of it through the other senses is secondary and derivative. While this cannot be conceded, it must be admitted that, in some respects, its testimony is more complete and decisive than that of any of its congeners. For example, its testimony, alike to the *form* and the *surface*, is alone decisive; and there is room to question whether any other sense, alone, could give directly the third dimension of space. Fortunately, therefore, for man, it is the one sense that is *never* wholly wanting.

Sec. VIII.—Comparative Functions of the Senses.

¶ I. **Taste and Smell relate to the Chemical Properties of Matter.**—In analyzing the comparative functions and values of the special senses, the first and most obvious fact that presents itself is their correlation to each other, and their special adaptation to the wants of man. Brought, as he necessarily is, and must be, in contact with matter, in all its varied forms and relations, it was indispensable that, by the aid of his special senses, guided by intelligence, he should be able to comprehend its nature and exhaust its values. This the special senses enable him to do, admirably supplementing and aiding each other. Taste and smell occupy themselves, almost exclusively, with the *chemical* properties of matter, i. e., with those relations and properties which fit it for the nourishment and support of the physical organism. They are, so to speak, divinely-appointed sentinels, placed as guards over the avenues of life, to prevent the intrusion of any hurtful or dangerous substances into the stomach and lungs. The subsidiary fact that they are sources of a high degree of physical pleasure, may properly be noted as not wholly irrelevant.

¶ II. **Touch relates specially to the Mechanical and Spatial Relations of Matter.**—Touch is preëminently the organ through which the external world, as such, is known to us. It is the one sense which seems never wholly to fail man, even when its congeners are wanting. It enables him to explore, at once, the surface and forms of bodies, and to determine their mechanical relations, which no other single sense, perhaps, could do. It is true that sight gives us a secondary and acquired perception of the properties of the surfaces of bodies, through the effects of lights and shadows, but any one, familiar with the power of perspective in the hands of a good artist, knows how illusive its judgments frequently are. But, with all its advantages, touch is limited to bodies near at hand, or, in fact, in contact with the physical organism, and left to it alone. Man's knowledge must ever be circumscribed to a narrow sphere.

¶ III. **Sight and Hearing are adapted to the Spatial Relations of Matter.**—Sight and hearing supplement touch by revealing *the distant;* the one adapting itself to the phenomena of light, the other to a corresponding series of phenomena, independent of the light and the day. How immensely they extend the sphere of human knowledge will readily be conceived if we compare the condition of one born deaf and blind with our own.

Sight is designed to give us, *primarily*, color and its relations, and, *secondarily*, extension, in its trinal form, though its third dimension is perhaps an acquired perception of sight. This is indicated by the phenomena of the stereoscope, in which a flat surface is made to represent perfectly all the phenomena of an actual landscape. Our estimate of distance by the eye is clearly an acquired perception, and is the result, in the main, of our unconscious education in childhood. It is, in fact, a *judgment* based upon lights and shadows, distinctness and indistinctness, apparent size, etc., and varies widely in different individuals. That men perceive objects, i. e., color, by the eye, as extended, has been already shown by the fact that an *unextended* point is invisible; and is also further proved by the fact that, when two or more colors are present to the eye at once, they necessarily occupy diverse positions; hence, occupy space.

Hearing supplements the touch, not only as vision does, in the light or day, but in the night and the darkness also, taking cognizance of distant objects, by their peculiar action upon the organism, through the vibrations of a sonant medium. Its relations to space are far more obscure than those of sight or touch, and its indications of distance and direction are much less reliable. The beating of one's own heart, to the preternaturally-excited auditory nerve, may become the roaring of a distant railroad-train, and the hum of a beetle may be mistaken for the mutterings of a distant storm. Our perceptions of distance and direction, through the medium of sound, fall decisively into the class of acquired percepts, and are the results of education.

The question, sometimes raised, whether a sixth special sense is possible, may be discounted as not only wholly fanciful but as wholly insoluble by any data open to us. That such a sense is inconceivable from our present stand-point is undeniable, but that it is therefore impossible is a *non sequitur*. The limits of human conception are not identical with the limits of abstract possibility.

CHAPTER III.—OBJECTS OF SENSE.

Preliminary Discussion.

General Analysis and Classification.

At this juncture, an inquiry, not less difficult than important, presents itself to us, namely, What is the real object known in sensation? An analysis of consciousness reveals three possible objects, which may be assumed, severally, to be the object known as extended, viz.:

1. The external object, or excitant, as the book lying upon the table and seen by the eye.
2. The material element in actual contact with the organ of sense, viz., the ray of light reflected from the book to the eye.
3. The sensorium itself as excited by the contact of the external object.

The first and second of these are truly *objective*, not only as referred to the soul, or true ego, but also to the soul as inhabiting the sensorium. With reference to the sense of touch, it is obvious that the two coincide; while, with reference to sight and hearing, they are diverse.

The third, i. e., the sensorium as excited, may be termed, for the sake of distinction, a *subjective object*, or excitant; though, as will be seen in the sequel, with respect to the soul, or true ego, it is not less really *objective* than the book or the table.

Sec. I.—Objective Excitants.

Our previous analysis of the objects known or cognized in sensation, indicated, with reference to some of the special senses, both a *proximate* and a *remote* object of sense, as the book lying upon the table, and the ray of light in contact with the retina of the eye. In the sense of touch the two coincide, and can be discriminated neither logically nor chronologically. It is obvious that the proximate object is the real excitant of the sensation, although perception almost invariably ignores the proximate, and fastens upon the remote object. We are accustomed to say, "I perceive the book, the table, the chair," and *not*, "I perceive the rays of light reflected by these objects;" and it is not until the scientific consciousness emerges, that men begin to comprehend that their perception of the *remote* object is, in fact, mediated by the light transmitted from that object to the eye. There is another distinction that should be noted here, namely, between *normal* and *abnormal* excitants.

¶ I. **Normal Excitants, or Objects.**—These are such as act upon the organs of sense in accordance with their own proper laws, as light upon the eye, the vibrations of the air upon the ear, etc. These require no special consideration here, as their general nature has been sufficiently indicated in our analysis of the special senses.

¶ II. **Abnormal Excitants, or Objects.**—These are such as act upon the organs of sense outside of, or apart from, their ordinary laws; as when the phenomena of vision are produced by a blow upon the head, or by pressure upon the eyeball.

Sec. II.—Subjective Excitants.

Under the head of subjective excitants may be included all those cases in which the sensorium itself, as an extended physical entity, becomes the exciting or active cause of sensation, as when the hand meets its fellow-hand, producing the phenomena of *double* sensation. Each hand is thus, alternately, *subject* and *object*, *active* and *passive*. The sensorium itself thus becomes a legitimate object of perception through sensation; and is, unquestionably, the first material object by and through which we attain to the perception of body, or matter, and its attributes. *Double* sensations, therefore, as compared with *single*, furnish the decisive test by which we distinguish between *the material self, or organism*, and *a material not-self, or the universe;* and this distinction is so marked and peculiar that it cannot fail to impress itself upon the nascent intelligence of the infant, at a very early period of its unconscious education. Here, as in the parallel case of objective excitants, the distinction between normal and abnormal excitants must be distinctly marked.

¶ I. **Normal Excitants.**—These are such as manifest themselves in consciousness under its ordinary laws, as when one hand meets the other in touch, or our limbs or members become objects of vision, etc. In some of these instances, as in the case of touch, the result is a double sensation; in other cases, as in vision, the sensation is single.

¶ II. **Abnormal Excitants.**—Under this head may be classed all such forms of sensation as originate in the physical organism, but outside of, or apart from, the ordinary laws of sensation, as when the phenomena of vision are produced by congestion of the optic nerve, or of sound by congestion of the auditory nerve.

Sec. III.—The Real Object known in Sensation.

The question now recurs, What is the real external object *known* in sensation, in the perception of which we attain to the knowledge of a *real material* world?

¶ I. **The Remote External Object, or Excitant, considered.**—The fundamental conditions of perception limit it to the *now* and the *here*, and to *immediate*, and not to *mediate*, knowledge. It is obvious, therefore, that any remote external object of perception, as a book lying upon the table, or a bird singing in the tree, *is not known immediately or presentatively in itself, but mediately or representatively*; that is, the book is mediated to the eye by the ray of light reflected from it, and the bird by the vibrations of the atmosphere. Our knowledge of the remote object of perception is, therefore, mediated by the law or principle of causation, i. e., we infer its existence, necessarily and immediately, from the phenomena of sensation of which we are conscious, while of the book and the bird themselves we have no direct consciousness. It is idle to say, as some have done, that the soul is face to face with *the remote* excitant of vision, however thoroughly it may be assured of its existence. This is shown, conclusively, by the phenomena of abnormal excitants, both objective and subjective, as well as by the well-known phenomena of double vision, in which two objects are distinctly seen, while but a single object is present to the eye. In all these cases, the abnormal excitant is real and objective to the organ of sense; for a drop of congested blood in the optic nerve is as really foreign or external to the sensorium proper as the book lying upon the table. In such abnormal sensations, the error is not in the assertion of *a real objective* cause, or excitant, but in the determination of the actual individuality of that cause, which the mind, under its own necessary laws, projects outward into space. It is *right* in asserting *an objective material cause*, it is *only wrong when it seeks to localize that cause.* The remote external object *is not*, therefore, and *cannot be*, the real *objective* element *immediately* known in sensation.

¶ II. **The Proximate External Object, or Excitant considered.**—The question, when referred to this element of the problem, becomes at once more complicated and more difficult; for it more nearly accords in its relations with the obvious conditions of *immediate* or *presentative* knowledge, which require the object known to be face to face with the ego, or percipient subject. Yet it is obvious that even here there is a link in the chain hopelessly wanting. Sir William Hamilton has indeed doubtfully attempted to supply this missing link by the hypothesis, that the soul is everywhere present, completely and perfectly, in each special organ of sense, in the tips of the fingers, the retina of the eye, etc., etc., and that it perceives at precisely that point of the sensorium which is in contact with the external object. But this hypothesis is not only unsupported by any single known fact of consciousness or physiology, but it is in direct contradiction of well-ascertained principles and facts of cerebral physiology, which determine the fact that the brain is the seat or organ of all true mental action; and such, unquestionably, are the phenomena of sensation proper. Our cognizance, therefore, of the *proximate* as well as of the *remote* excitant or object of sensation is, and must be, mediated by the law or canon of causation; and it is not, and cannot be, the *real* object known *immediately* and *presentatively* in sensation.

¶ III. **The Sensorium itself considered as an Excitant.**— If we pass now to the consideration of the sensorium itself considered as an excitant, and as a physical entity apart from the true ego, or conscious self, we shall find that the difficulties which attend the preceding hypotheses, measurably at least, disappear, while it fills all the necessary conditions of the cognition of a true material body filling space, or possessing extension.

It is obvious, in the outset, that the sensorium, considered as an object of sense and an excitant of sensation, is properly discriminated from self, or the conscious ego, and becomes as really a part of the true not-self, non-ego, or material universe, for the time being, as a book or stone; and is, moreover, as good a type of body, or matter, as such. At the same time, it is equally undeniable that it comes within the sphere of consciousness, in a sense and to a degree that no other material body whatever can do. While, therefore, we may well hesitate to affirm that the soul, or conscious self, is face to face with the book lying on the table, or with the apple grasped in the hand, there is no such difficulty in conceiving it to be face to face with the sensorium in which it dwells and which it vitalizes, and through which it is constantly exerting its activity on the material world. In fact, the real difficulty, at first thought, would seem to be, to imagine ourselves *not* to have immediate consciousness of this term or factor in the complex called sensation and perception.

If, now, the question be raised, How does the soul cognize matter or body, as an extended entity, through its consciousness of the sensorium as at once *excited* and *excitant?* the answer would seem to be that, in the phenomena of double sensation, as when one hand meets the other, the soul can but discriminate between the two sensations. In thus discriminating, it necessarily localizes them, and at the same time, by appropriating both to itself, i. e., to the sensorium, it comes, vaguely at least, to the consciousness of that sensorium as a body possessing extension. Any solution of the problem must needs be hypothetical, since the actual process is hopelessly hidden from us by the veil of infancy—that no-man's land of thought, which defies all our attempts at actual exploration. It follows, therefore, that the sensorium must be conceived as lying within the sphere of consciousness as a material, extended, physical entity.

Again, consciousness of a sensation presupposes, necessarily, consciousness of self, or the ego, as affected, and no form of words can be devised that will express the actual facts of consciousness, which does not, both implicitly and explicitly, involve the assertion of a consciousness of self as affected. Every admissible form of expression, in such cases, asserts or affirms three things at least, viz.: 1. Self or the ego; 2. The existence of the sensation; and 3. The relation existing between self and the sensation. The use of the personal pronoun "*I*" in all languages, in such cases, is decisive on this point. To assert, as some have done, that we are conscious of the sensation, but not of ourselves as experiencing the sensation, is to use words without meaning; is, in fact, to assert or affirm an *impersonal* sensation, whatever that may be. The sophism sometimes interposed, that mind, *at rest* or *asleep*, is not conscious of itself, is utterly nugatory, for the mind is, confessedly, not at rest nor asleep in sensation. The question is not, whether an *inactive* consciousness takes cognizance of itself, but whether an *active* consciousness takes cognizance of *its actions only*, or *of itself as acting.*

The problem, transferred to the external world, would be, Do we perceive motion pure and simple, or do we perceive this or that body moving? To the latter question there can be but one rational answer: The perception of motion, apart from the perception of some body moving, is impossible. So the consciousness of a sensation, apart from the consciousness of self as experiencing the sensation, is also impossible. The terms are strict correlatives, and cannot be known separately or apart. The conclusion, therefore, is irresistible, that we do have immediate or presentative knowledge, not only of the true self, or ego, in sensation, but also of that self as inhabiting and vitalizing the sensorium, considered as a material entity and an integral part of the material universe.

¶ IV. **Mind active in Sensation.**—The fact should perhaps be noted discretely here, that the mind is essentially active, not only in perception proper, but in sensation proper also. Here, however, the distinction must be broadly taken between the physiological and psychical processes, and the fact, moreover, be distinctly remembered, that sensation is strictly a physical phenomenon. In perception proper, the fact is still more marked and obtrusive in its character; for in it the mind reacts upon the materials furnished in sensation, and is not only *essentially, but wholly*, active. In passing, the fact should be noted, that the opinion sometimes entertained of the passivity of the soul in sensation, doubtless originates in the failure to distinguish between its physiological and psychical elements.

Sec. IV.—Are Sensations ever false or unreal?

A question arises, at this point, that merits at least a passing notice, viz.: Are our sensations ever false or unreal? In the light of preceding discussions, this question may be answered unhesitatingly in the negative. In the case of phantasms, or illusions of the sight, the exciting cause may be concussion or congestion of the optic nerve, instead of a normal external object; but none the less is there *a real, material cause* of the phenomenon. In other words, the sensation on the one hand is real, and, on the other, there is a real, external exciting cause of that real sensation. The only error involved is in the assignment of its true cause. The abnormal relation between the cause and the sensation depends upon a well-known physiological law, that any special nerve, when excited either normally or abnormally, can only respond in the one way peculiar to itself. Hence, the optic nerve, when excited by compression or concussion, responds with the phenomena of vision; and so of the rest. The conclusion, therefore, is decisive, that sensations, as such, are never false or unreal, although our perceptions, based upon them, may be.

CHAPTER IV.—EDUCATION OF THE SENSES.

Sec. I.—Development of the Senses in Infancy.

The gradual development of the senses in infancy has been casually alluded to more than once, and yet it demands at least a passing notice here. The whole process is so veiled from exact observation by the mists that hang around that no-man's land of life and thought, that any attempt to investigate it is almost purely hypothetical. The data of the problem amount to little more than these: Given the potential organs of an utterly helpless sensorium, and the potential faculties of an equally helpless mind; required, the order, law, or principle, of their evolution. It is obvious that here there is room for an endless variety of hypotheses, from the most abject materialism to the most extreme transcendentalism, while any true *experimentum crucis* whatsoever seems to be unattainable. It is therefore idle, in a treatise like this, designed rather for a hand-book for students than as a guide to experts, to enter upon the discussion at all.

Sec. II.—Education of the Special Senses.

The subsidiary or derivative question of the proper education of the special senses is one of the most interesting and fruitful in the whole range of the science of mind, since it connects itself with all the practical interests of our daily lives. It must suffice here, however, to note the fact of the seemingly-limitless extent to which the senses may be educated. It were as easy as it were idle to fill page after page with illustrations, drawn from actual life, of remarkable perfection and power, on the part of individuals in the use of the special senses. It suffices to refer to the delicacy of touch and hearing in the blind; of sight in the artist, the artisan, and sailor; of taste in the gourmand, etc. The thoughtful student will find abundant illustrations in the sphere of his own personal reading and observation, rendering it needless to quote any here.

Sec. III.—Limitation of the Sphere of Sensation.

In the light of preceding discussions, it is hardly necessary to add here discretely, that the revelations of the senses are limited strictly to the properties or attributes of matter. None of them reach to or grasp substance, i. e., matter *per se.* Whatever knowledge man has, or can have, of that, must come from intuition, or the reflective reason, or both.

PERCEPTION: ITS SECOND ELEMENT.

INTUITION.

CHAPTER I.—NATURE, VALIDITY, AND CLASSIFICATION OF THE INTUITIONS.

Sec. I.—Nature of Intuition.

¶ I. Discrimination of the Intuition from the Sensation in the Percept.—Our previous analyses, if they have not wholly failed of their design, have marked with some degree of precision the essential nature and limitations of sensation, and have indicated at least the line of demarcation between it and intuition in the synthesis of the percept. Sensation, as we have seen, gives certain attributes of matter, as resistance by the touch, color by the eye, etc., etc.; but space, time, and cause, and other essential forms or categories under which we conceive matter, are neither sensations nor mere products or resultants of any single sense, nor yet are they complex resultants of all the senses combined. It will not do to say, as some have done, that we come *first* to the conception (or cognition rather) of this or that particular body; and then, by abstracting the body, come to the conception of space, as the residuum left after such abstraction; for we can neither know nor conceive body apart from or prior to a conception of *space* as a condition precedent of body. Nor will it do to say, in virtue of the succession of sensations, percepts, or events in our consciousness, that we are able, by abstraction, to remove the concrete entities constituting the succession, and thus arrive at the conception of simple *duration* or *time* in its ultimate form. We can cognize succession only on condition that we simultaneously cognize duration or time, the essential condition precedent to the existence of succession. So, by parity of reasoning, it will not do to say that, in virtue of the affection of the retina of the eye, I see a book lying upon the table, apart from the law of causation, which compels me to look beyond myself for an efficient cause of the subjective phenomena of which I am conscious. Space, time, and cause, are the products of no single sensation as a sensation merely, and cannot be evolved directly from any complex of sensations whatsoever; they must, therefore, be referred to the intuitive power of the consciousness, which evolves them *a priori* on the occasion of a sensation consciously experienced.

¶ II. **Definition of Intuition.**—To know, must rationally be assumed to be of the nature of mind, as an entity distinct from matter; and it is no more wonderful or incomprehensible that the mind, or soul, should think, feel, and will, than it is that matter should possess its own peculiar corresponding attributes. Intuition may be defined, with sufficient accuracy for our purposes, "*to be the mind's power of originating necessary concepts and primitive truths, on the occurrence of proper occasions for calling forth its energies of thought.*" It is true that the sensational school of psychologists have sought to resolve every form of thought and every element of perception into mere transformed sensations; and yet it is far more difficult for us *actually* to conceive that the vibrations of a ray of light are transformed into what we know, in consciousness, as a thought, than it is to conceive that to know is of the essence of mind, just as to fill space is of the essence of matter.

Another thought is pertinent here, namely: men sometimes deceive themselves and others by the use of words without meaning, or words to which they themselves attach no definite or intelligible meaning; and the thoughtful student will, with difficulty, avoid the suspicion that this attempted identification of perception and thought with mere transformed sensations is a striking illustration of this unworthy process. This much is certain, it is absolutely incumbent upon sensational psychologists to define precisely: 1. What they mean by a *transformed* sensation; 2. By what process the transformation is effected, whether chemical, mechanical, or spiritual; 3. Whether any new element whatsoever is added in the process, and, if so, what; and 4. Whether the transformed sensation or thought is simply an *imponderable* material element, or whether it has changed its whole nature. These questions have never yet been fairly met and answered, and, until they are, it is needless to add, the doctrines of sensualism are entitled to no respect.

¶ III. **Potential and Actual Knowledge.**—Psychologists stumble needlessly, sometimes, over difficulties which originate solely in their own neglect to distinguish between *potential* and *actual* knowledge. Locke demonstrated the falsity of the dogma of "*innate ideas*," as he conceived it; but his argument is worthless the moment any accurate discrimination is made between actual and potential knowledge, and our intuitive concepts and primitive judgments are properly classed under the head of potential knowledge, which the soul makes actual, by its own inherent energies, on the occasion of an appropriate sensation. It is easy to show, as Locke has done, that "man does not come into the world with a stock of *elaborately-worded and classified concepts and primitive judgments;*" but the fact remains that our actual processes of thought are utterly incomprehensible, if we do not recognize the hypothesis, "*that to know is of the essence of mind;*" and that the soul, therefore, possesses the power to originate these *a priori* concepts and axiomatic truths.

SEC. II.—VALIDITY OF INTUITION.

The question here naturally arises, Are the intuitive processes of mind valid, and are the results reached trustworthy? Or, in other words, What are the guarantees of intuitive truth? These questions necessitate a consideration of:

¶ I. **The Modes of Truth.**—Truth presents itself under two forms in proportion, first, as we consider it with reference to self, or the ego; and, second, with respect to not-self, or the universe. It becomes necessary, therefore, to consider the nature and relations of the two forms.

1. *Subjective truth.*—A proposition is subjectively *true* which is based upon the actual percepts of a human soul evolved in accordance with its necessary laws of thought. For example, an intelligent gentleman once said to the writer: "I saw a strange thing to-day as I was riding on the prairie. Off to my right, at no great distance, I saw distinctly two gentleman riding toward me on a road that joined the one I was following, some distance ahead. I looked at them carefully, to see if I could recognize either. My attention was then called in another direction for an instant, and, when I looked again, I saw but *one* man. When I met him, he assured me that he had had no companion, and there was no way in which his fellow, if he had had one, could have disappeared. The second man was seen as distinctly as the first, and yet was simply an optical illusion." The primary statement, "I saw two men," was *subjectively* true, but, as afterward appeared, was *objectively* false; nor are such cases rare, although their philosophy is but imperfectly comprehended. Any conclusion evolved, therefore, from *apparently real* data, in accordance with our necessary laws of thought, may be regarded as *subjectively* true.

2. *Objective truth.*—This consists or inheres in the exact correspondence of our subjective concepts and beliefs with the actual facts of the external world, or with reality. It is obvious, therefore, as in the example noted above, that the two do not always coincide. Had my informant, in the case noted above, instead of simply turning his head for an instant, actually turned and rode away without looking behind him, he would never have suspected the optical illusion. The question, then, is to the last degree important: "How shall the accordance of subjective and objective truth be determined?" An unreal importance and significance are, however, sometimes given to it, by confounding simple *objective* truth with *absolute* truth. The latter has, and can have, in its strict sense, *no* standing in a *finite* mind, but is an exclusive attribute of absolute mind, i. e., of God.

¶ II. **The Criteria of Intuitive Truths.**—It is obvious, in the outset, for reasons already noted, that no absolute criteria of truth or falsehood are possible, else were absolute truth possible to man. So far as the senses are concerned, the test of truth is necessarily the concurrent testimony of two or more special senses, where the subject matter is amenable to more than one of them. Where but one special sense is available, its testimony may be strengthened and confirmed, in the individual instance, by varying the conditions of the suspected or tested sensation, as the gentleman did, in the case noted, by a repetition again and again of the act of vision, and thus more certain results may be reached. At times, also, the testimony of sense may be confirmed or corrected, *a priori*, by the reason, where sufficient independent data exist for its legitimate action. Failing the possibility of both these methods, the fact must be remembered that the sensation itself, even in such cases as that of double vision noted above, is real, and that the error, where error does in fact exist, is in the determination and assignment of the real objective excitant, or cause of the sensation. The possible element of error involved in sensation does not, in the slightest degree, invalidate our perception of *an objective* cause of our subjective sensations, but only the correctness of our actual determination of that cause.

Intuitive truths distinctively considered, in order to their rational acceptance, must possess two attributes, or characteristics, viz.: first, universality; and, second, necessity.

1. *Universality.*—This attribute, as a criterium of intuitive truths or primitive judgments, amounts precisely to this, namely: any concept or truth, in order that it may challenge a legitimate place as a veritable intuition of the soul, must meet with *universal* recognition and acceptance among men as men, when intelligibly presented to the individual consciousness. For example, if any tribe or race of men could be found who possessed a knowledge or concept of body, but no corresponding knowledge or concept of space, the latter must at once be discounted as an *accidental*, and not an *intuitive*, concept.

2. *Necessity.*—As a criterium of intuitive truth, this involves the conception of the impossibility of conceiving the opposite, i. e., the contradictory proposition; for example, I not only conceive it to be true that things equal to the same thing are equal to each other, but I find myself utterly unable to conceive the contrary to be possible, and would turn away in disgust from the folly and self-conceit of any one who should attempt to prove the contrary.

Any proposition uniting in itself these two marks, or attributes, must be accepted as an intuitive truth. To cavil at it, or reject it, were simply to stultify consciousness, and unsettle all the laws and conditions of thought. Any doubt, feigned or felt, under such conditions, must be invalid, since the existence of such doubt can only be known through the testimony of that consciousness whose necessary processes and products it proposes to impeach—a proceeding utterly inadmissible, since no legal maxim is better established than that "a man shall not discredit his own witness."

The whole problem of the relations of subjective to objective truth, on the one hand, and to absolute truth on the other, may be summed up in this simple statement: absolute truth as such, is impossible to man, since it lies without or beyond the sphere of the finite—objective truth, based upon the necessary laws of thought, and the nature of mind, is possible to man, and our knowledge of the external world, as a fact, is just as real as our knowledge of self, or the ego; and, in the perfect synthesis of subjective and objective truth, human knowledge culminates.

Sec. III.—Classification of Intuitions.

Previous discussions have already shadowed forth the classification of intuitions, that must here be made, discretely and decisively, into the two general categories of—1. Intuitive concepts; and, 2. Intuitive beliefs or primitive judgments; which must first be evolved discretely, and then carefully investigated.

¶ I. **Intuitive Concepts.**—Under this general head must be included:

1. *The category of being*, including the dual concepts of self and not-self, i. e., man and the universe.

2. *The category of limitation*, including the concepts of space (extension), of time (protension), and of cause (intension).

3. *The category of relation*, including the concepts of the true, the beautiful, and the good. To these must be added, finally, the resultant concepts of man, nature, and God; or the finite, the infinite, and their relations to each other.

¶ II. **Intuitive Truths or Primitive Judgments.**—Under this general head must be included:

1. The laws of thought, or the canons of logic.

2. The axioms of mathematics; and,

3. The categorical imperative of conscience, viz.: "I ought to do this, or I ought not to do that."

All of these, as will appear in the sequel, respond fully to the criteria of intuitive truths.

CHAPTER II.—INTUITIVE IDEAS, OR PRIMITIVE CONCEPTS.

SECTION I.—THE CATEGORY OF BEING.

Our previous analysis of the content of a typical percept evolved, immediately and necessarily, the category of being in its twofold forms of self and not-self, i. e., the subjective and objective elements in the percept. It now becomes necessary to examine them discretely and exhaustively, in order to the evolution of their generic values as elements of thought. The general method of the co-evolution of these related concepts has been, perhaps, sufficiently illustrated, so that we pass at once to consider them severally.

¶ I. **Self, or the Personality.**—The typical percept, as we have shown, distinctly involves, or includes, implicitly but necessarily, an affirmation of personal existence, and not obscurely of personal identity also; each of which requires discrete investigation.

1. *Personal existence.*—It does not require any extended argument to prove that personal existence is presupposed in every act of consciousness, and is an indemonstrable first truth underlying every other truth. Descartes's famous "*Cogito, ergo sum*" was not, fairly interpreted, an attempt to demonstrate the fact of existence by the fact of thought, but a simple enunciation of the truth here propounded, that the fact of conscious personal existence underlies the possibility to man of all other possible facts whatsoever; and is an *implicit*, if not an explicit, postulate of every affirmation which it is possible for him to make. In this case, *to deny* is *to affirm* the thing denied. I may conceive a time in past duration when, personally, I did not exist; I may conceive spaces where I do not now exist; and I may conceive a time future, in which I shall not exist; but I *cannot* conceive myself as *non-existent now* and *here.* The postulate of personal existence is, therefore, fundamental, and, so far as any thing human may be, absolute.

2. *Personal identity.*—This is likewise an implicit condition precedent of perception, though not, like personal existence, of strictly the *first* or *typical* percept. Man must come to the consciousness of personal existence at least once and again, before he can come to the consciousness of personal identity, whose essential conditions necessitate two or more disparate acts of consciousness, and its essence consists in the identification of the subjective personality in these disparate processes. At this point it becomes necessary to distinguish and classify the diverse forms of identity known to us in the actual experiences of life, and analyze their relations to true personal identity:

(*a*) *Physical identity*, or the identity of the essential particles of matter constituting a body, as a rock or a crystal.

(*b*) *Organic identity*, or the identity of physical organism, as in the plant, tree, or animal, in which, notwithstanding constant change in the integrant particles of matter, the organic unity of the body as a complex whole remains; and,

(*c*) *Spiritual identity*, or the unity of consciousness, which is wholly independent of physical identity, and, in fact, coexists with organic identity, but yet seems to be independent of it. Our concept and corresponding affirmation of personal identity is, at first, a confused affirmation of the second and third forms—not, however, distinctly discriminating against the first, which subsequent scientific researches exclude. This fact suggests a general remark, as pertinent here as anywhere, that we must not fall into the error of assuming that either our intuitive concepts or primitive judgments are, in the early stages of consciousness, either clearly defined or sharply discriminated from other kindred forms of thought; this process takes place only at a later period in the evolution of the reflective or philosophic consciousness; and this fact alone gives color of probability to the objections of the sensational school of psychologists, to the theory of intuitive knowledge, namely, that "children and savages not only do not possess these intuitive ideas and judgments, but that they are unable even to comprehend them when formally stated." It is precisely in this *formal statement* that the fallacy lies. If they would refute the theory fairly, it is incumbent upon them to show some tribe or race of men to whom these concepts and judgments in their *concrete, enveloped*, or *practical* form, and not in their *developed* or *abstract philosophical* form, are unknown. This they never yet have done, and it is safe to say will never be foolish enough to attempt to do. The child or the savage is as thoroughly conscious of his own personal existence and personal identity as the philosopher, though he may be utterly unable to analyze his consciousness or define his thought; or even to comprehend it when defined by another in the abstract terms of science. All attempts to account for the existence of this implicit faith in his own personal identity which is characteristic of man as man, by referring it to *experience, association of ideas*, etc., etc., ignores the obtrusive fact that it is itself a *condition precedent* alike of the memory and experience which are supposed to originate it.

¶ II. **Not-Self, or the Universe.**—Every percept, as we have seen, involves the correlated concepts of self as the percipient subject, and not-self, or the universe, as the object perceived; known, not separately and independently, but simultaneously, in the synthesis of perception. Analysis of this complex reveals:

1. The essential distinction between the *subjective* and the *objective* in human thought. The simplest form of the affirmation of a typical percept clearly involves this philosophical distinction. For example, if I say, "I perceive a book," the personal pronoun "I" is the direct representative of the *subjective* personality; while the book, with equal directness, represents not-self, or the *objective* universe.

2. Man's physical nature, i. e., the sensorium, is both subjective and objective. Viewed in certain relations, it is, as it were, absorbed into the true self, or ego, and is discriminated from the universe. Viewed in other relations, and more especially from the philosophical stand-point, it is rightfully discriminated from self, or the true ego, and is, as a true ob-

jective element, identified with not-self, or the universe; and it is in this identification of our physical nature with not-self, or the universe, that the soul, or true ego, attains to an *immediate* knowledge of matter and its *essential* attributes. This thought leads us, finally, to consider—

3. The real objective element known in sensation. This has already been shown to be, not the *remote* object of sense, as the book lying upon the table, nor yet the proximate object, as the ray of light acting upon the retina of the eye; but the sensorium itself, as excited by the impact of the ray of light, and responding by its own subjective affections, producing in the soul, or true ego, the phenomena of a genuine psychical sensation and perception. Our complex physical and spiritual natures, thus strangely and perfectly united, enable us to grasp, in the unity of consciousness, with equal facility, both the physical and spiritual worlds; equally allied to each, consciousness stands face to face with both.

¶ III. **Substance and Attribute.**—Subsidiary to the category of being, i. e., to the concepts of self and not-self, and as a condition precedent to the rational comprehension of either, there arise the correlated concepts of substance and attributes, taken originally, in a confused general sense, to represent the distinction between the properties or accidents of an entity, and the entity itself. Through the senses, it is obvious that the mind cognizes, primarily, only specific qualities. For example, an apple is presented to me: by the sight, I cognize its colors, etc.; by the smell, its odor; by the touch, its weight; by the taste, its savor, etc. Now, if this be assumed, for the moment, to be a *first* or *typical* sensation, the questions would at once arise: "Are these separate sensations independent of each other, i. e., *independent* entities, or are they *dependent*, inhering in a common substratum or substance?" The answer, as a matter of fact, universally given by the intelligence of the infant, is always, necessarily and universally, hence *intuitively*, that the special sensations represent special attributes or properties of a common entity or substance.

In its subsequent reflective movements, consciousness idealizes these correlative concepts, and postulates them as the symbols, respectively, of *phenomenal* and *real* existence. The same necessity of thought which compels the soul to unite the several attributes known in sensation in a complex unity called body, matter, or substance, constrains it, at a later period in the development of the reflective consciousness, to seek, underneath and beyond the diversity of changing or phenomenal existence, for an unchanging essence or substance.

The category of substance and attribute, as present to the consciousness of man, is dual, and not singular, involving the perception or affirmation of—

1. *Spiritual substance*, as represented in consciousness by the true self, or ego, as contradistinguished from both the physical organism and the external world. This consciousness postulates as of its own *essence*, discriminating it as an entity, *sui generis*, whose phenomena are: 1. *Thought;* 2. *Feeling;* and 3. *Volition*, which need only be named here. And—

2. *Material substance*, or matter, represented in consciousness by the physical organism as discriminated from the true self, or ego, by its own peculiar attributes, such as extension, impenetrability, etc., etc., whose proper discussion belongs elsewhere.

Sec. II.—The Category of Limitation.

In the synthesis of the complex typical percept, it will be remembered that our analysis revealed, not merely the category of being, but that it revealed it under the conditions of space, time, and causation, or the category of limitation, which must now, in turn, be discretely considered.

¶ I. **Space, or Extension.**—No concept or idea whatsoever is more universally and obtrusively present to the consciousness of man than that of space, involving at once the localizing of *being* and of *action*. The question "Where?" is ever upon our lips, when any thing, either act or event, is named; and, as it is with us to-day, so has it ever been with man as man. Whence, then, comes this concept, and what is its real nature?

1. *It is not an object of sense.*—We cannot see, hear, touch, taste, or smell it, nor yet any of its attributes, for body or matter is in no sense an attribute of space. Its sole relations to it are (*a*), that it occupies space; and (*b*), that it furnishes the occasion upon which the soul, intuitively and necessarily, affirms the existence of space as a condition precedent of the concept of being.

2. *It is not a mere abstraction from the idea or concept of body.*—The simple and sufficient proof of this assertion is found in the fact that a conception of space is, as before stated, an *essential condition precedent* of the conception of body. The truth obviously is, that the mind of the infant, confusedly but decisively, comes to the perception or conception of body in space; and not, first, to that of body and then of space, or *vice versa.* Our primitive percepts and concepts are, alike, *concrete* and *confused*, and not *discrete* and *determinate.*

3. *Space is not an entity, but a condition precedent of being.*—This statement has already been incidentally made, but requires discrete enunciation here, as it has been strongly contested. To conceive space as an entity, as some have done, is to confuse and contradict all our rational concepts of entity or being. To assume, with Kant, that it is a *simple formal condition* of thought, and not of being, is to deny its existence altogether. The only remaining alternative is the affirmation of space, not as itself an entity or being, but as a condition precedent of being. We can conceive a time when being was not; may imagine a time, perhaps, when being shall cease; but we can neither conceive nor imagine a time when space was not. We may abstract body in thought and leave space, but we cannot, in turn, abstract space and leave *not-space.* The abstraction of space, in other words, is unthinkable; it is, therefore, to man a true absolute.

¶ II. **Time, Protension.**—Space presents itself, under a

trinal form, as possessing three dimensions; time, its inseparable congener, is conceived as possessing but one. It is the unceasing flow of measureless duration, marked from the stand-point of the human consciousness. Its affinity to space, or extension, is indicated by the cognate word protension, occasionally applied to it. Time and duration are sometimes discriminated from each other, and the word time applied exclusively to that portion of measured duration which is marked by the revolutions of the heavenly bodies, and represented by days, months, and years; while the word duration is reserved for the measureless flow of time, which we call eternity.

That time, like space, is a universal, necessary, and therefore intuitive concept, needs but little proof. The attempt to derive it from our experience of successive acts of consciousness, fails, from the simple fact that the idea of succession is impossible apart from the conception of time, in which such succession may occur. Nor is it, for like reasons, in any sense an abstraction from the idea of succession; for any attempt to conceive the residuum of such an act of abstraction, either positively or negatively, must simply result in the conception of self as the underlying substratum of the consciously perceived phenomena.

Time, like space, is not an entity, but a condition precedent of being and succession, i. e., of motion or action. Like space, it is to man, so far as any concept can be, both infinite and absolute; and its non-existence is, therefore, unthinkable.

¶ III. **Cause, Intension.**—1. *Analysis of the concept.*—The same perverse ingenuity which led Kant to reduce space and time to the condition or rank of subjective forms or conditions of thought, has led to the denial of the real or objective validity of the category of causation, reducing *that* also to a mere condition of thought; and we are assured that we know and can know nothing of causation proper, and that that which we denominate causation is nothing more than the invariable relations of actual succession and resemblance that we perceive between objects and events; and that the variableness of this order, in the one series of cases, and its invariableness in others, leads us naturally to the assumption of a causal nexus or link in the latter case, which necessitates the consequent or effect. Causation, on this hypothesis, is a mere resultant of invariableness of succession, i. e., of antecedence and consequence between any two events whatsoever. On this hypothesis, which explicitly denies the legitimacy of any assumption of power in the antecedent to produce the consequent, it is obvious that the strength of our belief in the causal nexus must be *in direct proportion* to the *frequency* and the *invariableness* of the succession. This, however, is not true, for no successions known to man are so frequent or so invariable as those of day and night, summer and winter, life and death; yet no man, woman, or child, ever mistook the antecedent for a cause, and the consequent for an effect, in these successions, nor in a hundred others that might be named; while in numberless instances of successions, occurring but once in the experience of the individual, he unhesitatingly affirms the antecedent to be the cause, and the consequent the effect, with a faith that is absolute. In the face of such facts, it is idle for any man to insist upon such an hypothesis. The truth is, it cannot be stated and sustained by formal argument, by its most earnest advocates, in any form of words which does not implicitly deny it, and the man who professes to believe it stultifies his faith by every voluntary act of his life.

It should, perhaps, be added, discretely, that the concept of causation is not an induction from experience, as it is itself a condition precedent of all experience, for it is only in virtue of the law of causation that we come to the knowledge of either the proximate or remote external object of sensation. The conclusion is therefore irresistible, that, as a strictly *universal* and *necessary* concept of humanity, it is *intuitive*, and must be classed among the primitive affirmations of consciousness.

2. *Real import of the canon of causation.*—This has

been variously stated by different authors. It may, perhaps, be announced with sufficient distinctness as follows, viz.: "Every *event* must have an adequate or sufficient cause." This avoids at once and decisively the sophism that the canon of causation postulates an infinite succession of causes, and rationally predicates a first or uncaused cause of all things; *that* is not *an event*, and therefore does not postulate a cause, and is, consequently, *not* an exception to the universality of the canon of causation. It may, therefore, safely be regarded as absolute within its own proper sphere.

A question has sometimes been raised in reference to the unity or multiplicity of causes acting in the production of a given effect; and it has been asserted that causes are *never* singular, but *always* dual or multiple, i. e., concurrent. The only element of this problem worth discussion grows out of the confounding of the *conditions* of an event with its *cause* or *causes;* for causes *may*, not *must*, be dual and concurrent. There may be many concurrent conditions necessary to the operation of an efficient cause, but it is to confound all logical relations to rank them all together, and denominate them the coördinate causes of the resultant effect.

3. *Classification of causes.*—Aristotle classified causes under four general heads or divisions, viz.:

(*a*) Efficient causes; that is, real causes.

(*b*) Material causes; that is, the material out of which a thing is made.

(*c*) Formal causes; that is, the plan, or fashion, or model, according to which a thing is made; and,

(*d*) Final causes; that is, the end, purpose, or design, for which a thing is made.

For some purposes, this classification is convenient, but it is obvious that the second and third are not causes, but conditions, according to the distinction made in the preceding paragraph, while the fourth refers to the subjective motives in view of which the will puts forth its volition to act. At the present day, the first and fourth are the only forms that are practically recognized.

Sec. III.—The Category of Relation.

Consciousness, dealing as it does continually with the category of being, under the conditions of the category of limitation, universally, necessarily, and therefore *intuitively*, attains to the affirmation of the category of relation, i. e., to the concepts of the true, the beautiful, and the good, which must now, in turn, be subjected to discrete analysis.

¶ I. **The True.**—Prominent among the relations of things intuitively perceived by the human consciousness, is that relation which we denominate *the true*, or *truth.* Like all other intuitive concepts, its origin is hidden by the veil of childhood, and we can only conjecture the conditions under which it is evolved in consciousness, and assumes its legitimate place in the hierarchy of thought. The universality and necessity of the concept cannot be denied; all men, savage and civilized, young and old, recognize it. There are none so young, if capable of thought, to whom it is strange; none so ignorant among the lowest savages, that they do not possess it. Truth is, indeed, the proximate goal, at least, toward which all legitimate thought normally tends. Its opposite, falsehood, if ever the conscious object of the processes of human thought, is so abnormally, and, for special ends, sought in and through its agency, and not for itself.

1. *Analysis of the concept.*—The concept of truth involves, necessarily, the concept of a primitive judgment determining the agreement or non-agreement of two percepts. Concepts, as such, are *real* or *unreal;* judgments are *true* or *false.* Popularly, however, the *real* and *unreal* are confounded with the *true* and *false;* and this is, perhaps, a natural resultant of a curious logical paradox that will be noted in the sequel, namely, "that every concept implies a prior act of judgment; while, technically, a judgment is nothing more than a formal comparison of two concepts." This paradox, as it doubtless occasions, probably also justifies, the popular application of the terms true and false to concepts as well as to judgments; although, strictly con-

sidered, the terms *real* and *unreal* are alone appropriate to concepts, and *true* and *false* to judgments. In the intuitive concept of the true, or truth, we have the basal element of the moral nature of man, that which decisively distinguishes him from the most intelligent of the animal races.

2. *Nature of error, or falsehood.*—In any analysis of error or falsehood, it is necessary to discriminate accurately between the *natural* and *moral* elements, as well as between subjective and objective truth.

A statement is *subjectively true* when it accords with the facts as they are actually present to the consciousness of the speaker.

A statement is *objectively* true when it accords with the reality of things, independently of fallible human perception.

It is obvious, therefore, that, as between these two forms of truth, three cases, generically considered, are possible—viz.:

(*a*) A statement may be true, both subjectively and objectively; that is, true in the highest sense of the term.

(*b*) A statement may be subjectively true, but objectively false; true *morally*, but *not actually;* and,

(*c*) A statement may be *subjectively* false, but objectively true; or, *morally* false, but *actually* true.

Shutting out deliberate moral falsehood, which belongs exclusively to the sphere of ethics, this analysis enables us to determine the nature and conditions of error, or *natural*, not *moral*, falsehood; namely, it is *incomplete, imperfect*, or *partial* truth, seen or perceived out of, or apart from, its proper relations. Man necessarily sees any truth whatsoever from a *personal* stand-point and in a partial aspect. His conception of it is, therefore, necessarily one-sided and defective; he is liable, consequently, to see its component elements out of their true relations and proportions, the near obscuring or hiding the remote, just as the mote on the object-glass of the astronomer's telescope may hide a world, or be mistaken for a world. Perhaps no man ever held to error pure, simple, and unmixed with truth. It is the single grain or germ of truth, which the soul of the errorist has grasped and made the centre of his false system, which gives it all its vitality. He, therefore, who would combat error successfully, must seek to detect the underlying germ of truth around which the false system has crystallized, and rescue *that* from its unhallowed associations, and then the final destruction of the system is sure.

¶ II. **The Beautiful.**—Above and beyond the conception and cognition of the true, any careful analysis of the facts of consciousness reveals another and kindred concept, viz., the beautiful. This concept, like all other primitive products of consciousness, is simple and indefinable, and can be known only in our personal experience of it. Yet no one needs a definition of a term which sheds radiance and joy alike around the lives of prince and peasant—of the child and the philosopher.

1. *Analysis of the concept.*—In looking upon a landscape, we are conscious, above and beyond the perception of the mountains, valleys, streams, rocks, trees, shrubs, grass, and flowers, which constitute it, of a perception of something, in the individual objects, in their grouping, in their coloring, or in their relations, that is not mountain, valley, rock, tree, or flower; which fills the soul with emotions that thrill, exalt, and intensify it in the highest degree. This perception, with its accompanying emotion, we denominate the beautiful. It obviously involves an *external objective* element acting upon the mind through the senses, and a *subjective capacity*, to which the objective element appeals; and this subjective capacity, as already noted, includes both an intellectual element, a perception or cognition, and a sensible element, the emotion of beauty.

2. *Characteristics of the concept.*—Fixing our attention upon the intellectual element, and relegating the emotion to its proper place among the sensibilities, we find it to possess certain characteristics which determine its nature and origin.

(*a*) *It is universal.* This is a truth so obvious, even to the careless observer, that to state it is to prove it. Here the child and the savage are never at fault; whatever other idea or concept may be wanting, that of the beautiful never is; it is as universal as humanity.

(*b*) *It is primitive, simple, and indefinable.* Various attempts have been made to reduce it to some more simple and ultimate form, thus assuming it to be at once complex and derivative. It has, for example, been ascribed or referred *to novelty, to utility, to variety in unity, etc., etc., as generative principles;* but every attempt of this character has failed, hopelessly, to satisfy even the more obvious conditions of the problem. It is notorious, for example, that many things are exceedingly useful which not even the most tasteless of men could be persuaded to imagine beautiful. So, again, many things are *novel,* in the highest degree, and yet hideously ugly; and so of the rest. It may well be questioned whether these theories, not excluding the higher *spiritual theory* which resolves beauty into the manifestation of spiritual ideas or existence under *material* forms, are not based upon a misconception of the nature of the concept. If that is, in fact, as a majority of the ablest psychologists of the day concede, an *intuitive* concept, it must needs be *simple, primitive, indefinable, necessary.* To attempt to define it by a determination of its underlying elements is at once to exclude it from the category of *primitive, necessary,* or *intuitive* concepts; and yet, very strangely, authors who most strenuously assert its intuitive character, spend page after page in the attempt to resolve it into its elements. Tried by the decisive criteria of *universality* and *necessity,* it must be adjudged to be an *intuition* of the human soul, as simple and indefinable as its congener, *the true.* Different individuals and races of men vary in the clearness of their perceptions of the beautiful, and in the vividness and strength of their emotions of beauty, but in none are either wholly wanting, save in cases whose developments are manifestly abnormal.

It may, however, be argued that if beauty be indefinable men cannot possess any common standard whatever. This does not follow, and were just as valid as an objection against any other primitive concept whatsoever, and is therefore worth less. It, in fact, ignores the *real* element of unity involved, namely: the identity of humanity under all its varied manifestations, both normal and abnormal. Varieties of taste depend much more, as will be seen in the sequel, upon differences of *culture*, and the influence of *fashion*, than upon differences of mental nature, whether intellectual or sensitive.

3. *Cognition of beauty—taste.*—This is a complex element, involving both the intellectual perception, and the emotion of beauty, and is perfect in proportion—

(*a*) To the natural strength and delicacy of these elements; and,

(*b*) To the completeness and perfection of their culture.

The intellectual and emotional elements are not necessarily in direct proportion to each other. In uncultivated minds, the emotion ordinarily predominates; in cultivated, the intellectual element. The latter is the essential element in what may be termed critical taste, in which the consciousness reacts upon itself, and seeks to determine the laws of harmony and beauty, and to separate intelligently the discordant from the accordant elements, and to ascertain the relations of the *actual* beauty, cognized in the object, to the higher *ideal* beauty shrined in the depths of the soul. He who would enjoy beauty in its highest sense, must lose the critic in the man; he who would criticise beauty, and pursue it to its secret hiding-places, must lose the man in the critic.

Supplementary Topic.

Sublimity.—Closely allied to beauty is the sublime. It must, in fact, be ranked under the generic head of beauty, since it cannot, with propriety, be assigned to a coördinate rank with it and the other concepts of the category of relation, nor yet be assigned to any other department of mind. Like simple beauty, it is at once a perception and an emotion, but the emotional element ordinarily strongly predominates. Few men, comparatively, are capable of cognizing the sublime, as an intellectual element apart from the corresponding emotion, which, by its overpowering intensity, swallows up and obscures the perception; hence few are able, in the light of consciousness, to distinguish the intellectual act at all. As contradistinguished from beauty, as a coördinate species under the common genus, it is discriminated or marked by the concepts of vastness, power, etc., etc., which enter into the concept of the sublime, but not into that of the beautiful. The sublime may therefore, without impropriety, be defined to be beauty elevated and intensified by the elements of vastness, power, etc., etc. Accordingly we find that Niagara is alternately beautiful and sublime, in proportion as we include or exclude from consciousness, for the time being, the hidings of resistless power that are evermore present there. The same analogies may be traced in all the forms of natural as well as moral beauty and sublimity, but it is needless; our object is rather to suggest thought than to furnish it; to guide the student in his own psychological researches, than to unfold to him the imperfect and unauthoritative results of our own.

¶ III. **The Right, the Good.**—The terms right and good are here placed side by side, not, on the one hand, because they are regarded as strict synonymes, and therefore interchangeable; nor yet, on the other, because the right is in any sense, as is sometimes affirmed, a derivative conception, dependent upon the good, as its ultimate ground, basis, or principle; but because the term right, in its ordinary use, expresses a part only of the essential generic concept which we desire to note and investigate here. The term good, taken alone, is, as we conceive it, even less significant; hence, in a *determinate* synthesis of the two, we have sought to express the real idea involved.

1. *Analysis of the generic concept.*—Any discrete analysis of the facts of consciousness, as they are evolved in our daily lives, cannot fail to distinguish among the relations there existing one peculiar in its nature and attributes, in that it belongs not to things, but to men, and that in man it fastens exclusively upon his *intelligent voluntary activity.*

Here, perhaps, the true original distinction between the terms good and right decisively emerges in consciousness. We say of an apple or orange, it is *good* or *bad;* of the intelligent voluntary action of a man, it is *right* or *wrong;* and this discrimination is, so far forth at least, universal, that men never apply the adjectives right and wrong to things, as the apple or the orange. Secondarily, however, they have learned to transfer the epithets *good* and *bad* from material to spiritual things, and use them interchangeably with *right* and *wrong*, as attributes of moral or voluntary action. In fact, good and bad, as descriptive adjectives, when transferred to the plane of humanity, should have been restricted to *the men themselves*, and should *not* have been applied *to actions at all*, to which the adjectives *right* and *wrong* should have been exclusively reserved. This distinction has, however, not been intelligently maintained, and the result has been, that men have fallen into the error of seeking to account for the concept of the right, by reducing it to the rank of a mere derivative from the idea of the good. If this analysis be correct, the term *good* may be taken as representing a genus, in which the term *right* represents a distinct and peculiar species, *sui generis*, including, *only* and *exclusively*, *intelligent voluntary action.* If this distinction be accepted as real and legitimate, it goes far toward determining the two remaining problems which demand a solution, namely: (*a*) the nature, and (*b*) the origin of these correlated concepts.

2. *Nature and origin of these concepts.*—Various theories have been propounded in reference to the nature and origin of these concepts. Practically, the only theories that are worth noting may be reduced in essence to two, and but two; their minor modifications may be discounted in an elementary work like this, which necessarily deals with principles, and not details.

(*a*) *The theory of benevolent utility.* This bases the idea of the right upon that of the good, and identifies the latter with the happiness begetting or producing. It affirms that that is right which is good, and that that is good which tends to the production of happiness; or, reducing the theory to its ultimate analysis at once: "That is right which tends to happiness; that is wrong which produces unhappiness." In opposition to this theory, we posit four propositions, viz.:

First. That it confounds, at once and decisively, the intuitive distinction that men make in the application or use of the terms good and right—a use whose presence and reality can be traced through all ages and all languages. If the right were nothing more or nothing else than the good, the words ought to be, *uniformly* and *universally*, interchangeable, which is not true. The fact is undeniable that the term right carries with it a peculiar *content* or meaning which the term good does not, which restricts its use to voluntary action. It is not denied that the term good is actually applied to voluntary action, but when so applied few would venture to assert that it conveys all the actual significance of the term right used in the same relation. The first movement of the proposed identification is, therefore, a failure.

Second. It resolves both the right and the good into selfishness. Some advocates of the theory of utility have sought to evade this objection, by positing a *benevolent* and not a *selfish* utility as the condition of the right or the good. But if the legitimacy of this postulate be conceded, the theory still fails, decisively, because it does not and cannot supply, or account for, the *authoritative* element, *the categorical imperative of conscience*, which is the essential *characteristic* of our concept of the right. Tell a man that he ought to do thus and so, because it will make the Choctaw Indians or the Chinese happy, and the response you would receive would inevitably be, "Let them take care of their own happiness, that is none of my business." Tell him that he ought to do it, because it will minister to *his own* highest happiness, and he will still answer you, unhesitatingly, "I prefer another, even if it be a lower form of happiness;" and your mouth is closed: you cannot legitimately tell him, from the stand-point of either a *benevolent* or a *selfish* utility, that he "*ought to do right*," for he would tell you, "There is no *ought* in the case, it is a mere calculation of possible happiness and misery."

Third. In its last analysis, it resolves right and wrong into simple volitions of the Divine Being; prior to which nothing was either right or wrong, good or evil. It also legitimates the hypothesis that, in other worlds, God may have, conceivably, made happiness dependent upon hatred, adultery, and *falsehood*, and misery result from justice, mercy, and truth.

Finally. If an appeal to revelation is admissible, it must be added that the theory confuses and contradicts all those passages of Scripture, on the one hand, which declare God's ways to be just, equal, and right; and turns to mockery, on the other, those in which God challenges man to test His truth, goodness, and mercy. For to ask, as God has solemnly done, by the mouth of the prophet, "Are not my ways equal?" (i. e., just or right) "saith the Lord," is, on this hypothesis, simply to perpetrate the *farce* and the *mockery* of asking, "Are not *my* ways *my* ways? saith the Lord."

(*b*) The second alternative theory represents right and wrong as necessary attributes or immutable relations of intelligent voluntary action. These concepts may be conceived, in their ultimate analysis, as sustaining toward God and all truly voluntary beings, i. e., to all moral agents, a relation analogous to that which space and time sustain to material existence. According to this theory, God has so arranged the relations and consequences of human action, that conformity to the right shall in the end result in good, and non-conformity to right result in evil. It need hardly be said that this accords better with the spontaneous consciousness of man, in all ages, as expressed in the crystallized forms of language, than its rival, but it should be said, emphatically, that it alone harmonizes with the facts of consciousness. Every student may test this, decisively, by proposing to himself, or to another, a course of alternative action involving grave interests. Two questions at once arise, viz., first: Is the proposed act *right?* and, second, Will it be *useful* or *profitable?* i. e., Will it pay?—Now if the doctrine of utility, either benevolent or selfish, be true, and the happiness-begetting, the good and the right are identical; then these questions are not *dual* and *diverse*, but *one* and *identical*, a conclusion which it is safe to say no man in his soul believes or feels. It is perfectly safe to add that no moralist, even of the utility school, ever practically confounds them in actual life, however little he may regard right, or however strong may be his devotion to his pet theory.

The decision of the nature of these concepts carries with it the determination of their origin as primitive, necessary, universal, and therefore intuitive concepts or affirmations of consciousness, the only and all-sufficient basis of the moral nature of man and the moral government of the universe.

Sec. IV.—Coördination and Correlation of these Categories.—Evolution of the Concept of God.

The next step in the process of mental evolution is necessary and immediate, namely, the coördination and correlation of the categories of being, limitation, and relation, and the evolution of the resultant concepts.

At this point a remark is necessary by way of explanation, namely: no definite order of the evolution and development of the necessary percepts, concepts, and beliefs of the human soul can be assumed; the actual process is hidden from us by the veil of childhood. The logical processes only are open to our inspection, and, in reference to them, there is room for diversity of opinion. They necessarily involve, moreover, a commingling of diverse mental elements, together with a manifold repetition of each; and the mind attains to the clearness and distinctness of reflection only after years of weary effort. It is obvious, for example, that the mental evolutions we have attempted to sketch have involved memory, imagination, and judgment, which still, formally at least, lie before us in the unexplored regions of thought.

¶ I. **Evolution of the Correlative Concepts of the Finite and Infinite.**—The soul, conceiving body, as it necessarily does, under the conditions of space and time, by a like necessity conceives any particular body whatsoever as *circumscribed*, *limited*, *bounded*, in a word as *finite*; but these terms are essentially correlatives, and cannot be conceived or comprehended apart from *the uncircumscribed*, *the unlimited*, *the unbounded*, *the infinite*. The knowledge of the two terms or poles of a true contradiction is one; the two cannot be known apart. The question is not, here, whether the imagination can actually grasp infinite space or duration; for it is obvious that it cannot, just as it cannot grasp indefinite space, as the Pacific Ocean, which is as really unimaginable in fact as infinity; but whether the mind can conceive, in the sense of know, or recognize, the existence of infinity as a fact, just as it recognizes the existence of a (to it) practically boundless finite, as the Pacific Ocean, or the solar system. We here repeat the statement, that we may emphasize it, a practically boundless finite is as absolutely inconceivable (in the sense of unimaginable) as a true infinite. The thoughtful student, who studies carefully the ponderous volumes that have been written to prove that man cannot know, because he cannot conceive, i. e., cannot imagine the infinite, will hardly escape the suspicion, at least, that their learned authors have egregiously failed in the outset to determine definitely what they themselves mean by *conception*, *positive* and *negative*. The truth is, the cognition or intuition of the finite and infinite, as attributes of matter on the one hand, and of space and time, on the other, is necessary and immediate. Nor are these concepts alien even to the mind of a child. Said a little girl to the writer, one starlight night, "What is there beyond the stars?" the answer was, "Other stars!" "And what," she asked again, "is beyond these?" The answer was, again, "Other stars!" She was silent a moment, and then came the decisive question: "And what is there beyond the farthest star?" The thought of limitless, boundless, *infinite* space was struggling for expression in that almost infantile soul, that as yet could only lisp its thoughts in the broken speech of childhood. The conception of the infinite was as real and as vivid in the soul of that child as in the soul of a philosopher. The conclusion is irresistible that the concepts of the finite and infinite are universally and necessarily evolved in the presence of the percepts of consciousness.

¶ II. **Application of the Concepts of the Finite and Infinite to the Category of Being.**—The soul no sooner comes into the conscious possession of these correlated concepts, than it at once *intuitively* and *necessarily* proceeds to apply them as attributes to the correlated elements or factors of the category of being, and to evolve the logical resultants of this process:

1. Application of the concepts of the finite and infinite to self and not-self, i. e., to man and the universe. As applied to the former, the consciousness is immediate, direct, and obtrusive, that self, or the personality, is limited and finite—limited, in space, to the here; in time, to to-day and yesterday, i. e., to a present conscious existence, and to a brief past existence whose flow memory readily spans. No consciousness is clearer or more determinate in the soul than that of the limited sphere of its own personality.

As applied to the universe, these concepts result no less decisively in the cognition of its limited and finite character; for it is precisely in its consciousness of self and not-self, as mutually acting and reacting upon each other, mutually limiting and limited, that the soul, as we have seen, comes to the consciousness of its own existence. In cognizing not-self, or the universe, it cognizes it as limited by self; i. e., again, cognizes it as finite. Nor should the fact be overlooked, in this connection, that this application of the concepts of the finite and infinite to the category of being, is equally legitimate and equally necessary, whether considered with reference to space and time, extension and protension, or to cause or intension. In every case alike, the correspondence is perfect, and the inference immediate.

2. *Evolution of the concept of Infinite Being, i. e., of God.*—The soul cannot rest in either term of a correlative pair or duality, singly and alone; it must pass, by the very necessity of its being, to the opposite or complementary pole of thought. It comprehends the finite only on condition that it grasps the correlated concept of the infinite firmly and intelligently. Accordingly, in this concrete instance, it does not and cannot rest in the two complementary, mutually limiting and mutually limited *finites*, viz., man and the universe; since neither can account for the other, and much less can it account for itself. Nor can the mind, in the presence of finite being, escape or avoid the concept of Infinite Being; nor, having attained to this new concept, can it fail to apply to it consciously the category of limitation, and evolve the affirmation that this Infinite Being, as filling at once infinite space and endless duration, is infinite cause also; i. e., the uncaused cause of that finite being known in the depths of consciousness, and represented by self and not-self, man and the universe. The soul, in this synthesis of its intuitive concepts, comes at once to the concept of an adequate cause of the existence of self and not-self, of human intelligence and the material universe, of the human personality and material modality. But, as the cause or creator of human intelligence and of the human personality, the inference is necessary and immediate that this Infinite Being, God, is Himself an intelligent personality, and not a blind, unconscious soul of the world.

¶ III. **Application of the Category of Relation to this Infinite Personality.**—Another step remains, and that, like those which have preceded it, is immediate, direct, and necessary; namely, the application of the category of relation i. e., of the concepts of the true, the beautiful, and the good, to this infinite personality necessitating the affirmation of infinite truth, infinite beauty, and infinite goodness, as the necessary or essential attributes of this *absolute* personality, i. e., of God; the ultimate term or goal of human thought. Starting from the simple and familiar facts of *consciousness*, we have evolved simultaneously or successively (as the several cases demanded) the concepts of self and not-self, man and the universe, of space, time, and cause; of the true, the beautiful, and the good; of the finite, and of an infinite being filling space and duration, the uncaused cause of all things, infinite in truth, beauty, and goodness—God over all, blessed for evermore!

SEC. V.—RESULTANT CONCEPTIONS.

Apart from these primary relations, there are other secondary ones which emerge, when, in the processes of the reflective or philosophical consciousness, man, nature, and God, the integers of human thought, are coördinated with each other. In order to logical completeness, this coördination must now be undertaken and the resultant concepts generically (not specifically) determined.

¶ I. **Evolution of the Relations of the Finite to the Finite.**—These relations may, for the sake of clearness or distinctness, be discriminated into three generic classes or groups, viz.:

I. *The relations of nature to nature* (including man as an integral element of the cosmos), originating the general concept of *science*, or, perhaps we should say, of the *hierarchy of the sciences*,

II. *The relations of nature to man*, originating the general concept of *industry or art*, using those terms generically rather than specifically; and,

III. *The relations of man to man*, originating the concept of *government*, in its broad, generic sense, as the representative of *society as a vital organism.*

¶ II. **Evolution of the Relations of the Finite to the Infinite.**—These relations may be considered under two general classes, viz.:

I. *The relations of man and the universe to God*, originating the science of metaphysics; and,

II. *The relations of man as an intelligent, voluntary personality to God*, originating the science of theology. In this, human thought culminates and reaches its *Ultima Thule*, in which alone it can find perfect rest and complete satisfaction.

CHAPTER III.—INTUITIVE AFFIRMATIONS OR PRIMITIVE JUDGMENTS.

Preliminary Remarks.

The student will remember that the intuitive affirmations of consciousness appeared under two forms, viz., intuitive concepts and intuitive judgments. The first have been, perhaps, sufficiently considered; it now only remains to consider the second, under the general heads previously indicated, viz.: 1. The canons of thought; 2. The axioms of mathematics; and, 3. The categorical imperative of conscience.

SECTION I.—THE CANONS OF THOUGHT.

The remark is appropriate in the outset, that no attempt is here made to present an exhaustive summary of intuitive concepts and judgments; those only have been seized upon and coördinated, which, from their relative importance, were deemed indispensable to some degree of analytic clearness in the discussion of psychologic processes. Among the primitive judgments, it is obtrusively evident that what have been termed the canons of thought, or sometimes, technically, the canons of logic, are fundamental, as in a certain sense underlying and conditioning all the others. They have been variously stated and classified by different authors, the variety of statement not, however, affecting their real meaning or force, but only their forms. In the present instance the statements of Sir William Hamilton have been substantially followed.

¶ I. **The Law of Identity.**—This may most readily be interpreted algebraically by the equation: A=A. Otherwise it admits of a twofold statement, according to the use intended, viz.: 1. Any thing whatever is exactly equal to itself; or, 2. Any whole is exactly equal to the sum of all its parts, and *vice versa*. It obviously affords the logical basis of *all affirmation and definition*, as well as of all *true analysis*, which consists, simply, in resolving the concrete or logical whole into its constituent parts or elements.

¶ II. **The Law of Contradiction.**—This law is expressed logically under the general formula, "What is contradictory is unthinkable." Algebraically it may be expressed somewhat obscurely by the equation: A=Not-A=0, or A—A=0. This law is evidently the exact counterpart of the law of identity, though independent of it. In its practical use, it is the principle of all negation and distinction.

¶ III. **The Law of Excluded Middle.**—This enounces the condition of thought that compels us, of two repugnant or contradictory attributes or notions, which cannot coexist with each other, to think either the one or the other as existing. Hence arises the general axiom: "Of contradictory attributes, we can only affirm *one* of a thing: if *one* be *explicitly affirmed, the other is implicitly denied.*" It admits also of a secondary statement, which is, at times, logically convenient, viz.: "As between the terms or poles of a true logical contradiction, *there can be no middle term.*" This law, which Sir William Hamilton strongly states and defends, he himself has most strangely violated, in his celebrated review of M. Cousin's philosophy, where he postulates the conditionally limited or finite as a (thinkable) mean, between two contradictory extremes, viz., the unconditionally unlimited or infinite, and the unconditionally limited or absolute, a procedure in direct violation of this law, and therefore itself logically unthinkable.

As, by the laws of identity and contradiction, we are authorized to conclude, from the truth of one contradictory proposition, the falsity of the other; so, by the law of excluded middle, we are authorized to reverse the process, and conclude, from the falsity of one contradictory proposition, the truth of the other. One or the other *must* be true: A either *is*, or *is not*, B. The law of excluded middle is, therefore, the principle or basis of all disjunctive judgments.

¶ IV. **The Law of Reason and Consequent.**—Thought, however, still requires another limitation in order to its legitimacy; it must not be capricious or lawless; and this final limitation is found in the law of reason and consequent, or, as it is sometimes called, the law of the sufficient reason. Its simplest expression is found in the formula, "Infer nothing without a ground or reason."

"The relations between reason and consequent, when comprehended in a pure thought, are the following:

"1. When a reason is explicitly or implicitly given, then there must be a consequent, and, *vice versa*, when a consequent is given, there must also exist a reason.

"2. Where there is no reason, there can be no consequent; and, *vice versa*, where there is no consequent (either explicitly or implicitly), there can be no reason." (Hamilton's "Logic," pp. 60, 61.)

A single remark may be pertinent here, namely; the law of reason and consequent is broader than the law of cause and effect, and includes the latter as one of its specific forms.

To these four simple and self-evident laws all the processes of thought must be subordinated; and these laws, regulating all else and lying at the foundations of all intelligence, are simple *intuitions* of the conscious soul, having no other guarantee than their simple self-evidence; *they are unproved and unprovable.*

Sec. II.—The Axioms of Mathematics.

Subordinate to the primary laws of thought, we meet on the threshold of the science of mathematics with a series of self-evident propositions or axioms, upon which rests the whole grand structure of that science, which, from their intrinsic importance, demand at least brief, discrete notice.

¶ I. **Examination of their Essential Forms.**—As ordinarily stated in works on geometry, they are, obviously, only special and secondary forms of the canons of thought; especially of the laws of identity and contradiction. For example, take the first, second, and third axioms; I quote from

Robinson: "1. Things which are equal to the same thing are equal to each other;" "2. When equals are added to equals, the wholes are equal;" "3. When equals are taken from equals, the remainders are equal;" and it becomes evident that they are derived immediately from, and are in fact but variant forms of, the law of identity: that any thing is equal to itself, or a whole is equal to the sum of all its parts. So of all the rest, however enunciated.

¶ II. **Mathematics only a Special Form of Logic.**—The preceding paragraph reveals, at once, the fact that the whole science of mathematics, with all its grand developments, is only a special form of the science of logic; and is, in fact, nothing more than the canons of logic specially applied or adapted to the relations of extension and force. This fact, however, does not justify in the slightest degree M. Comte's rejection of logic, and his assumption of mathematics as the only true canon of thought. He should, moreover, with his acknowledged mental acumen, have discovered that all the objections which he posits against logic lie with equal force against mathematics.

Sec. III.—The Categorical Imperative of Conscience.

A third form of intuitive judgment which demands notice here, is that known as "the categorical imperative of conscience," and is expressed under the formulas, "I ought to do the right"—"I ought not to do the wrong." These correlative judgments underlie the whole moral nature of man, and, conjoined to the moral emotions and impulses, constitute that complex element which we denominate conscience. This judgment, as an unquestionably universal and necessary element or product of consciousness, must be accepted as *authoritative* and *intuitive*, and as evolved, *a priori*, on its own proper occasions. It is the true intellectual element underlying the moral emotions, and always accompanying the intellectual perception of the right. It cannot be discredited save at the cost of discrediting consciousness and stultifying reason. Any attempt to discriminate between primitive judgments, with a view to accredit some and to discredit others, in obedience to the necessities of any pet theory in physics, metaphysics, or morals, is unphilosophic, and can only lead to deceptive results. So also the attempt to exclude conscience from the sphere of intellect, and relegate it exclusively to that of the sensibilities, is false in principle and fatal in practice; and that analysis of the facts of consciousness which fails to discover the categorical imperative of conscience among the primitive judgments, must be adjudged radically and dangerously incomplete.

PERCEPTION: SYNTHESIS OF ELEMENTS.

COGNITION.

CHAPTER I.—NATURE, CONDITIONS, AND LIMITATIONS OF COGNITION.

Section I.—Nature of Cognition.

The general nature and conditions of cognition or perception have already, perhaps, been sufficiently indicated in general terms; but logical precision demands that they should be discretely enunciated here, in a synthesis of sensation and intuition.

¶ I. **Definition of the Term.**—Cognition may be defined to be "perception or knowledge based upon the synthesis and coördination of sensation and intuition in consciousness." Its precise place in the hierarchy of mind is thus definitely fixed, and it is relieved from the vagueness and indistinctness that too often shadow it, even in the works of able psychologists. It is believed that the propriety of this definition, and of the corresponding classification which it involves, has been sufficiently vindicated in the previous discussions, and needs no further support here.

¶ II. **Nature of the Process.**—Perception, cognition, or knowledge—for here the words are used as strictly interchangeable—is the expression of that notice which the consciousness takes of the *actual*, whether in the material or the spiritual world, through sensation and intuition. It is a knowledge of the *now* and the *here*. That this is true of the objects of sense needs no further elucidation; that it is equally true of the objects of intuition, will readily appear by a slight analysis. If we consider the category of being, self and not-self are obviously cognized, now and here; and if we consider the third term, God, the Infinite Being, He can no otherwise be known than as *now* and *here*, since He can never be absent in space or time. If the category of limitation be considered, space and time are never absent; while cause, if known at all, must be known either in itself or in its effects, but in either case it must be known as present, since the cause is potentially, at least, present in its effects. If the category of relation be considered, the judgment cognized as true—the object perceived to be beautiful—and the relations adjudged right or good, must alike be present to the consciousness; i. e., they must be cognized now and here.

Sec. II.—Conditions of Cognition.

Our summary would be incomplete without a formal restatement of that which has already been sufficiently declared, namely, the essential elements or conditions of cognition, viz., sensation and intuition, and their relations to the process.

¶ I. **Sensation.**—The fact has been distinctly evolved, and scarcely needs to be reannounced, that sensation is the occasion rather than the essence of cognition. Its office is rather to awaken and call the intuitive powers of the soul into activity than to furnish the more important elements of thought. It is true, in a certain sense, that sensation is said to furnish the material elements of thought, but this is true only of thoughts relating to material things in the proper sense of the term, since consciousness itself must furnish all the true spiritual elements, which are not and cannot be objects of sense. If, however, doubts still remain in the mind of the thoughtful student, they can best be satisfied by a careful analysis of the facts of his own personal consciousness. For it must be distinctly remembered that consciousness is the only decisive authority, and the final court of appeal, in all questions of psychology; here, authorities are of little value.

¶ II. **Intuition.**—Intuition, the second element in cognition, might perhaps, with some degree of propriety, be identified with cognition itself, sustaining to it, as it does, the double relations of a source of materials, and of the efficient agent in the evolution of the resultant cognitions arising out of the synthesis of the sensation proper and the intuition proper. The fact has been already indicated that the intuition, or rather the consciousness, in its exercise of its intuitive powers, necessarily employs the processes of *comparison*, i. e., of the judgment, and of course, to a limited extent, of memory and imagination also. This, however, is only a new proof of the indivisible unity of consciousness, and of the exceedingly slender thread on which hangs the idea of independent mental faculties.

Sec. III.—Limitations of Cognition.

For like reasons pertaining to distinctness of conception, it is here necessary to restate, formally, the limitations of cognition, viz.:

1. In the material world, cognition is limited to the *now* in time, and the *here* in space.

2. In the spiritual world, it is limited strictly:

(*a*) To the facts of consciousness known immediately and directly as actual phenomena of the present moment; and—

(*b*) To primitive concepts and judgments spontaneously evolved by consciousness in the exercise of its intuitive powers. Whatever is not legitimately concluded under one or the other of these categories, is not a legitimate object of cognition.

SEC. IV.—VALIDITY OF COGNITION.

To the oft-raised and much-mooted question of the validity or credibility of cognition or perception, the simple and decisive answer is, that faith is necessary, and skepticism or doubt self-destructive, and therefore irrational:

1. That faith is necessary and unavoidable is proved by the fact that no skeptic, of any age or any land, ever did *realize* or *actualize*, in *practical life*, his *theoretical* skepticism.

2. That skepticism or doubt is irrational, is just as decisively proved by the fact that it proposes to invalidate consciousness, by the testimony of consciousness, a proceeding so irrational that to state it is to refute it.

Here the appeal to common-sense is decisive, and is equally conclusive against the philosopher and the ignoramus.

CHAPTER II.—RELATIONS OF COGNITION TO CONCEPTION AND BELIEF.

SECTION I.—RELATIONS OF COGNITION TO CONCEPTION.

¶ I. **How discriminated logically?**—Logically, cognition is discriminated from conception by its objects. The first, as we have seen, deals with the real, or actual, whether material or spiritual. The second deals solely with the *ideal*, as it is evolved in thought.

¶ II. **How discriminated chronologically?** — Chronologically, cognition is distinguished from conception by priority in time. *Presentative* necessarily precedes *representative* knowledge; albeit the interval between them, in the rapid flow of thought, can be measured only *in thought*, and *not in seconds*.

¶ III. **How discriminated actually?**—Actually, the two are wholly incommensurable. The conceivable is *not*, as is sometimes affirmed, the measure, either:

1. *Of the actual*, as known in consciousness; or,
2. *Of the knowable.*

That it is not the measure of *the actual*, each successive

step of advancing science proves; that which men *did not*, and *could not*, conceive *yesterday*, becomes actual *to-day*, and *to-morrow* becomes the starting-point of a new and higher evolution, and, in this respect, "that which hath been, is that which shall be."

That it is not the measure of *the knowable*, may not at first sight seem so obvious to some minds, which have been accustomed to reject the inconceivable, *a priori*, as at once impossible and unknowable. That a self-acting steam-engine is, *a priori*, an impossible conception to an ignorant savage in Central Africa, needs no proof; that the thing itself is impossible, or that it is unknowable by the same savage, when he is brought in actual contact with it, will not be asserted. The fallacy underlying the sophism that "the inconceivable is unknowable," chiefly results from absolutely identifying conception with imagination, on the one hand, and with knowledge, on the other; when, in fact, imagination is not coextensive with conception, and conception is not coextensive with knowledge, but is only *a mode* of knowledge. Imagination is, in the main, limited to the sphere of the material universe, and is not capable of grasping even that, in its entirety, while thought transcends the material, and grasps the still wider sphere of the spiritual. The truth is, the sophism is the resultant, not of psychological investigation, but of *a priori* theorizing.

Not to multiply words, it suffices to say that decisive proof that the *conceivable* is not the measure of the *knowable* is found in the well-known fact that the man born blind cannot *conceive* color, though its existence, as a fact, can be decisively revealed to him.

3. *It is, however, the measure of the comprehensible.*—Men may and do cognize, as facts, many things which they can neither *conceive* nor *comprehend.* In such cases, their knowledge is of a very tantalizing and unsatisfactory character, but it is not, therefore, unreal. Thus, the man born blind cannot comprehend color, the man born deaf cannot comprehend sound, and so of the rest; yet the facts and even the

laws of these phenomena are familiar to him. Said an intelligent gentleman once, in the presence of the writer: "I cannot *comprehend* what music is, I cannot distinguish one tune from another, and the sound of the filing of a saw is just as pleasant to me as the sound of a piano." Yet the man was not deaf, and he was well acquainted with the mathematical laws of music, but the thing itself was incomprehensible. Owing to some defect in his hearing, his imagination had no power to respond to his logical knowledge of the term music.

Sec. II.—Relations of Cognition to Belief.

¶ I. **How they are discriminated logically.**—Logically, cognition is discriminated from belief, by the fact that the *former* is an *immediate* knowledge, the *latter* is always *mediate*. Objects known in perception are known in their relations to the sensorium; objects known in belief, or by reasoning, are known only in and through other objects or conceptions previously known—i. e., they are *mediately* known.

¶ II. **How they are discriminated chronologically.**—Chronologically, perception or cognition precedes belief, and furnishes the data for the concepts which are compared in the propositions and the syllogisms upon which beliefs are based.

THE INTELLECT: ITS SECOND MOVEMENT.

CONCEPTION.

Preliminary Discussion.

Summary of Results.

¶ I. **Materials of Thought furnished in Perception.**—Our preceding discussions have evolved, clearly and sharply, the generic fact that all the materials of thought used in intellection, in any of its stages or processes, are furnished in perception either through sensation or intuition. It only remains to inquire how the consciousness reacts upon and fashions this material into formal concepts and evolves its several values, actual and potential, by the processes of reasoning.

¶ II. **Conditions of this Evolution.**—It is obvious that, in order to the evolution of all the actual and potential values of the materials of thought given in perception, two processes are indispensable, viz.:

1. That it shall be stored up in memory as in a mental treasury, ready at all times to be reproduced at the bidding of consciousness, like coin in the vaults of a bank; and—

2. That it shall be grasped, comprehended, and conceived in all its varied relations, actual and potential, by the processes of the imagination and the synthetic judgment; and thus reduced to the form of specific concepts, bearing much the same relation to the crude material of perception that the *coined* gold of the mint does to the *crude* bullion from the mine.

Section I.—Conditions and Limitations of the Concept.

¶ I. **Materials of the Concept.**—For materials, the concept depends upon the elements of thought furnished in perception and stored in memory. We conceive the *absent*, and not the *present*—the *remembered*, and *not* the *perceived* object. However widely the ideal world of thought is seen to differ from the actual, it is, as will appear more clearly in the sequel, dependent upon it for the elements upon which its ideals are based, thus reversing in man the processes of the Divine Mind, in which the ideal universe must have preceded the *real*, and the *possible* have pioneered the *actual*.

¶ II. **The Processes of Conception.**—The term "processes" is here used, determinately, instead of process, to mark the fact that conception is generically a synthesis of the diverse movements of imagination and the synthetic judgment. We say it is *generically* so, recognizing the fact that in some forms of the concept the presence of the imaginative element is *potential* rather than *actual;* conception therefore involves:

1. The processes of imagination, which acts upon the *sensible* material stored in memory, evolving from the *real*, as given in perception, its corresponding *ideal.*

2. The processes of the synthetic judgment, which acts upon the *rational* or *supersensible* material furnished in perception, originating its corresponding ideal.

A discrete remark must, here, be distinctly made, viz: that while imagination is, practically, limited to *sensible* objects, the synthetic judgment is not limited to the *supersensible*, but grasps the *sensible* with almost equal facility; and is involved in the evolution of every true logical concept, whether it represents the sensible or the rational.

¶ III. **Resultant Forms of the Concept.**—From the dual processes of imagination and judgment, two resultant forms of the concept emerge, viz.:

1. *Concepts of material objects and relations.*—These involve true mental pictures drawn by the plastic finger of fancy. This form of the concept may rest, practically, in this imaginative process, or it may be submitted to the complete logical processes of the synthetic judgment also, and may be termed, distinctively, *the comprehensible.*

2. *Concepts of non-material percepts ;* of which *no* mental picture is possible, giving rise to the knowable merely.

Sec. II.—The Office of the Concept.

¶ I. **To reduce our Percepts to Possession.**—The first and most obvious office of the concept is to reduce our percepts to possession, and make them available in our processes of intellection. The materials of perception much resemble a mass of crude ore from the mine, whose real value, as it lies in a heap in the treasure-house, is utterly indeterminate, and almost wholly unavailable; and, in precise analogy to the processes of the smelter and the assayer, are the processes of the imagination and judgment, to which the crude material of thought is subjected. Logical concepts are the stamped coin of the realms of thought.

¶ II. **To mediate their Forms.**—The second office of conception is to mediate the *forms* of our percepts, and prepare them for the use of the elaborative faculty and the processes of reason. True logical concepts alone meet the necessities of accurate syllogistic reasoning.

¶ III. **Conception the Measure of the Comprehensible only.** —The fact has been already sufficiently stated that conception is not the measure of either the actual or the knowable, but only of the comprehensible.

CONCEPTION: ITS FIRST ELEMENT.

MEMORY.

General Analysis.

¶ I. **Memory defined.**—Memory, like other primitive mental processes, is best known in the personal consciousness of its exercise, and needs, for its practical definition, little more than the use of such forms of words as will indicate to the student the distinctive process of consciousness sought to be defined. Scientifically, however, it demands such a collocation of terms as will, in thought, *include* all the essential elements of the complex act of consciousness, and *exclude* all others. It may, perhaps, with sufficient accuracy, be defined to be *that power or faculty of consciousness by which it retains, reproduces, or recollects, its own acts or affections.* At first thought, this limitation of memory *to acts and affections* of consciousness would seem to be too narrow; yet it cannot be extended, since other things, if remembered at all, are recollected only in and through the acts and affections of the personal consciousness. I recollect, for example, the parting words of a loved friend, only as they affected my personal consciousness, acting upon it through the organs of sense.

¶ II. **Analysis of an Act of Memory.**—In an act of memory, two parts or movements must be distinguished and noted, viz.:

1. *The act of retention*, in which consciousness grasps and

stores away, as part at least of its *potential* treasures, each act and affection of its own conscious being.

2. *The act of reproduction*, in which consciousness reproduces, in thought, the act or affection thus stored away. Reproduction, as an act of consciousness, obviously manifests itself under two distinct forms, viz.:

(*a*) *Involuntary*, in which the thing remembered is reproduced independently of the will, in obedience to what are termed the laws of association of ideas. This form is properly termed *remembrance.*

(*b*) *Voluntary*, in which the thing reproduced in thought is recalled in obedience to an act of the will, for some definite reason or purpose. This form is properly termed *recollection.*

Section I.—Retention.

¶ I. **Nature of Retention.**—This is sufficiently indicated by the term used, viz., "to retain," i. e., to grasp firmly, to hold. It expresses accurately the true psychological process involved. The fact is familiar, indeed almost commonplace, but the process, like all other elementary phenomena of consciousness, is utterly inscrutable and incomprehensible. It is in vain that cerebral physiologists tell us of the repetition of nervous vibrations, or of cerebral movements repeated until they have become habitual, or of movements once beginning that can never be lost. These and other like physiological theories, if the truth of such vibrations and pulsations were absolutely demonstrated, would solve no one of the mysteries that hang around the purely *psychical* process of retention. After such demonstration, we should be no more able to bridge the gulf between the physiological fact of the nervous or cerebral movement and the psychical fact of *retention*, than we are to close the chasm between the pictured image on the retina of the eye and the purely psychical sensation of color. The truth is, all speculation on the mode or philosophy of retention, from the stand-point of the science of to-day, is utterly futile; as to what the future may reveal, it is idle to speculate.

¶ II. **Conditions of Retention.**—These obviously are, formally at least, twofold in their character, pertaining, first, to the subjective consciousness; and, secondly, to the objective element or specific fact, or relation, or thing, remembered. We are to consider, therefore—

1. *The subjective elements:*

(*a*) *Natural inequality of mental power.* The natural inequality of the powers of memory in different individuals is so marked a phenomenon in human experience that it needs no proof, and is never controverted, save from the standpoint of some favorite *a priori* hypothesis of *the natural equality of men in all things*, which does not condescend to notice the actual phenomena of mind, only as it spends its strength in vainly attempting to account for the very great inequalities actually manifest among men apparently equal to each other in all other elements of mental power but this.

(*b*) *The power of attention.* Inattention is fatal to the power of retention; that which the mind fails *to grasp strongly*, it *cannot retain firmly;* but the mind can only grasp that strongly to which it attends closely. Every thoughtful student will, however, verify this truth so readily in his own experience that it is idle to offer illustrations of it here.

2. *The objective element*, i. e., *the thing remembered.*—Here the fact must be noted that a percept or thought is, as *a thing remembered*, a true *objective* element, having its own intrinsic character and relations, which determine, in part at least, the facility or difficulty with which it is retained. The facility of retention is, from the objective stand-point, proportioned to, or affected by:

(*a*) *The intrinsic character of the thing remembered.* The mistake must not here be made of confounding character with value, for some things of high intrinsic value seem to escape us, no matter how earnestly we desire to retain them; and some of no value whatever, or, on the contrary, perhaps hurtful and polluting, cling to us like the fatal shirt of Nessus, whether we will it or not. Character in the thing remembered, by the law of similarity or contrast, responds to the character of the mind, and thus the object is fastened in the memory.

(*b*) *The form of the thing remembered.* This is an element of great power, and its influence is, practically, but slightly comprehended. Two men may speak or write exactly the same thought in but slightly differing forms of words, and yet the one will, together with his thought, soon be forgotten; while the other will rivet his thought to the soul of his hearer or reader as with triple links of steel. Here the difference is simply one of the forms of expression, and depends but slightly, if at all, upon the interest of the hearer or reader. Thoughts or facts, in order to be retained, must be *individualized.*

(*c*) *The relations of the thing remembered.* Some things connect themselves more nearly with our habitual trains of thoughts—our feelings—our prejudices—or our interests—than others, and are consequently more readily retained. The relations here posited are not usually those of *intrinsic*, but of *factitious* interest; the boy will remember the funny story or filthy jest long after he has forgotten the problem of Euclid.

¶ III. **The Office of Retention.**—The office of retention as an element of memory has already been sufficiently declared in the preceding discussions. It is its central or basal element, and may not inaptly be termed the very key-stone of the arch of conscious intelligence. Strike this from the soul, and its existence becomes a meaningless blank, without past—without future—void of hope, and unconscious of fear. To such a being, life would not, and could not, attain to the dignity even of a dream.

Sec. II.—Reproduction.

¶ I. **Involuntary: Remembrance.**—Reproduction, or the reproductive power of memory, as already noted, appears under two forms, the *involuntary*, or simple *remembrance;*

and the *voluntary*, or *recollection.* Remembrance, as the basal form of reproduction, demands primary notice.

1. *Nature of remembrance.*—This process, as familiarly known in our daily consciousness, may be defined to be the recurrence spontaneously, in thought, of mental acts and affections experienced in past life. Their appearance, however, though independent of personal volition, is not fortuitous, but is regulated by well-ascertained laws.

2. *Conditions of remembrance.*—The generic conditions of remembrance, viz., the laws of association of ideas, have already been noted. It only remains to evolve their several forms, and to determine their psychologic import and relations.

The general principle involved is this: "All experience proves it to be a law of mind that one thought is so related to another that, when one is reproduced voluntarily or involuntarily, it instantly recalls others in some way related to it." Our thoughts are not stored away in memory, as independent isolated entities, like ears of corn in a crib, but as chains bound together, link by link, according to determinate laws. Psychologists have sought to determine these laws and reduce them to their ultimate principles, and various statements and reductions of them have been made; practically, perhaps, the following is as satisfactory as any other, viz.:

(*a*) *Contiguity of time or place.* The simple principle here involved is this: two objects or thoughts cognized in relations of contiguity of time or place, naturally tend to suggest or recall each other in memory. For example, the writer, when a boy of eleven years of age, was called upon to make a long journey alone, on horseback, over the then almost uninhabited prairies of Illinois. In connection with certain peculiar landmarks of lonely trees and isolated groves, certain trains of thought passed through his mind. Years elapsed ere he passed over that road again, and these trains of thought had long been forgotten, amid the sterner realities of manhood, until, at length, he looked upon those lonely trees and groves again, and the long-buried trains of boyish thought came back, fresh and vivid as things of yesterday. Here the link was obviously simple contiguity of place.

(*b*) *Resemblance or contrast.* A second law of association is based upon the correlative laws of resemblance and contrast. A face or a person seen to-day recalls by its resemblance an acquaintance of other years; so, on the other hand, one fact or object suggests or recalls another, in virtue of the strong contrast existing between them; a very short man recalls a very tall one, and *vice versa.* Instances of both forms or modes of the law may readily be multiplied to any desirable extent. The relations of resemblance and contrast, though apparently diverse, are generically one, since the knowledge of contradictories is one.

(*c*) *Cause and effect.* The third law of association may fitly be denominated the law of cause and effect, as it is based essentially upon that familiar relation. Some psychologists have preferred the wider terms reason and consequent, but the difference is really unimportant, since, in an ultimate analysis, cause and effect are the real elements involved. The presence of a cause or reason naturally suggests the idea of its effect or consequent, and *vice versa.*

As we have before remarked, various attempts have been made to reduce these laws to a single generic form, with more or less of apparent success; but one fatal defect attends every hypothesis thus far presented, namely: the proposed single law fails to account for the actual phenomena with the readiness and clearness that the separate laws do, and can only be applied to account for certain special cases, by the exercise of an amount of logical ingenuity not at the command of the tyro in psychology. The utility of the proposed reductions is not, therefore, very evident.

¶ **II. Voluntary: Recollection.**—Voluntary reproduction, or recollection, introduces into the problem of memory a new factor, the human will, which decisively changes its conditions and relations, and demands consequently explicit examination.

1. *Conditions of the process.*—In remembrance, the stores of memory are recalled casually, in an order dependent, partly upon the subjective states, and partly upon the accidental objective relations of the personality; but in recollection, the attempt is made to recall such memories only as are adapted to the present wants of the consciousness. An analysis of an act of voluntary memory, or recollection, reveals the following elements, viz.:

(*a*) A present conscious want or need of a particular fact or train of thought.

(*b*) A consciousness, more or less distinct, that such a fact or train of thought is laid aside among the treasures of memory; and—

(*c*) A voluntary nisus, or effort, to recall the desired fact or thought, by the aid of the laws of association of ideas. It is obvious that, without at least a partial actual grasping of the thing wanted, in memory, there could be no consciousness of its existence and no attempt to recall it. Nor is it difficult to account for the presence of this vague consciousness: the very mental necessity which demands the recall of the desired fact or thing, tends, in obedience to the laws of association and remembrance, to suggest it to the mind, and thus bring it to the notice of consciousness, and under the power of the will.

2. *Methods of recollection.*—These vary widely with different individuals, but are, in general, a voluntary application of the laws of association of ideas. Thus, for example, if we wish to recall the name of an individual, we may fix our thoughts upon the names of his friends, upon the places where we have met him, upon occurrences with which he has been connected; or, failing these, if we remember the initial letter of his name, we may recall all the names we can recollect beginning with that letter, and so of other methods which it were idle to enumerate. The one principle common to them all is a voluntary application of the laws of association of ideas.

Sec. III.—Power of Memory.

¶ I. **Capacity of Memory.**—There seems practically to be scarcely any limit to the capacity of memory. Seneca, the Roman philosopher, tells us that he could repeat two thousand names, read to him a single time, in the order in which they were given. Muretus tells us of a learned Corsican who actually repeated an almost incredible number of words, Latin, Greek, barbarous, significant and non-significant, disjoined and connected, which were repeated to him only a single time; and not only so, but he also repeated them in the alternate order, giving the first, third, fifth, and so on, without a single mistake. This man claimed that he could thus repeat thirty-six thousand words. It is related of the celebrated Blaise Pascal, that, "until the decay of his health had impaired his memory, he forgot nothing of what he had done, read, or thought, in any part of his rational age." These are extraordinary cases, that scarcely recur in centuries, yet no observant student will fail to recall, in the circle of his own observation, instances of remarkable powers of memory, strikingly illustrating the topic under discussion.

¶ II. **Varieties of Memory.**—The varieties of memory are manifold, although they are the permutations of but a few simple elements. Some minds respond more readily to one law of association, and some to another; while others respond with equal readiness to all. Some memories are marked by their great tenacity of retention, although their processes may be slowly elaborated; while others are quite as distinctly noticeable for their readiness and their unreliable character.

The memory of the youth differs in its qualities and characteristics from that of the adult, and both differ from the memory of the aged. These differences obviously depend chiefly upon the complex relations of the soul to the physical organism, and are affected largely by its growth, maturity, and decay.

Curious instances of partial memory sometimes present

themselves to the psychologist, in which certain special groups of facts are grasped eagerly, retained tenaciously, and reproduced readily, while others, seemingly more important, elude the mind altogether. Such cases must be accounted for in part by the influence of the laws of attention, and in part by personal idiosyncrasies, not as yet clearly comprehended.

¶ III. **Is any Thing ever wholly forgotten?**—A question of some practical interest emerges here, namely: "Is any thing ever wholly forgotten?" It is obvious, in the outset, that no absolute affirmative answer is possible; but the fact must be noted that "the preponderance of testimony is decidedly in favor of the negative hypothesis." Numerous well-attested instances are on record of persons rescued from drowning, who, during the brief moments of strangulation preceding insensibility, recalled, as in a panoramic view, the whole record of their past lives, including incidents and acts forgotten for years. So, also, the celebrated Dr. Rush tells of Swedish and German immigrants to Pennsylvania, who, in middle life, lost all knowledge of their native languages, so that they could neither speak nor understand them; but who, in the decrepitude of their second childhood, recurred to their long-lost native tongues, and who, in some cases, could then neither speak nor understand any other. These, and other similar cases that might be quoted, strongly confirm the hypothesis that nothing which man has ever known can be finally forgotten, and that the waters of oblivion are, *in fact*, as in form, a poet's dream.

SEC. IV.—CULTIVATION OF MEMORY.

Any discussion of the phenomena of memory which fails to note its susceptibility to culture, is radically defective in view of its intrinsic importance as an essential element of mental power. It is true that the hypothesis has sometimes been advanced with much earnestness, that "great powers of memory are inconsistent with real mental strength or greatness." When, however, the facts are analyzed upon which the hypothesis rests, they indicate, fairly interpreted, nothing more than this, that great powers of memory may coexist with moderate powers of intellection, while no fact is better ascertained than that many of the greatest minds earth has ever produced were not less remarkable for their powers of memory than for other intellectual excellences. Their brilliant memories are ordinarily unnoticed, simply because they are eclipsed by the magnificence of their higher rational faculties.

¶ I. **Artificial Systems of Memory.**—Mnemonics, or the science of memory, has at times attracted much attention, and various systems of artificial memory have been devised, based upon one or more of the laws of association of ideas, by which men have been enabled to remember more perfectly special facts or classes of facts; but these special modes are not available for the ordinary uses of memory, and it may fairly be questioned whether equal care and pains devoted to the general cultivation of the faculty itself would not practically yield more valuable results.

¶ II. **True Principles involved in the Culture of Memory.**—True scientific culture of the memory is based upon a thorough comprehension of its laws, especially of the laws of association, and upon an intelligent exercise or discipline of its powers. These two elements, in their complete synthesis, are indispensable to the perfection of the result. Science alone cannot make the artist, nor yet will mere muscular skill and flexibility of manipulation suffice; so he that would develop to the utmost his powers of memory must first comprehend its laws, and then reduce his knowledge to practice by untiring effort. One fact must not be overlooked: he who would have a *good* memory must trust it; and not only so, he must *compel* it to respond to his demands upon it. He who trusts to pen or pencil, rather than to memory in its legitimate sphere, will soon have nothing else to rely upon.

CONCEPTION: ITS SECOND ELEMENT.

IMAGINATION.

SECTION I.—NATURE AND RELATIONS OF THE IMAGINATION.

¶ I. **Analysis of an Act of Imagination.**—Imagination is, essentially, an *act*, and *not an affection.* It grasps the materials presented to it, holds them up in new lights and new relations, combines and recombines them, seizes upon every single element presented to it in the complex wholes of perception, and evolves them anew in forms, relations, and combinations, unknown in the *actual* world, and thus creates its own peculiar world of the *ideal.*

¶ II. **Materials of Imagination.**—For the materials necessary to its processes, imagination depends *immediately* upon memory, *remotely* upon perception. We imagine the *absent, not* the *present.* We *perceive* the thing at which we look—we *imagine* the thing which we remember. Imagination, therefore, may without impropriety be defined to be, in its *lowest* sense, mental vision of the absent or the distant. In its higher sense, it may be defined to be mental vision of the *ideal* or *possible*, as contradistinguished from the *actual.* The fact must, however, be distinctly noted, that imagination is incapable of *absolute creation*, i. e., of originating *new material*, as well as new forms of thought. It cannot evolve a new element not derived, in fact or form, from perception through memory.

¶ III. **Its Relations to other Faculties.**—The relations of imagination to memory and perception have already been sufficiently declared. It remains only to note its relations to the processes of judgment and reasoning. For these, its office is to mediate the materials furnished by perception. The soul needs to know, not merely *what is*, in the limited sphere of cognition present to its senses, but also *what may be*, in the wider sphere of the ideal, in order to satiate its God-given thirst for the true, the beautiful, and the good. He, therefore, who speaks slightingly of imagination, only betrays his own ignorance of its real functions in the realms of thought, and of the glorious possibilities which it reveals to man.

SEC. II.—OFFICE OF THE IMAGINATION.

¶ I. **To mediate the Form of the Percept.**—This process has already been indicated in general terms, but must here be marked and discriminated more specifically. It presents itself, in the phenomena of mind, under two forms, depending upon the nature of the materials used in the mental evolution, viz.:

1. *It involves or includes the formation of a true mental picture or representation of objects* (i. e., *of sensible objects*) *known in perception.*—We thus readily recall the face of an absent friend, a familiar landscape, or the parts of a complex machine; and the remark has often been made, with a keen philosophic perception of this special function of imagination, that "a man can describe a landscape more graphically, from the vision of it in imagination, than from actual present perception of it." The reason is, imagination seizes upon precisely those salient features of it which are best fitted to represent it in words to a person who has never seen it, and omits all minor details which serve in the actual landscape only to confuse and perplex him who attempts to describe it from his actual present perception of it.

2. *It involves or includes the formation of a notion or idea of supersensible objects and relations which do not admit of representation in a true ideal or mental picture.*—The line of demarcation is here so narrow between the *imaginative* and the *logical* concept, that it is difficult to discriminate them, articulately; nevertheless, the existence of a true imaginative concept is indisputable. Such ideals, as honor, courage, virtue, etc., etc., are too well known to need other than simple mention, in order to their recognition, and they are not, in any sense, mental pictures of sensible objects; nor are they, on the other hand, mere logical concepts

resulting from the abstract processes of the synthetic judgment. The absolute limitation of imagination to sensible objects, sometimes affirmed, cannot, therefore, be accepted as legitimate. The error probably originated in the fact that imagination, in the sense of a *mental picture* or vision of an object, is possible only of sensible objects.

¶ II. **To evolve from the World of the Actual given in Perception the World of the Ideal.**—The range of thought here opened is a very wide one, including alike the dreams of the painter, the sculptor, the mechanist, the poet, the novelist, and the moralist, in a word—

> "All those charms and virtues which we dare
> Conceive in boyhood and pursue as men,
> The unreached paradise of our despair."

It touches every field of human thought, throws its resplendent light around every human conception, glorifies alike the poet's dream of earth and the Christian's dream of heaven. It is an equally welcome visitant to the cottage of the peasant, the palace of the king, the study of the sage, and the cell of the devotee. It is equally indispensable to the highest results of mechanism, of art, of science, of literature, of morality, and of Christianity.

SEC. III.—RELATIONS OF THE IDEAL TO THE REAL.

¶ I. **Of the Idea to its Object.**—The problem of the relation of an idea to its object has perplexed metaphysicians for ages, and has given rise to almost endless theories and disquisitions. Some have affirmed the identity of the two, making the idea nothing more than a sensible material image of the object, taken up by the organ of sense, and in some incomprehensible way cognized by it. Such theorizers strangely ignore the fact that the perception of one material object by the mind is just as incomprehensible as that of another, and that these figments of sensation, if their existence were demonstrated, could solve none of the mysteries of the process.

Others have affirmed that the idea or concept is a picture of the external object as it actually exists, independently of our perception of it. This hypothesis, however, cannot, in the present state of science, be maintained. Light or color, as an *objective* reality, and light or color as *cognized* by the soul, are two totally different things. Science is rapidly tending to a demonstration that the one is nothing more than a peculiar vibration of a medium (an aura, or ether) diffused through all space, a something which has no resemblance whatsoever to the subjective phenomena which we recognize in consciousness as light or color.

The truth would seem to be, therefore, that the idea or concept is a simple mental picture of the percept, whose relations to the external object we have already sought to determine. In other words, the concept is a mental picture of the *external* object, *not as it is in itself, or per se, but as it is mediated by the percept.*

¶ II. **Of the Ideal to Science.**—The term science is here obviously taken in its most comprehensive sense; and the generic fact that demands discrete enunciation is, *that imagination is indispensable to the processes of true science.* Mathematics may here be fitly taken as the analogue of all the sciences in this relation; and the uses of imagination in its processes are so obvious as scarcely to need illustration. The most noticeable fact, for example, that attracts our attention, as we open a work on geometry and analyze its pages, is, that the points, lines, angles, curves, etc., etc., with which the geometer deals, are all *ideal.* The truth is self-evident that it is beyond the power of man to actually describe a geometrical point, line, angle, or curve. Geometry *as a science* is, therefore, *purely ideal;* and the same is true, if possible, in a still higher sense, of the calculus, which has been not unfitly denominated the poetry of mathematics. The same laws of evolution apply to philosophy, astronomy, and all the other sciences, though the facts may be less obtrusive. The use of hypotheses in science may, in fact, be thus accounted for, and is itself an apt illustration of the value of the ideal element in the evolution of the *exact sciences.*

III. **Of the Ideal to Art.**—The term is here, likewise, used in its broadest generic sense, to include industry, mechanism, architecture, sculpture, painting, poetry, and music. Into each and all of these the ideal enters as an element of the highest practical import, as at once a stimulus and an aid to successful effort. The relation of the ideal to æsthetic art is so obvious that it needs no comment; but its relations to mechanism and to practical industry are not less real nor less important. Take the inventor, for example, who seeks to apply the laws of Nature, by the aid of machinery, to productive use, and imagination, i. e., the constructive or creative power of thought, is not less indispensable to him than it is to the poet. The imagination of Watt, the inventor of the steam-engine, was not less wonderful than that of Milton, albeit it found its exercise in conceiving in thought the relations of boiler, cylinder, piston, lever, pulley, etc., etc., in that wonderful creation of mind, the steam-engine. The grand creations of modern industry existed as ideals in the soul before they were actualized in the wood, the iron, and the brass, just as "Paradise Lost" existed in the imagination of the great poet before it was transferred to paper, or as the dome of St. Peter's dwelt a thing of beauty and sublimity in the soul of Michael Angelo before it spanned nave and transept in Rome's grandest temple.

¶ IV. **Of the Ideal to Morals and Faith.**—"The relations of the ideal to the real become yet more intensively important when we pass to the spheres of morals and faith, i. e., into those relations which man as an intelligent moral agent sustains to his fellow-man and to his God." Here the soul, in its purest, noblest, loftiest flights, in its most earnest efforts, and in its most glorious victories, is but struggling upward to *an ideal*, purer, nobler, higher, more sublime, than man has ever actualized—the ideal of God, and of the life of God—in the soul of man. It has been well said that no man is better than his faith, and it need hardly be added that his faith, in this sense, is but his ideal of humanity and God; I say, of humanity and God, for not only are the terms strictly correlative in the spheres of morals and faith, but the corresponding fact must be noted that we conceive the infinite only in its correlation to the finite.

It may not be amiss to add that imagination, in another aspect, is a powerful element in the moral and religious life of the individual. He who has but little power (like the man of feeble imagination) to individualize and actualize, in thought, the purely *moral* and *spiritual* relations of man, is necessarily a man of but feeble moral impulses and of wavering faith. On the contrary, the man who has the power of vitalizing and actualizing those conceptions—the purest and loftiest that ever move the soul—until they dwell within him with an intensity of life that overbears the lower and meaner impulses of the physical nature, dwells in love, for he dwells in God, and God in him. Nor is there room for the cavil here, that this is to idealize God and a future world; for it is the resultant of a complementary truth, that we know even the *material* world only as we idealize it; and that our perception of the *spiritual* world, through intuition, is just as direct, just as comprehensible, and just as valid, as our cognition of the material world through sensation. For, if man is *half dust*, and therefore allied to *material* things, he is *half deity*, and therefore allied to *spiritual* things. In the relations, therefore, of the *material* to the *spiritual*, imagination finds its most glorious realm, where, transcending reason in its loftiest flights, it dwells in light ineffable, hard by the throne of God and the Lamb.

Sec. IV.—Is the Imagination a Creative Faculty?

The question is often mooted, Is the imagination a creative faculty? Its solution is easy, if the fact is kept steadily in view that the terms "create" and "creation" are used in a double sense: 1. To indicate absolute creation both of *matter* and *form;* and, 2. To indicate *relative* creation; that is, the evolution of *new forms* from preëxisting materials. In the first sense of the term, it is obvious that imagination *is not* a creative faculty; it has no power to call into being *totally new* elements of thought. In this respect it cannot transcend the sphere of perception, through sensation and intuition, from which it derives all the elements of its grand creations. If we analyze, critically, the most aberrant fantasies of the dreamer or the madman, we shall fail to discover any new element of thought whatsoever.

In the second and derivative sense of the term "create," it is just as obvious that imagination is a creative faculty; and that the soul is filled with *ideals*, of which the *real* has never furnished the pattern. Nor is there room to say that such a limitation of imagination dwarfs it, and robs it of its brightest jewels. It does not, since it leaves it the three grand concepts of man, the universe, and God, as the inexhaustible factors of its glorious creations; and eternity itself shall not suffice it for a duration in which it may exhaust their values, and sit down to weep, Alexander-like, because it has no more worlds to conquer.

Sec. V.—Culture of the Imagination.

¶ I. **Value of the Imagination.**—In the light of the preceding discussions, but little need be said additionally, in reference to the value of imagination as an element of thought; he only is likely to undervalue it who is ignorant of its true relations to the higher processes of mind. That its functions may be abused, is the necessary correlate condition of its use as a *human* faculty. We know, alas! by bitter experience, that there is no gift of God to man so pure, so noble, so exalted, or so perfect, that he cannot abuse it. Ordinarily, the liability to abuse is in direct proportion to the intrinsic value of the element when legitimately used. That imagination, therefore, is peculiarly liable to be abused, is only a demonstration, on the one hand, of its intrinsic value, and, on the other, of the imperative necessity that its abuse should be forestalled and prevented by true scientific culture.

¶ II. **Conditions of its Evolution and Perfection.**—The imagination, like other faculties of the mind, is amenable to the influences of culture, and the results attained in any specific case will be in direct proportion:

1. To the philosophic adaptation of the method of culture to the end proposed; and—

2. To the skill and perseverance with which the chosen methods are carried out in practice.

In the first case, the philosophic educator will discriminate accurately between *general* and *special* culture. The wide range of the faculty itself, as indicated in our previous discussions, should be a check upon the hasty inductions so frequently made, that this or that person has *no* imagination, because he has no taste for poetry, music, or some other æsthetic art. His imagination may be *special*, and not *general*, and in its own peculiar field may possess extraordinary power and fertility. True *special* education of the imagination, philosophically considered, should be based upon the *general*, and should be scientifically adapted to the special forms of the faculty which it is proposed to develop. He, for example, who would develop the æsthetic imagination, must study the masterpieces of poetry, painting, sculpture, architecture, music, etc., etc.; while he who would cultivate a scientific or mechanical imagination, must familiarize himself with the grand creations of this wonderful faculty in these scarcely less fruitful fields.

¶ III. **Limits of its Capacity.**—Here no limits can be fixed. God *may* have said to the human imagination, "Thus far shalt thou go, and no farther," but, if He has, we know not where He has fixed the line. Practically, to man, the *ideal* world is infinite in extent, as it is in beauty and richness.

CONCEPTION: ITS THIRD ELEMENT.

THE SYNTHETIC JUDGMENT.

Preliminary Discussion.

SUMMARY OF RESULTS AND ANALYSIS OF RELATIONS.

¶ I. **Incompleteness of the Ideal Concept.**—The ideal concept, as contradistinguished from the logical, is marked by its *individuality* and *consequent incompleteness.* The imagination deals exclusively with the *concrete;* it does not and cannot represent the *abstract* or *general.* Thus I can imagine this, that, or the other individual man, readily and exactly, but *I cannot imagine*, though *I can conceive*, the genus man apart from any individual man. Here the primary distinction between the *ideal* and the *logical* concept emerges at once into consciousness.

¶ II. **Numerical Variety and Complexity of our Percepts.**—The *numerical* variety of our individual percepts is almost endless, and the attempt to grasp them all by simple enumeration and discrete examination would be almost fruitless, and quite hopeless. Life is too short and memory too weak for the multiplied burdens which must rest upon them, if the ideal concept were the ultimate form under which mind must deal with, and act upon, the wealth of material it acquires in perception. Memory must sink back overwhelmed, and reason recoil in despair from the attempts to grasp this indefinite and ever-increasing multitude of *singular* objects.

¶ III. **Influence of Poverty of Language.**—Were it possible, which it is not, for memory and reason to deal with this multitude of percepts in their individuality and isolation, there is another and perhaps insuperable difficulty in the way, viz., *the poverty of language.* It would be impracticable, if not impossible, to supply *individual*, i. e., *proper* names, for the multitude of objects known in perception. Without endorsing the more than problematic hypothesis that man can only think in words (an hypothesis sufficiently disproved by the fact that men born deaf and dumb do think prior to education, technically so called, and hence prior to any knowledge of words), the truth may safely be admitted that continuous, extended, and fruitful trains of thought are necessarily mediated by words, or language, and that every individual percept must sooner or later be fixed by an appropriate sign, in order to its preservation in memory, its representation in imagination, and its analytic development by the varied processes of the reasoning faculty proper. Hence we infer the necessity of a new mental evolution to mediate between the individuality of the *ideal* concept and the *generality* of the processes of analytic reasoning.

¶ IV. **Evolution of the Processes of the Synthetic Judgment.**—Corresponding to this *a priori* necessity of thought, we recognize the fruitful actual processes of what has been termed the synthetic judgment, viz., *abstraction*, *generalization*, and *classification*, whereby the mind is able, from its multitude of individual percepts, to evolve a comparatively limited number of *genera* and *species*, and thus reduce their multiplicity and variety to the unity of a few comprehensible logical concepts. The poverty of language is, at the same time, obviated by our power of applying a few specific names to many individuals, and a few generic names to many species.

Section I.—Abstraction.

¶ I. **Analysis of the Process.**—The very familiarity of this process is the sole cause of the difficulty that seemingly inheres in the statement of it. Every thoughtful student will readily recognize it among the daily phenomena of his own experience, so soon as the meanings of the terms used are brought home to his consciousness. In considering any complex object of perception, we are conscious of a tendency to fix the attention upon one attribute, or set of attributes, to the neglect or exclusion of others, equally or perhaps more important intrinsically. So, also, if several objects are presented to us simultaneously or successively, we naturally fix our attention upon those attributes in which they agree, or *vice versa*, and neglect or exclude the rest. In either case we realize the process of abstraction in our actual consciousness. Metaphysicians have refined upon the question whether the attributes attended to, or those excluded, are the ones that are properly abstracted; but the question has little or no significance, and is wholly one of propriety of language.

¶ II. **Final Cause and Relations of the Process.**—The final cause of this process is, obviously, the simplification of the processes of human thought, by the rejection of useless factors, which do not vary or affect the results reached in the particular instance. Without at all endorsing the popular heresy, that "the mind can attend to but one thing at a time," the fact may be postulated that the clearness and precision of our mental operations is, in proportion, inversely to the number of factors involved. Abstraction enables us, in this respect, to reduce any given problem to its minimum, by exscinding all attributes or conditions not relevant to its solution. This is an item of no slight importance in the development of thought and the complex evolutions of science.

Sec. II.—Generalization.

¶ I. **Analysis of the Process.**—Abstraction, as we have seen, is not in itself an end, but a means to an end. In its first and mediate result, it leads to the formation of a peculiar class of words, called *abstract* words. Technically, they are nouns, i. e., names, but they differ from ordinary nouns in this respect, that they are not the names of things or objects, but of attributes or properties of things. We reach them by the processes of abstraction described in the previous section, i. e., by neglecting certain attributes and fixing the attention on one or more of the remainder, the color, for example; and we then generalize this concept by the recognition of the fitness of the term representing it, to be applied as a common name to an attribute inhering in many different bodies. We thus pass from the concrete colored object to the abstract noun color, or the abstract adjective colored; and then, extending our thought one step farther, by a process of simple comparison of object with object, we attain to the conception that this abstract name is *generic*, i. e., that it represents a class of objects which, however much they may differ in other respects, agree in this, that they possess color. We have thus taken a second decisive step in the process of systematizing and simplifying our knowledge.

¶ II. **Final Cause and Relations of the Process.**—The final cause of the process of generalization has been already indicated. It is a second approximation to unity of thought, by seizing upon an abstract term representing a single attribute of a concrete object, and applying it as a common name or mark to many objects possessing this common attribute. A basis is thus laid for the next step in this logical process; namely, classification, which seizes upon the generalized abstract noun, as a mark or indice of separation, and divides all known objects, under the canon of contradiction, as possessing or not possessing this attribute.

Sec. III.—Classification.

¶ I. **Analysis of the Process.**—The process of classification, whether popular or scientific, is simple and direct. It seizes upon some attribute recognized as equally belonging to a plurality of objects, and reduces them to *unity* by their synthesis under this name taken as a common appellative. In the *popular* process, the similarity recognized is usually independent of any underlying philosophical principle, and the unity attained is *empirical* only. In the *scientific* process, the mind seizes upon some *essential* attribute or attributes, and applies that (or them) as a touchstone to the successive objects cognized, ranging under the proposed class all such as possess the common mark, however much they may differ in other respects, and excluding all others, however much they may resemble these in their other attributes. For example, if we start with the single word "thing" or "things," and conjoin to it the single attribute "existence," we at once include under it all *material* existence whatsoever. If we conjoin to that a second attribute, "organic," we exclude from the new or derivative class all *inorganic* things. If we conjoin a third attribute, "living," we again exclude a class, viz., *unvitalized* or *dead* organisms. If we conjoin a fourth attribute, "animate," we exclude the whole vegetable world. If we conjoin a fifth attribute, "rational," we again exclude more than a moiety of the whole. The process may thus be continued, in thought at least, till a final class is reached that shall consist of only a single individual. In this process, beginning with the highest class, i. e., with thing, being, existence, we denominate this the *summum genus*, predicating of it only a single attribute, viz., bare existence. When, however, we predicate a second attribute, we part this summum genus into the two proximate species, viz., organic and inorganic beings, existences, or things. Neglecting the second for the time being, we predicate of the first, i. e., of organic being, a third attribute, and thus part this proximate species of being, which now becomes a genus, into two proximate species, viz., living and not-living organisms. Again, neglecting the second, and applying the fourth attribute to the genus "living organisms," we part it into two proximate species, animate and inanimate; and so to the last, i. e., to a class containing only a single individual, which is the infima species.

Three distinct derivative concepts emerge from this analysis, viz., the extension, the comprehension, and the denomination of concepts, which will be considered in detail in the sequel, but which must be, meantime, distinctly noted here, viz.:

1. *Extension.*—This refers to and expresses the number of individuals or proximate species which a genus may include.

2. *Comprehension.*—This relates to and expresses the number of marks or attributes used to define a genus; as the attribute "existence" used to mark the summum genus "being" or "thing."

3. *Denomination.*—This refers to and expresses the pro-

cesses of naming a genus or species according to the marks or signs which part it from its proximate genus, on the one hand, and its proximate species, on the other.

¶ II. **General Principles of Classification.**—Certain general principles and relations emerge from this analysis, viz.:

1. Our knowledge, in all cases, begins with the *concrete;* i. e., with the individual person or thing. We first know, not man as a species, but this or that particular man. The child who first knows pa and ma, is apt to apply those names to the next man and woman it sees.

2. Our earlier classifications are necessarily rude, confounding genera and species, including many things that should be excluded, and, *vice versa*, excluding many things that should be included.

3. The number of conceivable species between the summum genus and the infima species is indefinite, if not infinite. We cannot, therefore, starting from the summum genus, actually reach the infima species.

CONCEPTION: SYNTHESIS OF ELEMENTS.

THE CONCEPT.

Section I.—Its Nature and Relations.

¶ I. **Relation of the Concept to the Percept.**—The relation of the concept to the percept has been incidentally declared in the preceding discussions; distinctness, however, demands their formal reënunciation here. Its relations may be marked as follows:

1. In time, the concept is posterior to the percept, inasmuch as it is dependent upon it for its material.

2. In extension, it is superior to it; i. e., it is applicable to many individuals, while every percept is, necessarily, individual.

3. In comprehension, it is inferior to it; i. e., more marks or attributes are united in a concept representing an indi-

vidual, or thing, than are included in the concept of the species containing that individual, or thing.

4. It is dependent upon it for representation in imagination. That faculty can grasp and represent only the *concrete*, and *not the abstract—the individual*, and *not the general*—this or that man, and not simply man as a species. But the first terms of these several couplets are distinctively percepts, the second, concepts; the latter are, therefore, dependent upon the former for representation in imagination.

¶ II. **Equivocal Use of the Term Concept.**—The term concept has been used in a variety of senses and with diverse limitations by different authors; and, from the poverty of language, the same author is compelled to use the term as the representative of different mental entities, as the imaginative and logical concepts. It is in this treatise used to express:

1. The percept as simply reproduced in memory.
2. As represented in imagination; and—
3. As logically evolved under the critical forms of the synthetic judgment, conditioned upon the processes of the imagination.

It is obvious that this threefold use involves a recognition of a *generic* and *specific* relation between the three forms, in which the last, as including both the others, alone expresses the idea in its generic completeness.

Sec. II.—Powers and Properties of Concepts.

The general properties of concepts, viz., extension, intension, and denomination, have already been noted, but may fitly receive more discrete examination here.

¶ I. **Extension of the Concept.—Division.**—1. *Its relations.* Extension has already been defined to be the relation of the concept to the number of individuals or species to which it may legitimately be applied. If we fix our thought upon the summum genus, that is, simple existence, it obviously includes all things, God and the universe, taken in their widest, i. e., in their *absolute* sense. On the other hand, in the infima species, the concept includes only individuals, which agree in the common possession of all conceivable attributes of being. In the summum genus, therefore, extension is at its maximum, while in the infima species it is at its minimum.

2. *Its resultant process. Division.*—This consists in the enumeration of the various coördinate species of which a proximate genus is composed. This process is one of much importance in the evolutions of science, and especially of natural history, where it receives its fullest and richest development. The rules governing this process may be stated as follows:

(*a*) The division must be made according to some single definite principle or ground.

(*b*) The constituent species, or dividing members, must exclude one another; and—

(*c*) The sum of the dividing members must exactly equal, taken together, the concept divided.

The reason of these rules is so obvious as scarcely to require discussion. Violation of the first involves utter failure of the entire process, and inextricable confusion of terms. Violation of the second involves the absurdity of cross-classification. Violation of the third gives us a whole unequal to the sum of all its parts.

¶ II. **Intension of the Concept.—Definition.**—Under the intension of the concept are included all questions of the comprehension and definition of the terms used.

1. *Comprehension.*—This, as we have previously noted, expresses the number of marks or attributes which distinguish a species from its proximate and remote genera. It must be discriminated from its proximate genus by at least one attribute, and from its remote genus by two or more. The intension of a concept is thus at its maximum in the infima species, and its minimum in the summum genus, and is, therefore, in *inverse* proportion to its extension. From this stand-point, again, it becomes obvious that, practically, if not theoretically, the infima species must coincide with the individual, or thing.

2. *Definition of the concept.*—This is nothing more than a formal enunciation of the actual intension of the concept, and is usually expressed, logically, by assigning the proximate genus which includes the concept to be defined, and the specific difference which separates it from that genus. Its rules may be enunciated as follows:

(*a*) A definition must enumerate all the essential attributes of the concept, and none other.

(*b*) *A definition must be adequate*, i. e., it must be narrow enough to exclude all species below, and wide enough to include all genera above. The fact must here be remembered distinctly that intension and extension are in *inverse* proportion to each other; that, in the infima species, intension is at its maximum, and extension at its minimum; and that, in the summum genus, extension is at its maximum, and intension at its minimum—consequently, the comprehension of a genus is less, i. e., narrower, than that of its proximate species.

(*c*) *A definition must be positive*, since the number of negative determinants is, or may be, infinite.

¶ III. **Denomination of the Concept.**—A concept is not complete until it is fixed in an appropriate mark or name. Until this is done, it is transient, and liable at any time to be lost from consciousness and memory. When, however, it is fixed in an appropriate mark, or name, it becomes, like the crude bullion under the processes of the mint, ready for immediate practical use, without the necessity of reëxamining the original processes by which it was first evolved. The discussion, technically, of names as such, is grammatical and logical, rather than psychological, and must, therefore, be discounted here. It suffices us to show the general relations of names and language to the processes of thought; for, while it must be admitted that thought is possible without words, yet the truth is obvious that, apart from language, the processes of thought must be narrow and imperfect.

SEC. III.—REAL SIGNIFICANCE AND VALUE OF THE CONCEPT.

Three general theories of the significance and value of the concept have emerged in the process of the evolution of the science of psychology; namely, realism, nominalism, and conceptualism.

¶ I. **Theory of Realism.**—This asserts a real existence or entity in Nature, corresponding to the concept, notion, or universal term; i. e., it asserts that there is, in Nature, a real archetype, or idea, or entity, corresponding to the general concept *man*—differing from the concept of this or that particular man known in perception. This strange doctrine was, perhaps, a legitimate outgrowth of Plato's doctrine of ideas.

¶ II. **Theory of Nominalism.**—Reacting from the manifest absurdity of realism, as thus discretely stated, psychologists passed to the corresponding extreme, and asserted that the concept is simply a name borrowed or abstracted from some concrete individual percept, and applied by accommodation to other percepts; and then, by a *fiction* of the imagination, taken as a representative idea equally applicable to any one or all of the associated or related percepts. This theory deprives the concept of all real content, except in so far as it escapes utter emptiness, by appropriating the actual content of some individual or concrete percept.

¶ III. **Theory of Conceptualims.**—This is obviously an attempt to mediate between these almost equally absurd extremes. It admits, with the realist, that the concept represents something more than an empty name; and, with the nominalist, that it is not the representative of an independent self-existent entity. It, therefore, postulates it as the representative of certain qualities or attributes existing simultaneously in two or more objects of perception, i. e., it postulates the concept as the representative of *a real relative*, but not of *a real absolute*, existence. The genus man exists in the perceived facts of the existence of this, that, and the other individual man.

¶ IV. **Real Import of the Controversy.**—It should be observed that the foregoing theories are designedly stated in their ultimate antithetic forms, and that all minor forms are neglected, simply from the fact that the underlying essential principle is the only element of real import in the controversy. Here, as usual, there is a germ of truth underlying both extremes. The realist is right in affirming that genera and species are something more than *mere names;* while the nominalist is just as certainly right in affirming that they have no independent existence as entities apart from the existence of the individuals composing them. The concept, or general term, really represents *the perceived relations* between the individual objects of perception, in virtue of their possessing certain common attributes. This relation is not, of course, *an entity*, nor yet is it a mere *fiction* of the imagination, but a real *perception*, not less valid than the perception of the several individual objects on which, in fact, it rests.

This suggests a final problem, viz., Are our concepts, as such, true or false? A little consideration will, perhaps, solve all the real difficulties of this problem. So far as concepts are, or are designed to be, representations of reality, they may be said to be true or false, in proportion to their agreement or disagreement with the archetypal object; but, so far as they are representative of the *ideal* only, they can be neither true nor false.

THE INTELLECT: ITS THIRD MOVEMENT.

BELIEF.

Preliminary Discussion.

General Analysis and Classification.

¶ I. **Summary of Results reached in Perception and Conception.**—The results of the mental processes thus far investigated may briefly be summed up as follows: Perception, through its twofold movement of sensation and intuition, reveals to us the world of *the actual*, not only under the forms of matter, but of spirit as well. Our knowledge of the latter through intuition is as immediate and direct as our knowledge of the former through sensation. Conception reveals to us the world of the *ideal*, making known to us the possible in all its varied forms and relations. But mind cannot rest in perception and conception, it seeks another and a higher sphere than either the actual known in perception, or the ideal known in conception; it seeks to know *the true*. To this end, it not only diligently compares the actual with the ideal, but it also compares idea with idea, and concept with concept, in order to evolve *the true* in all its native beauty and excellence, as the final cause of all intellection.

¶ II. **Evolution of the Processes of the Reason.**—The logical concept in its perfected form is not in itself *an end*, but only a *means* to an ulterior end. The soul seeks, as the final cause of all its processes, to reduce the variety and multiplicity of its percepts to unity. It makes its first approximation by the processes of the synthetic judgment; but our concepts, however generalized, are yet multiple and diverse, and the same psychologic necessity which impelled it to seek the reduction of the multiplicity of perception to the unity of conception, necessitates another and higher movement. The principle of this new movement is still *comparison*, or *the process of judgment*, but it now assumes the analytic rather than the synthetic form, and decomposes our complex concepts in order to evolve from their essential elements a still higher unity.

¶ III. **Analysis of the Reasoning Process.**—Reasoning involves two elements, namely:

1. Analysis, or the separation of a complex whole into its integrant elements; and—

2. Comparison, in order to the determination of the agreement or *non*-agreement of the related concepts.

This process is, in general, the converse of that involved in synthetic judgment, though the fact must be noted here, that no mental process, so to speak, dwells alone, or exists pure and simple, unmodified by other elements. The processes of conception, as previously detailed, involved analytic elements, which, although necessarily ignored in our analysis, were yet indispensable adjuncts of the movement.

¶ IV. **Forms of the Reasoning Process.**—The process of reasoning presents itself under two forms, which may be assumed as generic, viz.:

1. *The judgment, or proposition*, whose essential elements are a subject, predicate and copula; and—

2. *The syllogism, or chain of reasoning*, which consists essentially of three judgments, or propositions, so arranged or related that the third is an inference from the other two.

It is obvious that the two forms of reasoning thus enounced differ from each other, logically, in the fact that the conclusion in the one case is *immediate;* in the other, *mediate.*

¶ V. **Its Resultant Product, Belief.**—Every act of reasoning results in a belief, or a faith. This may, at first thought, seem paradoxical, in view of the fact that many acts of reasoning lead to a *disbelief* in the proposition offered for our credence; but this objection disappears at once when the fact is remembered that *disbelief* of one proposition, by the law of excluded middle, necessitates positive *belief*, or *faith*, in its converse. For example, I can only disbelieve the hypothesis that the soul is mortal, like the body, on condition that I believe the converse, that the soul is immortal. All reasoning, therefore, which does not result in faith, i. e., in *some* faith, is fruitless.

BELIEF.

CHAPTER I.—JUDGMENTS, OR PROPOSITIONS.

SECTION I.—ANALYSIS OF JUDGMENTS.

In the investigation of the operations of the judging faculty, or reason, the fact that mental processes are more tangible and important realities than mental faculties becomes obtrusively evident. So long as we had to do with sensation, memory, and imagination, the idea of a *special faculty* seems to be obtrusive; but when we consider intuition and the processes of reasoning, whether synthetic or analytic, it is far more difficult to fasten our thought upon the concept of special faculties. Intuition and reason seem to be rather essential functions of consciousness than special faculties of mind—a fact which, we think, justifies us in treating of processes rather than of faculties.

No mental act whatever is more familiar than a judgment; it enters implicitly, at least, into every mental process, and needs only to be named, to be realized in consciousness and comprehended. It is only necessary, therefore, to consider the elements of a judgment, or proposition; viz., the subject, the predicate, and the copula, discretely, and to evolve their several relations. A judgment is nothing more than a comparison of two concepts.

¶ I. **The Subject.**—In investigating a judgment, the subject, both logically and chronologically, demands attention first. It may be defined to be, *a concept of which something is affirmed or denied.* It is obviously, for the time being, the immediate and special object of thought or attention; and is, technically and necessarily, a *noun*, or name, or some word or words which, for the time being, represent a noun. The subject, as a concept, may be marked by a name, or by any collocation of words which may serve to bring definitely before the mind the concept intended; hence one sentence, or proposition, may be made the subject of another. It is hardly necessary to add that any form of concept whatever may be used as the subject of a proposition, whether it represent the actual or the ideal.

¶ II. **The Predicate.**—This, like the subject, is a concept, but, unlike it, is, ordinarily at least, not a noun grammatically considered, but an adjective, i. e., an attribute of a noun, which is declared to be congruent or non-congruent with the subject considered, *pro tempore*, as a substance capable of possessing attributes. The relation of subject and predicate may, however, seemingly be allowed greater latitude than the simple affirmation or denial of the relations of substance and attribute. We may, obviously, predicate of a subject three things, viz.:

1. What it is; i. e., we may predicate its essence, or identity.

2. What it does; i. e., we may predicate its acts; and—

3. What qualities it possesses; i. e., we may predicate its attributes. But, after all, essence, or identity, and acts, as predicables, come under the relations of attributes, *generically* considered. The discrete investigation of predicables belongs to logic rather than to psychology, and must, therefore, be discounted here.

¶ III. **The Copula.**—The copula, or connective of a judgment, is the word or words which declare the congruence or non-congruence of the predicate with the subject, and is, either explicitly or implicitly, some mode of the verb "to be," since all judgments may be reduced to the generic form, "A *is, or is not,* B." As a necessary resultant of this statement, or fact rather, there emerges at once a necessary ambiguity in the copula, namely, an apparent double affirmative, viz.:

1. The affirmation of the actual existence of the subject; and—

2. The affirmation of its congruence or non-congruence with the predicate. For example, I say, "Robinson Crusoe was wrecked on an uninhabited island;" or, "The phœnix is a beautiful bird," etc. In both cases alike, the copula carries with it the manifest assumption of the real existence of the subject, although no intelligent man would understand me to affirm the real existence of either Robinson Crusoe or the phœnix. This ambiguity is at once avoided by the recognition of the fact that the whole force of the copula, in a logical judgment, is exhausted in affirming the congruence or non-congruence of the predicate with the subject; the actual existence of either, as a fact, must be determined by independent evidence.

It is obvious that the agreement or disagreement of a subject and predicate in a simple judgment is, *logically*, *immediate*, and it is thus distinguished from the syllogism in which the conclusion is *mediate*.

SEC. II.—PROPERTIES OF JUDGMENTS.

Judgments, like concepts, possess certain properties or peculiarities which require discrete enunciation. Any analysis of our actual judgments, as present in consciousness, reveals three prominent properties, viz.: 1. Quantity; 2. Quality; and, 3. Modality.

¶ I. **Their Quantity.**—In the first case, we distinguish, obtrusively, two generic forms of judgments differing from each other in extension; as, All A is B, and Some A is B. In the first, the affirmation is universal, or without limit; in the second, the application of the predicate is restricted to some indefinite or definite part of A. Logicians distinguish a third form; as, John is a man, where the subject is singular. The first form has been denominated *universal*, the second *particular*, and the third *singular*. It is obvious, however, that a singular judgment is only a special form of the universal, since the predicate is applied to the whole of the subject; this class, therefore, may be discounted as useless.

¶ II. **Their Quality.**—A second obtrusive distinction is manifest in the quality of judgments. Some are affirmative, declaring the congruence of the subject and predicate; the rest are negative, declaring their *non*-congruence. Hence we have a second division of judgments, into affirmative and negative.

¶ III. **Derivative Classification.**—From the synthesis of judgments, considered in their duplicate relations of quantity and quality, four distinct forms emerge, viz.:

(A), Universal affirmatives; as, all A is B.
(E), Universal negatives; as, no A is B.
(I), Particular affirmatives; as, some A is B.
(O), Particular negatives; as, some A is not B.

Other secondary forms have been evolved, which need not be noted here. Logicians, for their own convenience, have agreed to symbolize these forms, as indicated above, by the vowels A, E, I, and O, and by these symbols they will be referred to here, as they are in all works on logic.

¶ IV. **Their Modality.**—Another distinction in judgments remains to be noted, viz., their modality, dependent upon their mode of statement:

1. Categorical judgments, i. e., judgments in which the affirmation of the congruence or non-congruence of the predicate with the subject is stated simply and unconditionally, i. e., categorically; and—

2. Hypothetical or conditional judgments, i. e., judgments in which the congruence or non-congruence of the predicate is expressed hypothetically or conditionally; as, If it does not rain, the day will be pleasant.

Sec. III.—Opposition of Judgments.

¶ I. **Forms of Opposition, or Contrariety.**—From the four primary forms of judgment, viz., A, E, I, and O, there result the general principles of opposition or contrariety of judgments, and the resulting doctrines of inference. The relations of contrariety have been expressed to the eye in the following diagram; or, to interpret the diagram, we recognize four kinds of opposition, or contrariety, viz.:

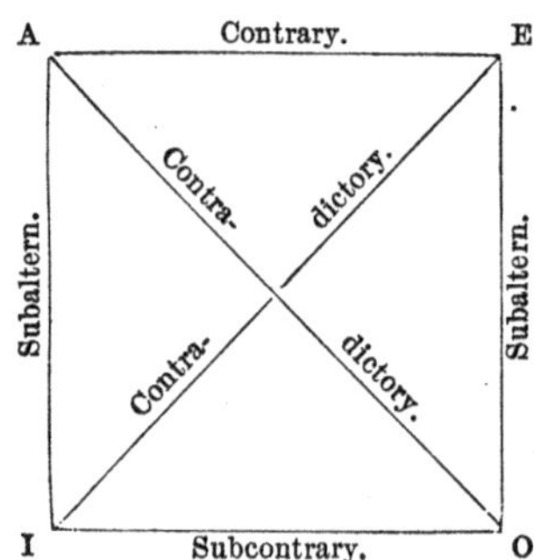

1. *Contraries*, i. e., a universal affirmative (A) opposed to a universal negative (E).

2. *Contradictories*, i. e., a universal affirmative (A) opposed to a particular negative (O); or a universal negative (E) opposed to a particular affirmative (I).

3. *Subcontraries*, i. e., a particular affirmative (I) opposed to a particular negative (O).

4. *Subaltern*, i. e., a universal affirmative (A) opposed (technically) to a particular affirmative (I); or a universal negative (E) opposed (technically) to a particular negative (O).

¶ II. **General Laws of Opposition, or Contrariety.**—The general laws of contrariety may be stated as follows:

1. *Contraries*, viz.: (A) and (E) cannot both be true at the same time, but may both be false; as, all men are learned (A), no man is learned (E).

2. *Contradictories*, viz.: (A) and (O), or (E) and (I), cannot both be true or both be false at the same time. One must be true by the law of excluded middle. For example, all men are learned (A), and some men are not learned (O).

3. *Subcontraries*, viz.: (I) and (O) may both be true, but cannot both be false at the same time; as, some men are learned (I), and some men are not learned (O).

4. *Subalterns*, viz.: (A) and (I), or (E) and (O). Of these the law is, that if the universal is true, the particular must be true also; and, *vice versa*, if the particular is false, the universal must be false also.

Supplementary Topic.

All Concepts involve a Primitive Judgment.

It is obvious, from the preceding discussions, that, although a *logical judgment* is a synthesis of concepts, yet a primitive act of judgment is necessarily involved in the evolution of every logical concept. Here, apparently, we are involved in an absurdity, making (as we do) the concept the essential element in every act of judgment, and yet postulating a prior act of judgment as a condition precedent to the existence of the concept. This mystery, however, disappears when we distinguish between *primitive* and *logical* judgments. The former class is based upon sensation and intuition, the latter class is based upon conception. The one deals with the *elements of thought*, the other with *developed thought*. The contradiction is, therefore, only apparent, and not real.

CHAPTER II.—THE SYLLOGISM.

SECTION I.—ANALYSIS OF THE SYLLOGISM.

¶ I. **Mediate Reasoning.**—Every valid mediate argument may be reduced to a syllogism or series of syllogisms depending upon the number of premises or steps by which the conclusion is reached. If it is mediated by two premises, or propositions, it may be reduced to the form of a regular syllogism; as, all men are mortal; John is a man: therefore, John is mortal—or, in a generic form, all A is B; C is A: therefore, C is B. In the latter example, A, B, and C, are simple concepts of any content whatsoever.

¶ II. **Analysis of the Syllogism.**—A slight analysis of this typical syllogism discloses two generic facts, viz.:

1. That every syllogism contains three and but three terms, or concepts, represented above by A, B, and C. These terms are called respectively the major, minor, and middle terms.

2. That every syllogism contains three and but three propositions, or judgments; called, respectively, the major and minor premises, and the conclusion. In the major premise, the major and middle terms are compared; in the minor premise, the minor and middle terms; and in the conclusion, the minor and major terms. The middle term is, therefore, nothing more than a common measure interposed between the major and minor terms, to ascertain their congruence or non-congruence with each other. The mathematical equivalent of this principle is found in the well-known axiom,

that "things equal to the same thing are equal to each other." The logical postulate, like the mathematical, is self-evident, and needs neither elucidation nor demonstration.

The inference, or conclusion, in a true syllogism is necessary. If the premises be admitted, the conclusion cannot be denied; we may, therefore, argue from the truth of the premises to the truth of the conclusion, or from the known falsity of the conclusion to the falsity of one or both of the premises. It is obvious that the truth of the major and minor premises, respectively, is simply a question of fact, to be determined, like any other question of fact, by appropriate evidence; the truth of the conclusion, on the other hand, is determined immediately by the correlation of the premises.

Sec. II.—Laws of the Syllogism.

The laws of the syllogism are simple and definite, and result necessarily from the principles already evolved. They may be enounced as follows:

1. *A syllogism must contain three terms, and no more.*—If four or more terms are used, no middle term would appear as a common measure, and, consequently, no conclusion could be reached.

2. *A syllogism must contain three judgments, and no more*, for a like reason.

3. *The middle term must be distributed* (i. e., *taken universally*) *in, at least, one of the premises.*—The reason of this rule is obvious; the two extremes, i. e., the major and minor terms, must be severally compared with it; and, in one case or the other, it must needs be taken in its widest sense, otherwise we cannot be sure that both have been compared with identically the same common measure.

4. *One premise at least must be affirmative;* otherwise there can be, in fact, no application of the middle term as a common measure. To affirm that neither the major nor minor term agrees with the middle term, is to postulate nothing whatsoever of their congruence or non-congruence with each other.

5. *The conclusion must follow the weaker premise.*—A negative is weaker than an affirmative, and a particular than a universal. It follows, therefore—

(*a*) That when one premise is negative, the conclusion must be negative also.

(*b*) That where one premise is particular, the conclusion must be particular also; and—

(*c*) That no term must be distributed in the conclusion which has not been distributed in one of the premises.

6. *From two particular premises no conclusion can be drawn*, since, in this case, there can be no assurance that the major and minor terms have been compared with each other at all.

No syllogism can be invalid which does not violate one or more of these rules; and it is, therefore, a matter of prime importance that the student learn to apply them correctly and habitually to all his processes of reasoning.

SEC. III.—FORMS OF THE SYLLOGISM.

Careful analysis of our mental processes reveals two generic forms of syllogism corresponding to the generic forms of the judgments upon which all syllogisms depend, viz., *categorical* and *conditional.* The latter, in turn, may be subdivided into hypothetical, disjunctive, and dilemmatic; all of which must now be explicated as illustrating important psychical processes.

¶ I. **Categorical Syllogisms.**—The general laws of the simple categorical syllogism have, perhaps, been sufficiently illustrated in the preceding discussions, which are based upon this, as the typical form involving the essential laws of the generic development; and the class is simply formally reannounced here, for the sake of distinctness of classification.

¶ II. **Conditional Syllogisms.**—A conditional syllogism is one of which the major premise, and the major premise *alone*, is a conditional judgment. There are three kinds of such syllogisms, corresponding to like forms of conditional judg ments, which supply the major premise. They are termed, respectively, the hypothetical, the disjunctive, and the dilemmatic. We give examples of each:

Hypothetical.	*Disjunctive.*
If A is B, C is D;	A is either B or C;
A is B:	A is B:
Therefore, C is D.	Therefore, A is not C.

Dilemmatic or Hypothetico-Disjunctive.

If A is B, C is either D or E;
C is neither D nor E:
Therefore, A is not B.

A very slight comparison of these three forms of conditional syllogisms will show that they depend, not like categorical syllogisms, upon the laws of identity and contradiction, but upon the corresponding canons of reason and consequent, and of excluded middle. The hypothetical syllogism depends upon the canons of reason and consequent, and simply postulates, from the *sufficient* reason, viz., that A is B, the necessary consequent that C is D.

The disjunctive syllogism, in like manner, depends upon the canon of excluded middle, which determines that, of two contradictories, one must be true and one false; as, in the example given, if A is B, it cannot be C.

The dilemmatic or hypothetico-disjunctive syllogism, posits, as its name indicates, the principles of both its congeners, and therefore applies both canons as the conditions of a valid conclusion; as, in the example given, where they determine that, if C is neither D nor E, A cannot be B.

The complete analytical development of these several forms of syllogisms belongs to the science of logic, but it seemed indispensable, to any tolerable comprehension of the processes and products of mental development, to grasp them in outline, at least, in this connection.

SEC. IV.—VALUE OF THE SYLLOGISM.

There has been much earnest discussion in reference to the real value of the syllogism, and objections have been made to it that in its use there is no real advancement or progress in knowledge, since the major premise necessarily declares *all*, and frequently *more* than all, that is declared in the conclusion, and that the whole proceeding is, consequently, puerile.

The fact is admitted, of course, that nothing can be inferred in the conclusion that is not involved in the premises; but the objection is nevertheless groundless, since it confounds *potential* with *actual* knowledge. Any man who has mastered the axioms and definitions of geometry possesses a *potential* knowledge of the whole science, but it would be absurd to say that he possesses an *actual* knowledge of it; so a man may have knowledge, severally and separately, of the possible major and minor premises of a hundred syllogisms, and yet never draw, in fact, a single one of the possible resulting inferences, and so convert his *potential* into *actual* knowledge. This single fact relieves the syllogistic process at once of the charge of puerility, and vindicates the propriety of its use, without entering upon those higher lines of thought which belong elsewhere. A few correlated thoughts, however, seem to demand enunciation, as illustrating the general topic, i. e., the value of the syllogism.

¶ I. **All Reasoning is syllogistic.**—The truth is not, perhaps, as generally comprehended as it should be, that all valid reasoning is syllogistic; that is, it is reducible, in its ultimate analysis, to the form of a syllogism. This is apparent from the very definitions of reasoning, which, however variously they may be stated, all agree in recognizing it as a process of *mediate* knowledge, i. e., a process by which we know one thing in and through another; but this is precisely the essential element in syllogistic reasoning.

Practically, men in reasoning do not use *formal* syllogisms, but enthymemes, i. e., syllogisms with one or the other of the premises suppressed, because of its familiarity to the minds of both speaker and hearer. But such enthymemes may readily be reduced to the form of regular syllogisms by restoring the suppressed premise.

¶ II. **The Syllogism guarantees Formal Truth only.**—The conclusion of a valid syllogism *must be formally true*, although it may be, and often is, *actually* false; for example, All men are Americans; John is a man: therefore, John is an American, is a valid syllogism *as to its form*, though its major premise is absurdly false. This, however, is no real objection to the syllogism as such, since it does not propose to furnish, or guarantee the truth of, its own premises, but only the absolute certitude of the conclusion, if the truth of its premises be admitted.

CHAPTER III.—REASONING IN GENERAL.

Preliminary Discussion.

Distinctness requires some notice of the more obvious divisions or classifications of reasoning. Here, however, we are met at the very outset by the difficulty that various classifications have actually been made from variant standpoints; all of which have become familiar, by name at least, to the popular mind, and must, therefore, be enunciated and correlated here. Reasonings may be classified according to their *subject-matter*, their *forms*, and their *final causes*, as follows:

SECTION I.—CLASSIFICATION OF REASONING WITH RESPECT TO ITS SUBJECT-MATTER.

Reasoning with respect to its subject-matter may be discriminated into two general divisions; viz., demonstrative or necessary, and moral or probable.

¶ I. **Demonstrative or Necessary Reasoning.**—This is sometimes called mathematical reasoning, simply because it finds its widest and most fruitful field of application in mathematics. We note:

1. *Its nature.*—Demonstration, in its technical sense, may be regarded as a series of consecutive syllogisms, founded upon *practically* absolute premises ; hence the comparatively narrow range of its use, limiting it almost entirely to the sphere of pure mathematics. There it meets all the necessary conditions of its evolution, viz. :

(*a*) Intuitive truths, or axioms, whose validity and truth are undeniable, which serve it for premises ; and—

(*b*) Necessary relations between ideally perfect lines, angles, circles, etc., etc., which serve it for factors.

2. *Its certitude.*—This is, obviously, humanly speaking, absolute; we cannot disbelieve its conclusions if we would. Consciousness vouches for the premises, and the laws of the syllogism for the conclusion. In fact, each step of the process, however extended, is self-evident, and doubt is, both theoretically and practically, impossible. It affords, of course, no degrees of certitude; its conclusions must needs be absolute.

3. *Its range of application.*—This is necessarily limited, because it demands *self-evident* truths for its premises, and *necessary* relations for its conditions; and these, in the sphere of human experience, belong exclusively to the spheres of intuition and conception, and not at all to that of sensation or the material world. Experience, therefore, in its ordinary metaphysical sense, does not and cannot furnish any data whatsoever for demonstrative reasoning. The lines, angles, and solids, to which the geometer applies his theorems, are not those inscribed upon the book or black-board, but those more perfect archetypes which exist in his conceptions of the ideal.

¶ II. **Moral or Probable Reasoning.**—Complementary to demonstrative reasoning, whose sphere is the region of necessary relations, is moral or probable reasoning, whose sphere is the wider realm of the material and the actual. It is, of course, not intended here either to affirm or deny any thing in reference to the actuality or non-actuality of the necessary intuitions or concepts of demonstrative reasoning, nor yet the existence or non-existence of *necessary* relations between material existences or entities. Our classification is dependent solely upon our *subjective conceptions* of the several entities and relations. Demonstrative reasoning is applied solely to necessary existences and relations; probable or moral, to contingent.

1. *Nature of moral reasoning.*—Moral reasoning deals exclusively with contingent facts and relations; i. e., with facts and relations which, however real, might have been, and may, hereafter, conceivably be, otherwise than we now actually perceive them to be. This form of reasoning depends for its materials upon experience; and its data are, therefore, contingent, like the experience upon which they rest; and the processes of the syllogism, as we have seen, guarantee only *formal* conclusions, and not *actual* truths.

2. *Certitude of moral reasoning.*—This, obviously, is relative, and dependent upon the certitude of the elements that enter into it. It consequently admits of all possible degrees, from the slightest preponderance of doubts to the most absolute certitude. I no more doubt, for instance, that man is mortal, than I do that all the angles of a plane triangle are together equal to two right angles; yet, to deny the last were absurd, to deny the first were simply to falsify known facts. In other words, I conceive mortality to be a *contingent*, and not a *necessary*, attribute of man; but the equality of the angles of a triangle to two right angles I conceive to be a *necessary* attribute of the concept triangle when discretely explicated to the mind.

3. *Range of application of moral reasoning.*—This is obviously wider and more varied than that of demonstrative reasoning. It includes all subjects of probation outside of the comparatively narrow sphere of the demonstrable. It is equally at home in the material and spiritual worlds—in the circles of business, and the halls of politics; in the student's cell, and in the sacred desk.

Sec. II.—Classification of Reasoning according to its Forms.

Reasoning, when classified according to its forms or modes of statement, may be discriminated as *a priori* and *a posteriori*.

¶ I. **Reasoning a Priori.**—1. *Its nature.*—This form of reasoning depends for its vitality upon the category of causation; and posits or concludes the existence of an *effect* from the proved or conceded preëxistence of an *adequate cause.* It is logically based upon the canon of reason and consequent; or, as it is sometimes called, the law of the sufficient reason. The process, and the principle of it, are alike familiar, and need no special discussion.

2. *Its certitude.*—The certitude reached by *a priori* reasoning never attains, under ordinary circumstances, that perfect satisfaction which the soul craves. It produces that peculiar mental influence expressed by the term *plausible.* Yet, perhaps, under conceivable conditions, it might attain to absolute certitude. So far as any cause tends to produce a certain effect, we may conclude the existence of the effect, provided no opposing or hindering cause has intervened to neutralize its influence. Thus I argue that a certain man must die because he has swallowed a large dose of arsenic. The conclusion is *plausible*, but other causes may have intervened to neutralize the poison or remove it from the stomach, and thus the argument may fail. The proviso, "If no sufficient contrary cause intervene," is ordinarily indeterminate, and shadows the certitude that would otherwise result from *a priori* reasoning.

3. *Its range of application.*—This is, in general, indefinite, and is practically indeterminate. Wherever a cause can be proved to exist, and operate in the material or spiritual worlds, we may fairly predicate the conclusion that *some effect*, determinate or indeterminate, must follow; but, if the problem be complex, the certitude reached may be of so doubtful a character as to be practically valueless. Its prin-

cipal generic use is to prepare the way for other more positive proofs, by showing the antecedent probability of the position assumed to be true.

¶ II. **Reasoning a Posteriori.**—This includes all other valid forms of reasoning whatsoever, such as reasoning from sign, from example, from testimony, etc., etc., which it is unnecessary to discuss here. Any legitimate form of reasoning, other than *a priori*, falls legitimately under this class. The degrees of certitude reached are, therefore, as varied as the range of application of the process, and this is almost unlimited.

Sec. III.—Classification of Reasoning with Reference to its Final Cause.

Reasonings, as discriminated from each other, with reference to their final causes or purposes, in each special instance, are divided into deductive and inductive.

¶ I. **Deductive Reasoning.**—The fact has been already noted that all reasoning, as such, is essentially deductive in its last analysis. The syllogism, as it is ordinarily stated in the quantity of extension, is the typical form of this mode.

1. *Its nature.*—This may be summed up in the general statement, that deduction is, essentially, the analysis of an extensive whole into its constituent parts, and the positing of the essential attributes or properties of the whole of its constituent parts. The process, therefore, hinges upon the necessary relations of a whole to its parts; of a genus to the species contained under it; and of a species to the individuals constituting it. That which is true of the genus must needs be true of its constituent species; and that which is true of the species must needs be true of the individuals composing it.

2. *Its certitude.*—This has already been discussed in the examination of the various special forms of deductive reasoning that have already passed under review.

3. *Its range of use.*—This is coextensive with the quantity of extension, logically considered, and is, therefore, al-

7

most unlimited in the domain of human thought. It is sometimes said, however, that it is limited to the *exposition* of truth, and that it is useless as a means of *discovering* truth; but it has already been shown that this objection is based upon a misconception of the relations of actual and potential knowledge. A thing may be potentially known, and yet actually unknown, and we may come into the *conscious* possession of this actually unknown factor, only by a course of deductive reasoning; and the gain is as real in thus transferring the *potentially* known to the sphere of *actual* knowledge as the economic gain of discovering and opening a new mine of gold to the owner of real estate.

¶ II. **Inductive Reasoning.**—If the foregoing estimate of the nature and relations of what is ordinarily known as deductive reasoning be accepted, the necessity is apparent of some other mental process by which the mind may attain to strictly *new* truths, and not merely to truths already potentially known. This necessity becomes yet more obvious when the question is raised, as it must be, "Whence do we obtain the major premises upon which all proper deductive reasoning rests?" It is obvious:

First. That only a moiety of them, at most, are the products of intuition, either immediately or mediately; and—

Second. That they cannot themselves have been obtained by other primary deductions.

It is sometimes said, indeed, that "they are obtained from experience;" but there is room for the suspicion that those who assign to them this origin do not always realize in thought the exact significance of the words they use, or define the nature and conditions of the experience they postulate, and so determine at once its possibility and validity. The real solution of the problem is found in the process of true logical induction, through which we obtain that moiety of the major premises of deductive syllogisms which are not intuitive concepts. It only remains, then, to consider the nature, certitude, and range of use of the inductive process.

1. *Nature of the inductive process.*—In one sense, no pro-

cess of mind is more familiar to us than this, since it has been an essential constituent element of our whole personal mental development, from the first faint dawn of consciousness until the present moment; yet, notwithstanding this fact, and notwithstanding its enormous development in the grand evolutions of modern science, logicians yet battle over its nature and vital principles. It is far easier to evolve the legitimate empirical laws which regulate its practical application, than it is to evolve its real nature.

The process, popularly stated, is as follows: As a naturalist, I meet a strange and hitherto undescribed animal; I note its marks and peculiarities; I meet a second, a third, and a fourth, similar to it in all respects. I class them together, assign them a common name, and posit, concerning all similar animals yet to be discovered, that, however much they may differ in minor points, they will all agree in certain essential marks or attributes constituting them a genus or species, as the case may be. It is obvious that, underlying this whole process, there is one essential postulate which is vital to it, namely, *the assumption of the uniformity of Nature, alike in her laws and her processes.*

2. *The vital principle of inductive reasoning;* viz., the assumption of the uniformity of Nature.—Without this fundamental postulate in some form, all induction, whether in its scientific sense or in its popular form of reasoning from experience, would be not only fallacious but absurd. What, then, is the content and what the origin of this assumption?

If it be carefully analyzed, certain elements emerge at once into view, and the somewhat vague and indefinite phrase "*uniformity of Nature*" becomes instinct with life and pregnant with meaning. It predicates or postulates:

(*a*) *The universality of the law or category of causation;* i. e., it predicates the assertion that Nature is the expression, *not* of a series of accidents and chances, but of a series of evolutions according to *both determinate and determinable laws*, which mutually involve each other, and also involve a second postulate, viz.:

(*b*) *The unity of this law of causation.* It does not suffice, as an adequate basis for legitimate induction, to assume merely that causation as such is universal; the assumption must also include the secondary conception of *determinate causation*, according to some consistent law or principle. Should we posit a multiplicity of creators differing from each other in nature, characters, and purposes, it is obvious that confusion, and not order, must reign in the universe, and prevent all determinate and determinable order. It postulates:

(*c*) *The intelligence of this causation.* That alone is *intelligible* which springs from *intelligence.* Induction necessarily predicates *a determinable determinate order* in the universe; i. e., *an order* intelligible under the laws and forms of the human intellect. It thus postulates a *community* or *unity* of intelligence between man and the universe; i. e., between *man* and *the efficient cause* of the universe.

It is not obvious how any one of these allied assumptions can be discounted or set aside, and leave any intelligible basis for induction. If causation be not *universal* in its range, the inductions of Newton, Kepler, and Laplace, were absurd. If the principle of causality were *not singular*, but *multiple* and diverse, the result would be the same; thought could never know when it was passing the line of another and hostile sphere of causation, acting under diverse laws. Finally, if causation is not intelligent, and that too with an intelligence in harmony with *the human*, induction would still be impossible and irrational, since two intelligences, whose mental processes depend upon different laws, and respond to diverse principles, could have no intelligible relations to each other.

The necessities of the inductive process thus lead us to the concept of an intelligent Creator of man and the universe, in whom alone we can attain to the conception of a *singular intelligent universal cause*, adequate at once to the necessities of human thought and of material existence.

If the legitimacy of this reference of the *vital principle* of induction (viz., the assumption of the uniformity of the processes and laws of Nature) to the category of causation be admitted, the origin of the postulate at once becomes evident. It is nothing more than a legitimate deduction from our necessary intuitive concepts. The alternative theory, which makes *it* and *the category of causation also* deductions from experience, fails in two essential conditions, viz.:

First. It does not and cannot account for the element of *necessity* implied, and in fact posited, in both concepts. Take *that* away from the law of causation, and it is utterly without meaning; take it from the assumed law of the uniformity of Nature, and any induction based upon *that* is just as devoid of meaning or value.

Second. It makes experience the condition, and in fact the cause, of its own existence. Take away from man the allied *intuitive* concepts of causation and the uniformity of Nature, and it is impossible for us to conceive how experience could begin at all; and, if a beginning were possible, there would remain no conceivable law under which it could be evolved. Invariableness of succession and resemblance, which certain psychologists affirm to be all we know of causation, cannot aid us here; for it is obtrusively evident that the only successions in Nature which are to man *absolutely invariable* are precisely those with which he *never* connects or associates the ideas of cause and effect. Such are the successions of *day* and *night*, of *summer* and *winter*, of *life* and *death*. It is almost idle to say that, notwithstanding the invariableness of these successions, no man, woman, or child, *ever*, in *any* of the cases named, mistook the antecedent for a cause and the consequent for an effect; but, on the contrary, all men have, just as invariably, postulated an efficient cause for each phenomenon outside of this invariable succession. Two inferences are thus necessitated, viz.:

(*a*) That the concept of causation is universal; and—

(*b*) That it does, in fact, include something more than the perception of invariableness of succession.

3. *Range of use of induction.*—Deductive reasoning, as has been already noted, is used chiefly for the evolution of

the content of general laws or propositions. The special function of induction is to supply or originate these general truths. The one is used to evolve *potential knowledge* and make it *actual*, by reducing it to possession; the other is used to discover *new* truths, to bring the *unknown* into the sphere of the *potentially* or *actually* known. The one is the instrument of *investigation;* the other, of *probation:* the one belongs to the scientist, who seeks to fathom the mysteries of Nature; the other belongs to the teacher, who seeks to unfold those mysteries to the minds of the multitude.

It would be interesting and profitable, were it pertinent, to investigate the scientific laws and processes of induction, as well as to evolve the inductive syllogism and determine its relations to the deductive, but such discussions belong rather to the domain of logic than of psychology; and are inconsistent with the limits of a treatise like the present.

CHAPTER IV.—REASONING: ITS RESULTANT PRODUCT, FAITH.

Section I.—Analysis of its Relations.

¶ I. **Final Cause of all Intellectual Activity.**—In the processes of reasoning, the intellect of man attains to its ultimate product, namely, *belief*, or *faith*, which must, therefore, be accepted as the *proximate* final cause of all intellection whatsoever. The steps or processes (to recapitulate them) have been three, viz.

1. *Cognition or perception of the actual*, both in the material and spiritual worlds. This, as we have noted, involves the perfect synthesis of sensation and intuition in the resulting percept.

2. *Conception of the ideal* (both imaginative and logical) in the synthesis of the processes of the representative faculties, viz., the memory, the imagination, and the synthetic judgment. The resultant products are concepts, both imaginative and logical.

3. *Reasoning*, *inductive* and *deductive*, based upon the

faculty of judgment, giving, primarily, knowledge of the *true;* secondarily, knowledge of the *beautiful* and the *good;* and resulting in belief, or faith, as the ultimate product and proximate final cause of all intellection. This, in turn, prepares the way for the normal evolutions of the sensitive and moral or voluntary functions of the soul. In other words, we cognize the actual, we conceive the ideal, and we believe or attain to faith in the true, the beautiful, and the good, that we may bring them within the sphere of our sensitive natures, and call our voluntary powers into action, in accordance with their own normal laws. Faith thus stands as a sentinel at the door of the *inner*, and in a certain sense *higher*, functions of the soul, to guard the citadel from the intrusion of open or secret foes. Faith, therefore, is the highest, as it is the ultimate, product of human thought, the end to which all intellection tends, and in which it terminates.

¶ II. **Faith is the Rational, as it is the only Possible, Condition of Human Activity.**—To men accustomed to sound the praises of *reason* and to underrate *faith* as childish, it may seem a lame and impotent conclusion, that faith is not only the *rational*, but the *only possible*, condition of human activity; but so it is, as a few additional considerations, in the light of our previous discussions, will clearly prove. We remark:

1. Perception or cognition gives and can only give knowledge of the *actual*, of that which *now* exists in the sphere of consciousness, and is known in the synthesis of sensation and intuition. That which we perceive we necessarily perceive *now* and *here;* and perception does not, and *cannot*, reveal to us, in any sense whatever, that which is absent in time or space. It tells us, and can tell us, directly, nothing of *the future;* of its hopes or fears, its promises or its possibilities—hence it is not, and cannot be, the legitimate incitant to action. Men never act merely from the knowledge of what now is; their acts must needs have their outlook and their excitants, as well as their final cause, in the future. But perception knows nothing of final causes, purposes, or ends, and so

can offer, *directly*, no stimulus to action. We say, can offer *directly*, i. e., *immediately;* for, *remotely*, perception of the actual, as the basis and condition precedent of both conception and belief, may be said to furnish a basis for action. Yet it may safely be postulated as an axiom, that he who will only act from knowledge will never act at all.

2. Conception gives only the ideal, the possible. It may, therefore, by presenting an *ideal* brighter and more beautiful than any reality which perception has ever revealed, stimulate man to grasp after it; but, if our activity have no other and no higher stimulus to effort than this, our efforts must needs be transitory and spasmodic. Humanity needs, in order to persistent and intelligent effort, a stimulus to action as constant and persistent as the effort required; and this does not, and cannot, come from a bare *ideal*, however beautiful or perfect. In fact, the very perfection of an ideal may paralyze the energies that it should stimulate, by taking away all rational hope of success. Men struggle after the *attainable*, never after that which obviously lies secure behind insurmountable barriers. The *unattainable* may be an object of despairing and anguished desire, but it cannot be of effort or of hope. Something more and something higher than a lofty ideal in the near or the distant future is necessary to awaken and sustain the energies of the human soul in its struggles after the ideal, which has for the time become its supreme good.

3. Rational faith alone remains to be considered as a possible basis for intelligent action, adequate to the necessities of man in this life. We emphasize the words *rational faith*, i. e., the resultant product of all our intellectual processes in their last and highest evolution. Two facts may be postulated as axiomatic, namely:

(*a*) That reasoning, in the proper sense of the term, is the *highest* as it is the *last* evolution of human thought; and that—

(*b*) Belief, or faith—for here the terms used are strictly interchangeable—is the highest as it is the ultimate product of the reason in man. The term faith, or belief, is here used as the true generic representative of the product of reason in its ultimate evolution, and includes every condition, from the slightest preponderance of probabilities to the absolute certainty of mathematical demonstration. Sometimes the term belief is reserved for the lower, and faith for the higher, degrees of certitude, especially in the sphere of moral or probable reasoning; and the term knowledge is appropriated to express the certainty of demonstration. But the latter distinction is objectionable on two grounds, viz.:

First. It implicitly assumes that *all* the conclusions of demonstrative are more certain than *any* in moral or probable reasoning—an assumption wholly untenable and false; and—

Second. That every step in mathematical reasoning is self-evident, which is untrue in the higher algebra and calculus. Here the assumed necessary superiority of demonstration fails; the term knowledge again becomes inapplicable, and the final product is belief, or faith.

SEC. II.—ANALYSIS OF ITS FORMS.

Faith, or belief, has already been declared to be *generic*, the resultant product of various processes of reasoning operating upon materials diverse alike in nature and value. It becomes necessary, therefore, to analyze this product, and determine at once its essential character and its relations. This is the more necessary, inasmuch as our previous analysis has shown that it is, in some of its forms, not only the ultimate product of thought, but that it enters into the initial processes of all intellection in perception. Our intuitions are frequently, and with propriety, called *primitive beliefs;* and we accept them with an invincible faith, on the ground of their self-evidence. Hence, sometimes, we are said "*to know*" them to be true, thus distinguishing or marking a higher apparent degree of faith, or certitude, by the term knowledge. It is not apparent, however, how any better distinction can be taken between the terms faith and knowledge than the one taken in this treatise, namely, the application of the term knowledge to perception and its resulting percepts; and the terms belief and faith to reasoning and its resulting conviction. This theory, it will be seen at once, postulates for faith, in its highest forms, a degree of certitude as complete and as satisfactory as any act of perception whatsoever can give.

Faith as a *generic* term covers a variety of mental states or products differing from each other in the processes by which they are severally evolved; and these processes, as to their form at least, are largely determined by the objects to which they are directed. The various modes of reasoning have, perhaps, been sufficiently investigated, and it only remains to analyze and classify our faiths with respect to their several objects. It is obvious that these must, in general, coincide with the normal ultimate elements of human thought; viz., self and not-self; or, following out our previous evolution, man, Nature, and God, as the expression of not-self. We here apparently isolate self illogically from man, but this is necessary from this stand-point, as will be seen in the sequel, since self as an object of faith differs generically from man, who in this relation belongs to the category of not-self. We proceed, therefore, to analyze faith in its relations: 1. To self, or the consciousness; 2. To Nature as the real finite not-self known in perception; 3. To man as the congener of self; and 4. To God.

¶ I. **Faith in Self, or the Consciousness.**—The first striking result of this special analysis is the explicit evolution of the fact that, although faith has thus far been defined to be the ultimate product of the highest form of intellection, namely, reasoning, it must also be recognized as a primitive fact of consciousness, both logically and chronologically antedating and conditioning all mental processes whatsoever. In other words, faith *in consciousness*, its *processes*, and its *products*, is an underlying condition precedent of all intellection whatsoever. No course of reasoning can supply its own premises; no process furnish its own data; no intellectual faculty supply its own Archimedean "*pou sto*," upon which to plant its machinery. That which is true of this or that special faculty of mind, is true of consciousness itself. Memory, for example, can neither furnish its own materials nor vindicate the correctness of its own processes. It trusts perception (i. e., the consciousness) for the one, it postulates the truth and validity of the other; i. e., in other words, it appeals to the primitive faith of consciousness (or the soul) in itself, its processes, and its products; and this appeal, it will be observed, is final, ultimate, decisive. If it be rejected as unsatisfactory, intellection is at an end; no other appeal is possible. We cannot legitimately, if we would, attain to that indefinable "no-man's-land" of universal doubt; for doubt can only exist on condition that the consciousness which doubts be accredited as a competent witness to the existence of the doubt postulated. But to accredit the consciousness is to discredit the doubt; while to accredit the doubt is to discredit the consciousness which doubts. An impossible condition, therefore, emerges at every attempt to discredit consciousness. The fact must, therefore, be postulated as axiomatic, necessary, and universal, *that faith in consciousness is the essential condition precedent of all intellection whatsoever.*

Faith in consciousness may be normally discriminated into certain elementary forms, which may profitably be noticed discretely, viz.:

1. Faith in itself; i. e., in its own conscious existence. This is, strictly, the primitive fact postulated in every phenomenon and every act of consciousness. It is alike undeniable and indemonstrable. To doubt it were to demonstrate it; but to doubt it is impossible, hence to demonstrate it is also impossible.

2. Faith in its processes. It is just as impossible to verify the processes of consciousness, in principle or in fact, as it is to verify the existence of consciousness to itself. It is true that, to a limited extent, we may verify the testimony of one sense by another, and one process by another; but this is true only to a limited extent. When, however,

the question is raised as to the credibility of sensation, or as to the verity or credibility of mental processes in general, the problem is insoluble, and doubt is impossible, because self-destructive. Here one faculty or process, antecedently, can claim no superiority over another. It is absurd to accredit sensation at the expense of intuition, or *vice versa;* or to accredit memory and discredit reason or the judgment, and so of the rest. This is not, of course, intended to preclude the proper verification or correction of one mental process by another, when such verification or correction is practicable, but to discredit the absurd attempts sometimes made to discriminate between the primitive coördinate faculties of the soul.

3. Faith in its necessary products. Under the head of necessary products of consciousness, must be included:

(*a*) *A priori concepts and affirmations*, such as space, time, causation, the axioms of mathematics, etc., etc. For our faith in these, or our affirmation of these, no other reason can be given than that we are so constituted that *we do* and *must* believe them implicitly; in other words, our faith in them is fundamental and absolute, and he who attempts to discredit them actually accredits them, either explicitly or implicitly, in every statement he makes, or act he performs.

(*b*) *In its secondary concepts and beliefs.* These obviously follow the law of their primitives, and stand or fall with them. Here, however, we must discriminate accurately between faith in this or that particular act or exercise of any special faculty, and faith in the average results and operations of the faculty itself. I may, for sufficient cause, distrust a special act of memory or judgment, without discrediting either faculty. So, also, I may distrust this or that act of perception, without distrusting the faculty itself. For example, in pure, syllogistic reasoning, I may doubt the conclusion, either because I doubt one or both of the premises, or I may doubt the conclusion because it disagrees with or contradicts other well-established conclusions; and, doubting the conclusion, I may come to doubt the premises, but I cannot, if I would, doubt the regular syllogistic process by which I have evolved the conclusion from the assumed premises. Whatever else may be false, that, at least, is true.

¶ II. **Faith in Nature and its Laws.**—Passing from the sphere of consciousness, we come, at once and necessarily, into that of Nature, which environs, contains, and conditions, the sphere of consciousness. Here we attain, at a period so early that we cannot fix the time, to a vague but real conception of a certain repetition, regularity, order, uniformity, or causation in Nature, corresponding to, and complementary of, the order of evolution of our personal conscious existence. The nature and character of this recognized order or uniformity in Nature has, perhaps, been sufficiently considered, under the heads of the category of causation and of induction, and the fact need only be formally restated—that the essential element underlying our conception of the uniformity of Nature is nothing more than the generic canon of causation. No man hesitates to affirm that, all efficient causes remaining the same, to-day will be as yesterday, and to-morrow as to-day; but, at the same time, he will have just as little hesitation in accepting the hypothesis that the *future* will be *unlike* the *past*, if the intervention of new and diverse efficient causes be either postulated or proved. That which the mind really affirms is not the *uniformity of Nature*, pure and simple, but the *uniformity* of its *coördination* under the general law or canon of causation. We may thus postulate, at once, *unity* and *variety* in Nature, as the *legitimate* resultants of this order; for we recognize as *real* the efficiency of personal human agents, acting upon Nature through the medium of natural forces, coöperating with or contravening the plans and purposes of the Divine Architect who called the universe into being.

Faith in Nature and the uniformity of her laws is essential to the evolution of the arts, of the sciences, of civil society, and, in a word, to the normal development of humanity. It is, in fact, a condition precedent of all legitimate improvement, whether intellectual, social, or moral. It is an evidence, therefore, of the Divine Wisdom, which has prearranged all things for man's good, that he is not left to learn this fundamental condition of all art, all science, all government, and, in a word, of all development, by the slow and doubtful processes of experience, which can, indeed, reveal what is and what has been, but which can in nowise tell us either what must be, or, apart from the assumed uniformity of Nature, what may be in the future. Experience can be a guide to the future only on the assumption of the uniformity of Nature, and that assumption it can neither originate nor verify.

¶ III. **Faith in Man.**—Passing onward and upward in our analysis, under the generic concept of not-self, yet far more closely allied to self than aught else with which we come in contact, we find our fellow-man our congener and kinsman in the relations of an identical nature and consciousness. Here the problem of faith, as viewed in relation to its object, involves new and complex elements. In reference to our own personal consciousness, the elements upon which faith fastened were comparatively simple and direct; their modes of action were familiar, and their products determinable. In reference to Nature, considered apart from man, the problem is limited by the processes and relations of material causation, and our faith fastens upon that law as the regulating principle of the grand cosmical movements that are going on around us; so that, however mysterious the combinations and complications may seem to be, we yet feel assured that, if we can but lay our hands on the hidden clew, we shall unravel them all, and find only glorious order and beauty, where the unbelieving soul sees only complexity and confusion. But when we turn to man, we come in contact with new elements; not only with an intelligence like to our own, but also with the powers of a free volition, or free moral agency, uncontrolled by the law of causation. Faith in man, therefore, as involving diverse elements, differs essentially from faith in Nature; but it approximates, by so much, to the faith we have in ourselves.

The essential elements distinguishing man as an object of faith, are: 1. His physical nature; 2. His intelligence; 3. His voluntary powers.

1. *His physical nature.*—In this, man is very closely allied to the proximate genera of animals; and inductions or analogies based upon their phenomenal life may, with considerable certainty, be applied to the animal life of man. Yet the links in the chain of causation, or rather the complexity of elements in organic life, is so great that the problems to be solved are far more difficult than they are in the inorganic world, and the results are, therefore, correspondingly doubtful.

2. *His intellectual nature.*—In this, he is so absolutely identified with us, by the possession of a consciousness so perfectly congenerical with our own, that we reason concerning it with a faith based upon our consciousness of the intellectual life within us, which tends naturally, if not inevitably, to dogmatism. We affirm of a neighbor, for instance, that "he does not and cannot believe this or that, or that he does not and cannot doubt this or that;" and we do this with a perfect sincerity and an undoubting faith that can only be generated by the consciousness that it would be impossible for us to so believe or doubt under the actual conditions of the problem. We thus unhesitatingly apply to our fellow-man the laws of our own free personality; or, in familiar language, we judge our neighbors by ourselves. It results necessarily from this principle that good men are naturally trustful and bad men are naturally suspicious.

3. *His moral nature.*—This, in the true sense, is the representative of the individuality or personality of the man; it is, therefore, a phenomenon *sui generis*, having absolutely no analogon in the sphere of experience. We can, in this respect, therefore, only judge our fellow-men in the light of personal consciousness and of observation of man. All arguments or analogies drawn from Nature or the animal world to the moral nature of man are necessarily deceptive, since they ignore conscience and the will, the absolutely essential

elements in the problem. But here, fortunately, we possess a golden key to this closed door, in the depths of consciousness and the phenomena of our own free personalities, so that we can, in fact, judge of the actions of men in masses or communities with even more certainty than we can judge of some of the more complex elements of Nature.

The ground or basis of our faith in man as man must, therefore, be sought in the depths of our personal consciousness; and *it is not*, as we are often told, the result of experience, but is coördinate with it, and in a certain sense antedates it. The truth is, faith in man is *instinctive*, or *intuitive*, and we learn by experience, not *trust*, but *distrust.* "Credulous as a child" has passed into a proverb, and justly too, for children instinctively trust men, and only learn to distrust them by the bitter lessons of a sad experience. Fearful, therefore, is the work of that parent who, by carelessness, or, worse, by so-called *innocent* deception, first teaches the child the bitter lesson of distrust; for, to the last, excessive credulity is wiser, better, happier, than excessive doubt or distrust. Better far is it for man to trust and be deceived a thousand times, than never to trust, and thus to dwell for ever alone, in a solitude worse than that of Sahara, and in an atmosphere more deadly than the miasms of the Campagna!

¶ IV. **Faith in God.**—In the affirmation of God and His infinite perfections, faith culminates, and finds absolute repose. In Nature it meets only with the finite, the limited, the variable, under multiple forms; while, by the very laws of its own being, it demands *unity* and *invariability.* In man, it finds a certain degree of unity, but it is the unity of limited, finite personalities, acting and reacting upon each other and upon Nature, which they limit, and by which they are limited; and thus the seeming unity of the individual is lost in the endless multiplicity of the race; and man and Nature alike demand a reduction to a higher unity, which shall contain both, and account for both, in the overwhelming fulness of its own self-sufficiency. Faith in God is a psychologic necessity to man—a fact proved, not only by actual analysis of the content of the individual consciousness, but also by decisive historic evidence, which proves conclusively that the generic concept, under some one or other of its possible forms, has ever been an actual fruitful element in the evolution of the historic forms of human society. Generically considered, the concept of God has originated, under the canon of contradiction, two schools, viz.: 1. That of atheism, which denies; and 2. That of theism, which affirms the existence of God.

I. *Atheism.*—This is not, as might be supposed, a simple, indivisible school or theory. It presents itself under at least two specific forms, each of which has been an object of faith, viz.:

(*a*) *The theory of chance*, in which the devotee affirms at once the non-existence of God, and the universal dominion of chance. This theory logically excludes, not only destiny or fate, but law or order also. It is needless to say that it is the resultant and concomitant of a very low order and degree of mental development, and emerges only from the sphere of ignorance. At the present day it commands no respect, and has no advocates.

(*b*) The theory of law, destiny, fate, the immutable order or relation of things, etc. Intelligent atheism is a *positive* as well as a *negative* faith. On its negative side, it denies either the actual existence of God, or, conceding the abstract possibility of His existence, denies the possibility of a revelation and authentication of that existence to man. On the latter hypothesis, if God is, He is to man as if He were not.

On its positive side, it affirms the universality of the dominion of law, using that term, not as the expression of the intelligent volitions of a personal lawgiver, but as the synonyme of the immutable relations of things, conceived as self-existent and eternal entities. It does not, however, postulate their eternal existence in this or that specific form, but in their ultimate generic or typical form. This hypothesis obviously ultimates in the affirmation, philosophically, of the endless recurrence of a series of cycles of evolution and disintegration, each cycle beginning and ending in a fundamental chaos, in which ultimate being and its laws alone exist, and consciousness is not. This theory, as will be seen in the sequel, is identical in fact with pantheism in its last analysis.

II. *Theism.*—This, as a generic concept or theory, opposed to atheism, may be resolved into three specific concepts or hypotheses, differing widely from each other in their natures, their relations, and their consequences. The specific ground of division parting the genus is personality. Theists, *generically* so called, may be classified into those affirming, respectively: first, the impersonality, and, second, the personality of God; or, in popular language, into pantheists and theists proper.

1. *Pantheism.*—doctrine of an impersonal God. This differs in little else than the name from the rational form of atheism. It postulates, like that, the universality and immutability of law throughout the cosmos, or universe, including in those terms *absolutely* all existence, material and spiritual, intelligent and unintelligent, necessary and voluntary, known and unknown, human and divine. Like atheism, it postulates also the eternity and self-existence of the germinal or ultimate element of all being; and this ultimate being, in its undeveloped, formless, unconscious self-existence, is God —*but a God unintelligent, unconscious, and impersonal.* Atheism posits the eternal relations, properties, and laws of the eternal substance or substances in the primal chaotic state, without attempting to determine the ultimate *unity* or *multiplicity* (though inclining to multiplicity) of substance or substances. Pantheism posits the ultimate unity of substance, and its *unconscious* self-evolution into the perceived multiplicity of the universe under the necessary attributes, conditions, properties, or laws of its own unconscious being. Atheism, therefore, in its rational form, sustains the same relation to pantheism which polytheism sustains to true theism, i. e., to monotheism.

Atheism admits the *illusory* intelligence and freedom of

the human personality, but cannot, in any wise, account for even that illusive existence. Pantheism affirms the self-consciousness, intelligence, and personality of its Deity; but only in the consciousness, intelligence, and personality of each one of its multiple human personalities. This self-consciousness, intelligence, and personality, are, however, but illusions, which, like bubbles on the ocean, appear for a moment, only to sink back and be reabsorbed into the bosom of *unconscious*, *unintelligent*, and *impersonal* Deity. Atheism and pantheism alike, therefore, fail to account for, or rationally justify to the human soul, its own conscious existence, states, and phenomena. Nor is the fact that intelligent men hold to both of these forms of faith as the satisfactory and only satisfactory solution of the cosmic problems that, from age to age, emerge into human consciousness, presumptive evidence in favor of either; for both the atheist and the pantheist habitually state their theories in language appropriate only to the theory of a monotheistic personal God, and which, of right, belongs exclusively to the last-named theory. They thus, consciously or unconsciously, throw around their several theories an illusive or deceptive meaning, which renders to the mind a satisfaction which the theories themselves, fairly stated in language strictly appropriate to themselves, could not give; just as the sensualistic school of philosophers (intentionally or unintentionally) cover the nakedness of their theory of causation, viz., "mere invariableness of succession and resemblance," by *the use of language, forms of expression, and applications*, which in all fairness belong *exclusively* to their opponents. It unquestionably requires an effort for any intelligent reader of the works of the great pantheistic writers of the day to stop, in the midst of the full tide of flowing thought, and divest his mind of the *illusive* significance of their beautiful descriptions of God and the universe—illusions which spring from their habitual use of forms or modes of expression, of words, and of allusions, which originated in the faith of a personal, self-conscious God, and which cannot be used, even by an avowed pantheist, without awaking ideas and concepts which the pantheist would formally disavow. This is obviously as unfair as it is unscientific; and the plea, sometimes offered in justification, that "there is no other language in which they can express their thoughts," is simply an admission that the theories of atheism and pantheism alike contradict the common consciousness of humanity. It is perfectly safe to say that neither atheism nor pantheism would need any other refutation than the habitual use of exact and characteristic language on the part of their professed advocates. Neither faith could long endure such an ordeal.

2. *Personal theism.*—This form also is generic, and presents itself under two divisions or species, viz., polytheism and monotheism, or theism proper.

(*a*) *Polytheism.*—This involves the assertion of a plurality of Gods, each of whom is conceived as a distinct and independent personality. They are sometimes conceived as entirely independent, and often as antagonistic, and at others as related by consanguinity or other forms of affiliation. It suffices, for the sake of logical completeness, to note this form of faith; discussion of it is needless, although it is held to-day by a majority of the human race. It has, however, no standing whatever among truly civilized and enlightened nations, and, in the nature of things, can have none. As obviously self-contradictory and absurd, it must be discounted at once, as a simple perversion of the natural elements of human thought, originating in *moral* rather than *rational* causes, and disappearing with the abnormal elements and conditions that called it into being.

(*b*) *Monotheism*, or *theism proper*, predicates the existence, the unity, the spirituality, the infinity, and the perfection of God, and affirms Him to be self-existent and self-sufficient, the uncaused cause of all being, whether material, spiritual, or mixed, and the sufficient reason of the universe, with all its actualities and potentialities.

This theory grounds itself immovably in the actual phenomena of the human soul as an intelligent, self-conscious free agency or free cause; and, in the midst of the atheism, pantheism, and polytheism of the ages, has carved out, in language, the reflection of these indelible, necessary processes of human thought and development, so that the atheist, the pantheist, and the polytheist, are alike compelled to robe their adverse theories in language borrowed from theism proper, and are thus constrained to pay unwilling homage to truth and the God of truth.

In the conception of God, human thought culminates, and faith attains to its perfect rest, and its maximum of energy and power. In Him alone it attains to that intellectual and moral "*pou sto*" in the heavens which Archimedes vainly sought, whereby it is enabled to move the earth, and to solve *potentially*, if *not actually*, all its mysteries. In Him alone it finds at once the sufficient reason for the phenomena of matter and of mind, for the laws of physics and of thought, for our faith in the uniformity of Nature, and our faith in consciousness.

It is sometimes said that the steps by which man struggles up to faith in God are, separately considered, weak and doubtful, and that the resultant faith must, logically, be correspondingly weak and doubtful; but this is a simple misconception of the process. As well might it be said to a shipwrecked mariner, who has climbed, tremblingly and doubtfully, from the top of a surf-beaten wreck, by a slender ladder of swaying ropes, in which sometimes but a single half-rotten cord interposes between him and death, that his position is still insecure, when he stands firmly at last upon the level surface of the granite cliff. *It is not true, psychologically, that a faith is no stronger, rationally, than the weakest link in the chain of thought that led to it.* That link may have been but a preponderating doubt, while the faith may have, rationally, the strength of a perfect demonstration. It is thus that the faith of the earnest thinker grasps the concept of God, and fastens upon it with an energy, a power, an intensity of conviction, and a self-evidence, that reacts upon the whole intellectual and moral life, and lifts the man to a higher plane of thought, inspires him with nobler impulses, and incites him to a purer life. This suggests a final thought, with which our analysis of the intellect must conclude, namely:

¶ V. **Relations of Faith to Character.**—No single phenomenon of human development is more marked or more remarkable than the influence of a special faith upon the development of personal character. History is full of examples of men who have grasped some special faith or truth with such energy and intensity that it has absorbed and appropriated all the faculties and powers of their souls, and changed, not only all the purposes of their lives, but the destinies of nations as well. It may be an hypothesis in science or in government, a dream of the ideal in art, or it may be faith in God, that thus absorbs and appropriates all the energies, all the powers, all the hopes, all the sweetness of life, into itself; but, whatever it may be, the fact remains that faith is, at last, the vital force that moves and moulds the world.

But, while the fact is so obtrusive, its philosophy is not so apparent. It is easy, indeed, to generalize concerning it, and to illustrate the power of the nearest object to seize upon the soul, just as the mote on the object-glass of the astronomer's telescope hides or obscures a distant world, but, after all, such analogies fail to satisfy us. In the light of preceding investigations, the solution of the problem resolves itself into two complementary thoughts, viz.:

1. That *concentration* is the essential element or condition precedent of the evolution of decisive power in the *finite human soul.* It is, consequently, a necessary law of the evolution of humanity, that it attains to its highest results, in any given sphere of research or action, only on condition of neglecting all minor elements, and of fastening upon some central vitalizing thought, concept, or faith. And—

2. That, in the analytic evolution of the ultimate elements of thought, as well as in the final resultants of our intellectual processes, we attain, severally and personally, to faith in God, as the final specific and generic faith of humanity, and

as the broadest, the highest, the intensest, and the most philosophic vitalizing element of human activity.

The man whose life is vitalized and intensified by any less comprehensive faith than this ultimate faith in God, must necessarily be limited, *de facto*, to a partial, imperfect, and incomplete evolution of his own *potential life;* while the man whose life is vitalized by a living faith in God, not only attains to a higher plane of thought, but also to a more comprehensive and equable development of his own *potential life;* with the additional advantage that, returning from this higher plane and intenser vitality, he may and will react with accumulated momentum upon any subsidiary purpose, or object, or faith, which may, for the time, legitimately claim his attention. Faith in God is thus, *psychologically*, as well as *theologically*, the central element in the evolution of a pure, an intense, and an ideally perfect humanity.

THE INTELLECT: SUPPLEMENTARY TOPICS.

Preliminary Analysis.

Before passing from the sphere of the Intellect to that of the Sensibilities, it seems to be necessary for us to pause and investigate certain normal and abnormal states or affections of the soul, which cannot, as yet, be reduced to any scientific coördination with the mental faculties or the ordinary processes of intellection, but which, from their frequency and importance, demand some notice, even in an elementary treatise. These special states and affections may, with sufficient accuracy, be considered under the heads of Sleep and its concomitants, and of Insanity.

DIVISION FIRST—SLEEP.

Preliminary Analysis.

EVOLUTION OF THE FORMS OF SLEEP.

¶ I. **Natural Sleep.**—No phenomenon of human life is more familiar or more grateful to man than that of sleep. It comes to relieve his weariness, to ease his pain, to soothe his sorrows, and to bring new life and new energy to his whole complex being, physical and intellectual. It needs, therefore, but to be named to be recognized.

¶ II. **Cataleptic Sleep.**—Nearly allied to the phenomena of natural sleep are those that manifest themselves in the phenomena of trances, animal magnetism, modern spiritualism (so called), etc., etc., which may not improperly be classed together, and called cataleptic sleep, and which, from their marked peculiarities, demand separate analysis.

CLASS I.—NATURAL SLEEP.

Preliminary Analysis.

¶ I. **Sleep both a Physical and a Psychical Phenomenon.**—It is needless here to offer any formal definition of natural sleep; it suffices to analyze its conditions, and to ascertain its relations. It is obviously both a physical and a psychical phenomenon, i. e., it involves, primarily, both the material and spiritual natures of man in its influences; not, indeed, that we have any positive evidence that mind, as such, ever intermits its activity, but that we know that sleep modifies, controls, and sometimes obliterates, that activity as a *conscious* fact. The phenomena of dreams, while they give us reason to suspect that mind is never wholly inactive, do not conclusively prove the fact, while they do demonstrate that sleep essentially modifies our actual mental processes, when we do recover them in consciousness more or less perfectly.

¶ II. **Final Cause of Sleep.**—Sleep, although it is a psychical as well as a physical phenomenon, is essentially an affection of the brain and nervous system, and its immediate final cause is the rest and recuperation of the cerebral and nervous energies. Mediately, it results in the corresponding rest and recuperation of the muscular and organic systems, also; while the cessation of the functions of the brain and nervous systems sufficiently accounts for the other physical phenomena, and for the cessation or interruption of the ordinary flow of the consciousness.

¶ III. **Classification of the Forms of Natural Sleep.**—In the light of personal consciousness and experience, the simplest and most natural classification of the ordinary forms of sleep is into—

1. *Perfect sleep;* i. e., into that state in which the proper functions of the cerebral and nervous systems enjoy perfect rest, the senses are locked in slumber, and the consciousness of the soul is, for the time, completely cut asunder by a dreamless sleep. And—

2. *Imperfect sleep;* i. e., a broken slumber, in which the rest of the cerebral and nervous systems is not complete, the senses are not wholly closed to the impressions of the external world, and the consciousness is partially active, producing the phenomena of dreams, etc.

CHAPTER I.—PERFECT SLEEP.

Section I.—Its Physical Phenomena.

¶ I. **Indications of Approaching Sleep.**—The indications of approaching sleep are familiar, and need but little illustration; the most prominent are—

1. General languor and weariness of the muscular and nervous systems; and—

2. Dulness and heaviness of the senses. This is peculiarly marked in reference to the eyes, though it is scarcely less obtrusive in regard to the hearing and the other senses,

¶ II. **Physical Conditions of Perfect Sleep.**—If we pass now from the phenomena of approaching, to those of perfect, sleep, and examine the conditions of the physical organism, we shall find—

1. *That proper organic action is uninterrupted* during perfect sleep. The heart, the lungs, etc., etc., maintain their several functions unimpaired.

2. *That all voluntary muscular activity is suspended.* —We must here distinguish between the action of the voluntary muscles, as of the limbs, and the involuntary, as of the heart and lungs. The action of the first is entirely suspended, or if, by chance, movement takes place, it is automatic, the result of local irritation of the nerves of motion, and is not a consequent of volition; while the action of the involuntary muscles goes on uninterrupted and unimpaired.

3. *Normal cerebral and nervous action are suspended.*—This statement is superfluously evident, in the light of the preceding statements that sleep is essentially an affection of the brain and nervous systems.

Sec. II.—Its Mental Phenomena.

¶ I. **Loss of Consciousness.**—Loss of consciousness is the first, as it is the immediate, mental resultant of perfect sleep, and seems to depend, like the loss of the powers of sensation, upon the suspension of cerebral action. It thus indicates, decisively, the intimacy of the connection between our physical and spiritual natures.

¶ II. **Loss of Voluntary Power.**—This is a simple necessary corollary of the preceding fact. The will is dependent upon the intellect, and cannot act wholly independently of it; where, therefore, there is no consciousness, there can be no volition or voluntary power.

¶ III. **Probable Activity of Mind in a State of Perfect Sleep.**—Here the whole question turns upon a simple balance of probabilities. On the one side, we have the simple fact of blank unconsciousness, and the materialistic hypothesis that thought is a simple function of the brain, with the resulting corollary that, when cerebral action is suspended, thought must cease. On the other hand, we have the phenomena of dreams and imperfect sleep, and the spiritual hypothesis that mind has an independent existence. The faith of humanity tends, and has ever tended, to the latter theory.

Sec. III.—Conditions of Perfect Sleep.

¶ I. **Regularity of its Hours.**—This is an underlying condition of perfect sleep, that cannot safely be disregarded. Its power is strikingly manifest in the animal races, especially in the arctic regions, where the day is continuous for months, but where, none the less, the animals have their regular seasons of repose. The same physical law is obtrusively evident in human physiology, and the evil results of irregular hours of sleep, and of the modern custom of turning night into day, are manifest in the increasing nervous irritability of the Anglo-American people, among whom such customs are specially prevalent. He who would sleep *perfectly*, must sleep *at night*, and at *regular hours.*

¶ II. **Quiet, or Freedom from Disturbing Influences.**—Quiet is here used in a purely relative sense, not so much as the synonyme of *silence* as of *regularity.* Noises, if regular and customary, as the clatter of a mill, or the beating of the ocean-surf upon the shore, do not break the rest of those accustomed to them; while the sudden cessation of these sounds would at once arouse the sleeper.

¶ III. **Health of Body.**—Sickness often predisposes to sleep, but not to natural or perfect sleep. Where pain, suffering, or disease intervenes, the perfect rest of dreamless sleep is broken; and, in turn, where the latter is not realized from any cause, languor, weakness, and eventually disease, are the natural resultants.

Sec. IV.—Hours of Sleep.

¶ I. **Hours of Sleep as affected by Age.**—The hours of sleep necessary to perfect health vary with the age of the individual. In infancy, the proportion of sleeping to waking hours is at its maximum, and this ratio, ordinarily, steadily diminishes and reaches its minimum at or a little after the meridian of life, and then again slowly increases to old age or second childhood. This law strikingly corresponds with the physical and mental necessities of the race, giving the largest proportion of time to rest and unconsciousness when time is relatively least valuable.

¶ II. **Hours of Sleep as affected by Occupation.**—Occupation has much to do with the number of hours of sleep demanded in order to perfect health. Some kinds of physical labor are more exhausting than others, and mental labor, proportionally, is more exhausting and requires more sleep than physical. The physiological principle involved is obviously this: the amount of sleep demanded is proportioned to the amount of cerebral and nervous exhaustion superinduced by the previous labor. The maximum, in this direction, it need hardly be added, is reached, *not by muscular*, but *by mental effort.*

¶ III. **Hours of Sleep as affected by Health.**—The influence of health and disease upon the hours of sleep has been already incidentally noted, and needs only to be formally reannounced here for the sake of logical completeness. Sickness, involving physical weakness, involves also corresponding cerebral and nervous exhaustion, and therefore predisposes to sleep; or, contrariwise, in cases of febrile excitement of the brain, causes sleeplessness.

CHAPTER II.—IMPERFECT SLEEP.

Preliminary Analysis.

¶ I. **In what it differs from Perfect Sleep.**—Imperfect differs from perfect sleep only in degree, if the radical principle alone be considered: but its phenomena are wholly diverse; and—

1. The senses are but imperfectly closed to external impressions.

2. Cerebral and nervous action are but partially suspended.

3. Muscular activity is not wholly suspended.

4. The unconsciousness is but partial; and—

5. The power of volition is not entirely dormant.

¶ II. **Causes of Imperfect Sleep.**—The causes of this phenomenon cannot, in every case, be ascertained with precision; ordinarily, it may be traced—

1. *To internal or personal causes*—such as the peculiar states or conditions of the physical organization, with its multiform conditions and complications; but still more frequently to the states, conditions, or affections of the mind. Any unusual excitement or preoccupation of body or mind is unfavorable to the existence of perfect sleep.

2. *To external disturbing elements.*—The nature and influence of these have, perhaps, been sufficiently indicated in our statement of the conditions of perfect sleep; and they are, moreover, so familiar to the experience of all, that any specific statement of them is useless.

¶ III. **Phenomena of Imperfect Sleep.**—The phenomena of imperfect sleep may be reduced to three general classes, viz.: 1. Dreams; 2. Nightmare; and 3. Somnambulism.

Section I.—Dreams.

¶ I. **Nature of Dreams.**—Dreams have already been declared to be a resultant of imperfect sleep, a fragmentary consciousness, of which, ordinarily, we have neither the beginning nor the end. The phenomena of dreaming are so familiar to the experience of all that they need no description here. They seize apparently upon all the elements of human thought, actual and ideal, and reproduce them in every conceivable form and combination, rational or absurd. For materials, they depend upon the ordinary elements of human thought, which wayward fancy combines, indifferently, into forms of matchless beauty, of unspeakable horror, or of incidents as staid and commonplace as are our daily lives.

¶ II. **Characteristics of Dreams.**—Among the more marked characteristics of dreams, are—

1. *Their incoherence.*—We connect in them, without a thought of incongruity, elements the most contradictory, and materials absurdly heterogeneous. Not only are the events of years crowded into single hours, but in the brief moments of disturbed slumber we live lives lengthened through untold cycles of years. At one time we find ourselves flying through the air, like wingless birds, or again walking spider-like upon the face of the water, as the writer has often done, without a thought of the impossibility or absurdity of the performance. We talk with men across the lapse of centuries, as unthinkingly as, in our waking hours, we converse with our nearest neighbor. No matter how wild the vagaries of our fancies may be, they occasion no surprise to the dreamer. For this incoherence, no other reason can be assigned than that the mind is deprived, at the same time, of the regulating power of the senses and of the will; it, therefore, acts under abnormal conditions.

2. *Apparent reality of dreams.*—Notwithstanding their incoherence, dreams are characterized by a seeming reality, that renders them, for the moment, most intensely actual to the dreamer, stirring the deepest emotions of his soul, and rousing it to the highest pitch of excitement and enthusiasm. He laughs, weeps, lives, moves, in a fairy-land, with as intense a consciousness of reality and actuality as possesses his soul in the stern contests of his waking life. This sense of reality must be attributed to the entire absorption of the soul in the fantasies that engross it, and which seem to come and go entirely independently of the volition of the dreamer, just as the perceptions of actual life impress themselves upon the waking consciousness. This seemingly independent existence is, obviously, their signet of reality to the soul.

3. *Prophetic aspect of dreams.*—There is no single phenomenon of dreaming better attested than the prophetic form which dreams sometimes take, foreshadowing actual occurrences, which could in nowise depend upon them, with a minuteness of detail that would do no discredit to one of the

old prophets. Many such cases have been recorded, and are as well attested as any other occasional psychologic phenomena. The writer recalls two marked cases in his own experience. In the first, he dreamed of a trip into (to him) an unknown region of country, his dream involving peculiarly-marked horses, cattle, scenery, and conversation. He related his dream on the morning after its occurrence, in detail, to a friend, and three weeks afterward realized it, even to its most minute features. Yet it involved nothing of any conceivable importance to himself or any one else; and was only remarkable for the multitude of its details, and for its minute fulfilment. In the second case, while driving in a carriage alone across an unsettled prairie, on a sultry day in July, on his way to his father's house, he fell into a light slumber and dreamed that, on reaching his destination, he met in a certain gateway a younger brother, with whom he had parted a few days before, a hundred miles away from the old homestead, who said to him, "Did you get our letters, and do you know that father is dead?" His dream awaked him, but he gave it little heed; it was not new to him to dream of the death of friends, and such dreams had never proved prophetic. But, when he reached home, in that very gate he met that brother with those sad words upon his lips; and his strange dream was a prophecy. His father had, he knew, been seriously ill, but for more than a week letters from home had relieved all anxiety, and his visit was wholly unconnected with his father's sickness. Any number of similar instances, equally well attested, might be quoted; but space does not permit. The two cases given, perhaps, fairly represent the principal generic forms of what may be called prophetic dreams, viz.: 1. Those which have not, and 2. those which have, or seem to have, a specific bearing upon the interests and happiness of man. The first was utterly without significance then or afterward, though the coincidences were minute and remarkable. The other connects itself with one of the deepest sorrows of life—the loss of an honored father. Such dreams are real and numerous; how are they to be accounted for?

First. Are they mere coincidences? This has been affirmed, but can hardly be sustained, in view of the actual facts. The coincidences are too numerous, too minute, and wonderful, to render such an assumption plausible or credible. This hypothesis, therefore, can hardly be accepted as a *rational* solution of the mystery.

Secondly. Are they supernatural? This we are not at liberty lightly to assume. There is, of course, *no absolute a priori reason* for asserting that God does not and cannot reveal the future to man in dreams now as in the elder days, if there be any sufficient reason for His doing so; but we may not, therefore, rationally assume that He does reveal the future to us, and much less that He reveals to us matters *utterly without significance or importance.* Divine revelation is a fact to be proved, and *not lightly* assumed.

Thirdly. May dreams, then, be prophetic, and yet not supernatural? Or, better, Is prescience, in any degree, or under any conditions, a *natural* attribute of mind? This would seem to be the only reasonable hypothesis. To deny the facts, blankly and peremptorily, were simply to unsettle all the foundations of faith in human testimony. To ascribe them to accidental coincidences is to tax credulity to its utmost. To ascribe them, *en masse*, to supernatural interposition, is to posit more in the conclusion than is warranted by the premises. The only alternative is to admit that *a limited prescience* is an attribute of mind, *simply as mind.* To the believer in revelation, who accepts the literal truth of God's Word, that "God created man in His own image," this hypothesis will not seem strange or incredible.

¶ III. **Reverie, or Day-Dreaming.**—Closely allied to natural dreaming is that state of mind called reverie, or day-dreaming, in which the soul abandons itself to the play and the dominion of its own idle and wayward fancies, and lives, for the time, an unreal and morbid life in dream-land, that unfits it for the sterner realities of actual life. Such states are conditioned, at once, upon morbid influences of body and mind; i. e., upon languor of the first, and upon lack of energy or will-power in the second. It is hardly necessary to add that such day-dreams are seductive and dangerous in their influence.

Sec. II.—Nightmare.

Nightmare seems to be only a peculiar and distressing form of dreaming, dependent upon congestion or stoppage of the circulation of the blood. It is, in some cases, extremely painful to the sufferer, who imagines himself placed in circumstances of horrible danger and suffering, and yet finds himself utterly unable to lift his hand or foot for self-protection, or even to cry out for help. In some extreme cases the symptoms become dangerous, and may result fatally if help be not at hand. It is closely allied in many respects to dreaming, differing from it in the fact that it always involves suffering to the dreamer. In some other respects it is more nearly allied to somnambulism, which must now be considered.

Sec. III.—Somnambulism.

¶ I. **Illustrations of Somnambulism.** — Somnambulism, though less common in human experience than either dreaming or nightmare, is yet a well-ascertained phenomenon of the abnormal consciousness. It occurs under conditions not well understood nor definitely determined. Two illustrations may be quoted from many well-authenticated ones, which may serve to give an idea of their more characteristic phenomena.

1. Dr. Abercrombie tells us of a young nobleman living in the citadel of Breslau, who was observed by his brother to rise in his sleep, wrap himself in a cloak, and escape by a window to the roof of the building. He there tore in pieces a magpie's nest, wrapped the young birds in his cloak, returned to his apartment, and went to bed. In the morning he mentioned the circumstance as having occurred in a dream, and could not be persuaded otherwise until he was shown the birds in his cloak.

2. The French Encyclopædia reports a case which fell under the notice of the Archbishop of Bordeaux. A young minister, a resident in a theological seminary, was a somnambulist, and the archbishop was accustomed to go every night to his room, after he was asleep, and watch him. He would arise, take paper, pen and ink, and proceed to the composition of sermons. Having written a page in a clear, legible hand, he would read it aloud from top to bottom, with a clear voice and proper emphasis. If a passage did not please him, he would erase it, and write the correction plainly, in its proper place, over the erased line or word. All this was done without any assistance from the eye, which was evidently fast asleep, a piece of pasteboard, interposed between the eye and paper, producing no interruption or inconvenience. When his paper was changed for another of the same size, he was not aware of the change, but, when paper of a different size was substituted, he at once detected the difference, thus showing that the sense of feeling was active, and was the guiding sense.

Other illustrations are on record, in which in this state persons have executed paintings, written poems, etc., etc., which they could not equal in their waking hours; and yet others, in which, in apparently profound sleep, with closed eyes, persons have climbed up and walked over the skeleton framework of lofty buildings, where they would not have dared to walk in daylight.

¶ II. **Analysis of these Phenomena.**—In all of these cases we recognize certain common elements, viz.:

1. *A power of abnormal perception.*—They performed, for example, acts involving all the functions of the most perfect vision, not only with closed eyes, but with opaque bodies interposed between the eye and the object.

2. *Abnormal skill or muscular power;* as in the case of persons walking upon narrow timbers in lofty buildings, or executing fine paintings with a degree of skill they did not possess in their waking hours. Here their abnormal perceptions and powers seemed to serve them better than the normal.

3. *Abnormal intellectual powers.*—These are distinctly indicated in a number of cases on record, but are not so distinctly marked or so obtrusive in their character as the other elements noted.

¶ III. **Philosophy of Somnambulism.**—It is easy to ask how these things can be accounted for, but extremely difficult to answer. There is a manifest analogy between them and prophetic dreaming on the one hand, and visions and clairvoyance on the other; and, as will be seen in the sequel, they all point, as with index-fingers, to a common hypothesis, viz., the existence of certain undetermined mental powers, giving knowledge of things not present to sense, nor known through the ordinary channels of perception.

CLASS II.—CATALEPTIC SLEEP.

Preliminary Discussion.

¶ I. **Illustrations of Cataleptic Sleep.**—The term cataleptic sleep is here used to express that peculiar condition of the system known—

1. As the trance-state, produced involuntarily by mental excitement acting on the individual under peculiar circumstances and conditions.
2. As magnetic sleep, produced by the agency or power of another person, with the consent of the sleeper; and—
3. Clairvoyant sleep, produced after the forms and by the processes of so-called modern spiritualism.

All of these forms are more or less familiar, and need little more than to be named to bring them to the consciousness of the intelligent student.

¶ II. **Analysis of its Physical Conditions.**—Cataleptic sleep involves in all its forms certain peculiar physical conditions, viz.:

1. It presupposes certain peculiarities of nervous organization in the sleeper. It is only occasionally that a person is found to fall accidentally or involuntarily into the trance-state; and, in the circles of animal magnetism and spirit-

ualism, it is well understood that only certain forms of nervous organization are susceptible.

2. It presupposes an efficient external cause acting upon the sensitive nervous organization. In natural trances, this may be a season of intense religious excitement; in animal magnetism, it is the will of the operator; in spiritual circles, it is claimed to be the agency of spirits.

¶ III. **Analysis of its Mental Conditions.**—It involves certain corresponding mental conditions, viz.:

1. Deficiency of voluntary or will power. This may be *permanent*, a natural characteristic of the individual; *temporary*, the result of disease or accident; or *voluntary*, the result, for the time being, of self-abnegation. But, whatever be the cause, the thing itself is a condition precedent of the phenomena.

2. Predominance, for the time being, of the sensitive over the intellectual and voluntary natures. No one who has intelligently investigated these phenomena can fail to recognize the facts here noted; they are obtrusively evident, and, in fact, in the circles of animal magnetism and spiritualism, it would be safe to add that the simple presence and resistance of one or two determined wills often suffice to defeat the ordinary manifestations in limited circles.

Another fact should be noted. Cataleptic sleep and its phenomena, not only presuppose intellectual and especially *voluntary* weakness (or better, deficiency of will-power), but they *superinduce both*, even to the extent of producing, in numerous instances, actual insanity or idiotcy.

¶ IV. **Classification of its Forms.**—Cataleptic sleep presents itself under two forms, viz.:

1. *Involuntary*, in which it is produced unconsciously to the subject of it, by the influences surrounding him and acting upon him. In such cases there is, obviously, no consent of the will of the subject; but there is, at the same time, no actual resistance, and the fact is well ascertained that the tendency to cataleptic sleep increases by repetition, and tends to become habitual, if not actually voluntary. Indeed, there

is much reason to believe that under the influence of habit the party may eventually acquire the power of passing voluntarily into this abnormal state.

2. *Voluntary*, in which the subject, of his own choice, yields himself up to the power of the influences designed to produce the result, and, so far forth, aids in its production, as in animal magnetism and spiritualism.

¶ V. **Classification of its Phenomena.**—The phenomena corresponding to these forms of cataleptic sleep, respectively, are:

1. *Visions*, in which the subject sees, with the vividness of reality, scenes which, for the time being, are a part of his real life, and which, afterward, he is able ordinarily to recollect with a freshness and distinctness which render it almost impossible to disabuse his mind of its intense conviction of their reality.

2. *Clairvoyance*, in which the visions of the dreamer are controlled, ordinarily, by the mind of another, and relate chiefly to things actual, seen under abnormal conditions. In clairvoyance, however, as well as in visions, the mind takes a wide range, and grasps the unknown world beyond with seemingly the same readiness with which it grasps things nearer at hand.

It is obvious that these distinctions between natural visions and clairvoyance, as well as those separating both from dreams, nightmare, and somnambulism, are somewhat arbitrary, and may eventually disappear; but premature identification of things involving, apparently, different conditions and attributes, is eminently unscientific.

CHAPTER I.—VISIONS.

Evolution of their Generic Forms.

¶ I. **Natural Visions.**—The form of natural visions has already been announced, and needs only to be formally noted here; it will be discussed hereafter.

¶ II. **Supernatural Visions.**—The believer in the Holy Scriptures necessarily and joyfully recognizes a second form of visions, viz., *the supernatural.* This form, it need hardly be said, is illustrated and attested solely in the Word of God, and must here be recognized among the proper phenomena of mind, wholly independent of the question of the actual or possible repetition of such supernatural revelations. A single remark on this point may, however, be hazarded, viz., the passage in the last chapter of Revelation (18th verse) has been taken in a wider sense than the context warrants, and we have, therefore, no Divine authority for asserting that no future revelations will be made to man.

Section I.—Natural Visions.

¶ I. **Illustrations of Natural Visions.**—It was once the privilege of the writer to see two cases of a remarkable character of cataleptic sleep, accompanied by natural visions. They occurred in a religious meeting in a country congregation, among an excitable people, accustomed to place no restraint upon the manifestations of religious emotion. The known characters of all the parties present precluded all suspicion of, and cut off all motives for, deception. The parties were a young lady and gentleman of the ages of nineteen and twenty-two years, respectively. The meeting was at a private house, with perhaps one hundred persons present, and was of a very exciting character. The parties both became very much engaged, shouted excessively, and finally, in a state of great physical exhaustion, but still conscious, were taken out of the room at nearly the same time, and carried into different rooms and laid upon beds, where they soon became insensible to all that was going on around them. The writer examined the young lady carefully, having been near her, and, in fact, watching her for nearly an hour, anticipating the result, as she had been similarly affected before. She lay, for the most part, quietly, her breathing easy and natural, her pulse regular, firm, and not hurried, her color fresh and rosy, as in health, her eyes open and natural in appearance, but *utterly insensible* to the impression of the strongest light, even when suddenly brought so near to the open eye as to endanger scorching the eyebrows. She was entirely insensible to sounds, however loud, sudden, or startling, and to pain, however acute, as was decisively tested by a gentleman present, who suddenly and without warning thrust a needle into her forearm until it grated against the bone, making a wound which was unmistakably painful four hours afterward, when, after her restoration to consciousness, she complained that some venomous insect had stung her there, pointing to the discolored spot made by the needle; yet, at the time, she manifested not the slightest consciousness of pain. Her eyes were open, and she used them, apparently self-consciously, as she did also her hands, making motions as if she were washing and wiping herself, using freely a napkin which some one placed in her hands; plucking fruit, as if from a tree, and eating it, etc., etc. All of these actions she fully and naturally accounted for in her subsequent relation of her visions, which were of Paradise, Heaven, and Hell. She detailed at length conversations had in these places with various persons; among others, with the young man still lying in a similar state in the adjoining room, a knowledge of whose condition we had carefully sought to conceal from her. He had never been similarly affected before, and on his return to consciousness related visions, in all respects, even to the conversation with her, the counterpart of hers, though he could by *no* possibility have known what she had related, and collusion between them was practically impossible, even had there been any motive for it, which clearly there was not. It is almost needless to add, their visions were wholly unverifiable in this world, and had no special significance of any kind, unless they could be accepted as testimony in regard to another state of being, which is clearly not warranted by the facts of the case. If true, we have no guarantee of their truth; and, if their truth were conceded, they added nothing to the more sure word of prophecy we already possess.

¶ II. **Conditions of Natural Vision.**—These have, perhaps, been fairly illustrated in the example given; and, obviously, are:

1. *Intense mental or spiritual excitement*, reacting upon:

2. *A highly-sensitive nervous organism.*

The young lady exactly filled these conditions, and became, so long as the writer was enabled to follow her subsequent history, increasingly sensitive to such influences, but without any apparent evil results, physical or mental. The young gentleman, though ordinarily strong and rugged, had recently been ill, and was still comparatively feeble, and, so far as is known to the writer, never had any recurrence of these strange phenomena. It is, perhaps, proper to add that both parties were of unblemished characters, and were, in ordinary life, modest and unassuming in their deportment, shunning rather than seeking notoriety; and to neither was there any conceivable motive for deception or collusion.

¶ III. **Elements of Natural Visions.**—The elements present in the visions of both these parties were simply the ordinary elements of their waking natural and religious consciousness, reproduced under new forms and combinations. The closest analysis failed to reveal any actually or potentially *new* element, or possible new truth.

¶ IV. **Significance of Natural Visions.**—These phenomena raise, at once, two secondary questions, viz.:

1. *Are they, in any real sense, prophetic?*—Can mind, under any circumstances, penetrate the veil that hides the invisible from us, and reveal its mysteries? and—

2. *Is prescience an attribute of mind*, as the phenomena of prophetic dreaming would seem to indicate?

It is obvious, in the outset, that we are not justified, by the facts thus far elicited and verified, in answering either question decisively in the affirmative; and, in the face of the actually-observed facts, it is just as obviously premature to decide either decisively in the negative, as two opposing schools of scientists have, for precisely opposite reasons, been disposed to do. On the one hand, Christian psychologists have been ready to reject all such facts and theories decisively, *a priori*, lest they might militate against the credit of Divine revelation, as expressed in the visions of the prophets and evangelists; while, on the other hand, skeptics and materialists have been just as ready to discredit them, *a priori*, lest they might result in proving the reality of a spiritual life and a Divine prescience.

Both processes are unscientific and unjustifiable, but, least of all, does it become Christian psychologists thus to ignore and discredit well-established facts. The theory of an inspired, supernatural, Divine revelation, upon which the faith of the Christian rests, postulates two conditions, viz.:

First. Prescience as an attribute of God; and—

Second. A natural point of contact in the soul of man, to which a Divine revelation may appeal.

But the hypothesis of the reality of natural prescience, as an attribute of the human soul, as indicated by dreams, visions, and clairvoyance, would seem to furnish just such a point of contact, between the Divine prescience and the human soul, as Christianity demands.

SEC. II.—SUPERNATURAL VISIONS: PROPHECY.

¶ I. **Illustrations of Prophecy.**—The student will not need to be referred to the Holy Scriptures as containing the *only* authenticated prophecies known to man. There stand the original, authenticated, supernatural visions of the old Hebrew seers, written and published to the world centuries before the occurrence of the events they minutely foretell, and the history of the world is the standing witness of their accurate fulfilment.

¶ II. **Conditions of Prophecy.**—The conditions of a Divine revelation are obviously three, viz.:

1. *Human.*—Revelation or prophecy presupposes, as has been already noted, a necessary point of contact in the human soul, to which it may appeal, such as natural prescience would afford, if it were an actual element or attribute of mind.

2. *Superhuman*, i. e., Divine prescience, acting upon the

soul of man, and communicating to it, in some way, a knowledge of future events, such as is in no wise possible to limited human prescience.

3. *The existence of a sufficient final cause* or *motive* for such communication.

Skeptics, who laugh to scorn the supposition that God has supernaturally revealed Himself to man, uniformly ignore the fact *that He does so only for sufficient reasons*, such as would impeach, at once, His wisdom and His goodness, were He to withhold such revelation. It is idle and foolish to say, as some do, that "God is so great, and man is so little, that revelation is incredible." God, who condescended to create man in His own image, would be false to Himself if He did not condescend to care for his welfare, and for the cravings of his spiritual nature, which longs for nothing else so much as it longs for a portion of the Divine prescience.

CHAPTER II.—CLAIRVOYANCE.

SECTION I.—EVOLUTION OF THE GENERIC PHENOMENA.

¶ I. **Involuntary or Accidental Clairvoyance.**—Perhaps no better instance can be given of this than one related of Baron Swedenborg. While visiting in Germany, in the midst of a large company, he passed into the clairvoyant state, and described a fire then raging in his own house in Stockholm, and endangering his library and most valuable papers. He detailed all the incidents of the fire with much minuteness, and announced its suppression and the safety of his property. Dispatches received from home, a few days after, confirmed his vision in all respects. This incident is said to be well attested, and offers a fair illustration of one form of clairvoyance, which, for the sake of convenience, may be termed the involuntary.

¶ II. **Animal Magnetism.**—Under the general phenomena termed animal magnetism, we meet with a second form of clairvoyance, in which the subject, having been put into a state of cataleptic sleep by the direct agency of another person, is enabled to see and reveal things wholly unknown to him in his normal state. Authorities differ as to the limits of this clairvoyance, one party restricting it to a knowledge of what is in the mind of, or is actually known to, the person or persons in magnetic connection with the clairvoyant; others affirm that it extends to any knowledge whatsoever present to the mind of any person in the room; while a third party extends it to a knowledge of things actual, whether present or absent, known or unknown to the parties present. Facts *seem* to sustain the first and second theories, but the third needs *both* rational limitation and confirmation to entitle it, not to credence, but even to scientific consideration.

¶ III. **Odism, as developed by Baron Reichenbach.**—Clairvoyance challenges acceptance in a third form, as presented in the works of Baron Reichenbach. In this case, however, the clairvoyance affirmed extends, not to the thoughts and actions of men, but only to a natural agent or power kindred to, but not identical with, *natural* magnetism, but perhaps identical with what is called *animal* magnetism, and which the baron has denominated "*Od.*" This mysterious agent, he affirms, is present to the senses, and especially to the sight, not of men generally, but of certain peculiarly sensitive persons, who are not only conscious of its physical influence upon their own persons, but are able in darkened rooms to see it flowing forth, in streams of light, from the bodies of men and animals; from magnets, and from many other natural objects; and are, moreover, able to determine the fact of its existence as a cosmical element in the planetary and starry worlds.

¶ IV. **Modern Spiritualism.**—The broadest and highest claims to clairvoyance, however, come from the circles of modern spiritualism, which *claim* for their *seers*, not only the power to read the thoughts, the histories, and the characters of men, and the secrets of Nature, but also to be able to transcend the sphere of earth-life, and to reveal the mysteries of the spirit-world. The latter half of their claim, like the natural visions of the young lady previously noted, were their pretended revelations less contradictory than they notoriously are, must await some method of verification not now known to the circles of spiritualism, before it can challenge *any rational credence whatever.* The mutual contradictions of even the most noted clairvoyants, in reference to the spiritual world, are so numerous, so radical, and so destructive, as to decisively rule their testimony out of court, by demonstrating a fatal and apparently ineradicable element of incertitude which totally vitiates all their spiritual revelations.

In their other forms of clairvoyance, they do not vary materially, in claim or in fact, from the animal magnetists, and their *apparently verified* phenomena do not appear in any respect to surpass the equally well-attested claims of their rivals.

¶ V. **How far Psychologists are bound to recognize such Phenomena.**—In the preceding analysis we have neither attempted to verify the phenomena nor to sift the evidence offered in support of them. It suffices our purpose to know that able, candid, honest men, including some who make pretensions to science, affirm their truth and reality, and offer to verify the phenomena by repeating the experiments. That there is something more in these strongly-asserted phenomena than blank deception must be admitted; that they are what their enthusiastic advocates claim for them, may safely be questioned. Science demands that the *real* phenomena be ascertained *definitely,* which never yet has been done in reference to any one of the forms of clairvoyance noted, and then that their true significance be determined.

Sec. II.—Comparative Analysis of these Phenomena.

¶ I. **They all involve the Affirmation of a Knowledge transcending the ordinary Knowledge of Men, and depending upon Peculiar Conditions.**—However much these forms of clairvoyance differ in detail, they agree in this; and agree, moreover, in the general nature of the knowledge affirmed, with the exception of odism as developed by Baron Reichenbach, which seems to give us a glimpse of the real agency common to them all, rather than an independent series of phenomena.

¶ II. They all agree in conditioning this knowledge upon marked peculiarities and susceptibilities of the complex human organism.

¶ III. They all predicate, in some form and to some degree, the peculiar generic condition known as cataleptic sleep, as a condition precedent of the clairvoyant phenomena.

SEC. III.—PHILOSOPHY OF CLAIRVOYANCE.

¶ I. **Theory of Animal Magnetism.**—This affirms the existence in man—

1. Of a peculiar magnetic influence, whereby one man can act upon another, and produce at pleasure the phenomena of magnetic or cataleptic sleep.
2. Of a peculiar power, while in this state, of seeing and revealing to others things unknown to himself in his ordinary or normal state.

As an hypothesis, scientifically considered, this is not inadmissible; *but it is as yet only an hypothesis absolutely unverified.* It is obvious, in the outset, that the name "animal magnetism" is, at best, based upon a hasty generalization, and upon doubtful if not deceitful analogies. The science—if, indeed, science there be—yet awaits alike its Kepler, its Copernicus, and its Newton. Baron Reichenbach, in his theory of odism, which is evidently only another and more scientific name for substantially the same element (if, indeed, element there be), has pursued a more purely scientific method than the charlatan professors of animal magnetism, who have usually only succeeded in filling their own pockets with pelf, and bringing the whole subject into contempt with scientific men.

¶ II. **Theory of Modern Spiritualism.**—This is more pretentious than that of animal magnetism, and affirms not a single natural element, such as animal magnetism or od, but the direct influence and power of disembodied human spirits, superinducing both physical and mental results and conditions outside of, and superior to, the ordinary powers of Nature. This theory is not necessarily unscientific, since science cannot disprove, and is not therefore authorized, *a priori*, to reject its two fundamental postulates, viz.:

1. That disembodied spirits do actually exist; and—
2. That such spirits may *conceivably* manifest that existence to embodied spirits, that is, to men.

It should be noted here that Christianity predicates the same postulates, among others, as conditions precedent of its own existence; and incidentally asserts more than once the fact of the actual manifestation of the spirits of *disembodied* to *living* men. Neither science nor Christianity, therefore, can justly, on *a priori* principles, reject the claims of modern spiritualism; but they may and should demand of it positive *scientific* verification of its pretentious claims upon human credence. They should, moreover, rigidly test its actual moral influences and relations by its fruits, personal, social, and moral.

¶ III. **Theory of Swedenborgianism.**—This, if the writer comprehends it, is yet broader than that of modern spiritualism; and comprehends the affirmation, not only of *secondary* spiritual inspiration, such as modern spiritualism posits, but also direct Divine spiritual illumination—the exact counterpart of the inspiration of the old Hebrew prophets. It is needless to say that this theory is broad enough to account for all the facts of clairvoyance, if the legitimacy of the baron's claim to be a prophet after the order of Isaiah or John be conceded. But precisely here the theory fails; the baron's claims sadly need the verification which would scientifically challenge the credence of mankind in his prophetic office.

¶ IV. **Relations of Clairvoyance to Dreams, Visions, and Prophecy.**—Clairvoyance, like its congeners named above, seems to be in fact but a manifestation of that occult power of the human soul which we have denominated natural prescience, and which is in man the feeble counterpart of that infinite prescience which belongs to God alone, and to which the latter appealed when He communicated the glorious visions that filled the rapt souls of Moses and Daniel, of Isaiah and John. Natural prescience does not infer or imply any thing supernatural in man; nor is there any thing unreasonable or unscientific in the hypothesis of its existence, especially in view of an earlier assertion, *that to know is of the essence of mind.* But this suggests a more radical thought, namely: there is nothing unscientific, necessarily, in the assumption of the supernatural in its actual relations to the natural, since human science culminates in the concept of man as an intelligent, free personality, capable of reacting upon Nature through its laws, i. e., capable of essentially modifying and changing the course of Nature at pleasure, by intelligently seizing upon its laws, the hidings of its power, and turning them against itself. The analogies of thought, therefore, demand the concept and affirmation of a like relation to Nature on the part of a *primary* personality, i. e., on the part of God. The moment the concept of a free personality, in the true sense, is admitted as scientific, the door is opened widely for the admission of all that we, *legitimately*, term the *supernatural.* The truth is simply this: *the mutual limits* of the *natural* and *supernatural*, conceived in the only strictly rational sense possible, *lie not at some unknown point of contact between man and Nature on the one side, and God and the spirit-world on the other; but at the point of contact between man as an intelligent, free personality, and Nature.*

In conclusion, the remark is hazarded that it is neither wise nor safe for Christian psychologists to neglect the phenomena of this strange border-land of dreams, somnambulism, visions, and clairvoyance. Its phenomena, however much they may have been distorted, magnified, and abused, are to some extent real, and are an open door through which we may look in upon the human soul and its mysteries, under conditions which, properly investigated and comprehended, cannot fail to add to our intelligent comprehension of its real nature and capacities.

DIVISION SECOND—INSANITY.

Preliminary Discussion.

EVOLUTION OF THE GENERAL FORMS OF INSANITY.

Among the saddest, and yet, alas! among the familiar forms of mental phenomena, must be reckoned disordered or diseased mental action. No community is free from its sorrowful influences, and no household is secure from the danger of its possible approach. It presents itself to us under three familiar generic forms, viz.:

1. Intoxication, or temporary insanity produced by stimulants;

2. Insanity proper, under its two specific forms of mania and frenzy;

3. Idiocy, or imbecility; all of which must now be discretely considered.

SECTION I.—INTOXICATION.

¶ I. **Phenomena of Intoxication.**—These are so familiar, and, alas! so frequent objects of observation, that they need no description. They may be seen and studied, almost any day, in the streets of our villages, towns, and cities. They present themselves under the three typical forms of insanity proper, viz.:

1. *Mania*, or aberration of intellect, more or less marked and decisive; in which all true intellectuality is, for the time being, lost.

2. *Frenzy*, or temporary madness, in which the intoxicated man rages like a true madman, dangerous alike to himself and to his fellow-men. And—

3. *Idiocy*, or utter imbecility—the final resultant of absolute intoxication, in which all the attributes of rationality are lost, and nothing but the semblance of disgraced humanity remains.

¶ II. **Nature of Intoxication.**—This is well ascertained,

physiologically, to be lesion of the brain, produced by alcohol, which is taken up by the blood, and carried unchanged to the brain, where, as alcohol, it fills the cavities, and acts continually as a disturbing and destroying element, whose influence is evil and only evil continually. Thus far reference has been had exclusively to drunkenness produced by alcohol, but there are kindred forms of intoxication, not less destructive, produced by opium, hasheesh, and, at times, by tobacco.

¶ III. **Relations of Intoxication to Insanity.**—These have already been indicated in the statement that it takes on the three typical forms of insanity, viz., mania, frenzy, and idiocy. The drunken man is as truly insane, for the time being, as the legitimate inhabitant of a lunatic asylum; and every successive act of intoxication is a direct, and may become a decisive, step toward permanent insanity under that most terrible of all its forms, delirium tremens, as well as toward a drunkard's grave. Each fresh draught of the intoxicating cup is a new link forged in the chain that is binding the besotted victim to the car of death and hell. Would to God that the words were here written in letters of fire, that every young man might not only read but realize them!—*that the first glass of wine is just as dangerous, just as deadly, and just as wicked, as the last fiery cup of alcohol which consigns its wretched victim to the drunkard's grave. The first he could have refused without an effort; the last he has no power to put from him.*

SEC. II.—INSANITY PROPER.

¶ I. **Its Phenomena.**—The phenomena of insanity proper, typified by intoxication, are themselves so common as to need but little illustration. Its forms are—

1. *Mania*, or *simple mental aberration*, either partial or total, temporary or permanent. Its forms vary from the hallucinations of the harmless monomaniac, affecting only special forms of thought or modes of mental action, to complete insanity, in which all rationality is lost, and mental ruin alone remains. Some of the forms of mania, and especially of

monomania, in which only a single faculty is disordered, are exceedingly interesting, but space does not permit their introduction here.

2. *Frenzy, or madness proper.*—This, like mania, may be partial or total, paroxysmal or permanent. It may exist only in reference to certain forms or modes of mental action; or it may be paroxysmal, and only supervene at intervals more or less regular, or otherwise recur only on occasion of certain provoking causes at irregular intervals; or it may, and frequently does, alternate with mania, or with states of apparently perfect sanity.

3. *Idiocy, or imbecility.*—This may be, and usually is, congenital, but it may also be the final and hopeless result of insanity proper. As a congenital phenomenon, it is usually accompanied and marked by obvious physical malformation or imperfection. Like other forms of mental aberration, it may be either partial or total, paroxysmal or permanent. In the latter form it is often the final resultant of permanent insanity, in which nothing remains of humanity but its semblance, the jewel within being hopelessly obscured, and the feebleness of a second and sadder, because hopeless, childhood having supervened.

¶ II. **Nature and Conditions of Insanity.**—These are strikingly indicated in the actual phenomena of intoxication, which represent in turn, for the time being, every phase of actual insanity, from monomania to idiocy. In other words, the drunken man is, for the time, voluntarily insane. This fact proves conclusively that insanity in all its forms results from simple malformation or lesion of the brain, and is not in any sense an affection of *the soul*, apart from physical organization. The phenomena of delirium produced by fevers, or blows upon the skull, all confirm the truth of this hypothesis. Lesion of the brain fully accounts for all the phenomena, and shadows forth the hope of a higher and better life, where mania, frenzy, and idiocy, are not, and intoxication is unknown. It is hardly necessary to add that this lesion of the brain may be the result of accident, of excessive labor, physical or mental, of the use of narcotic stimulants, of disease, or it may be congenital.

¶ III. **Its Lessons.**—The lessons taught us by these sad phenomena are simple, direct, and sorrowful. Reason, intelligence, hope, love, all that render life tolerable, desirable, hopeful, happy, hang upon the slender thread of cerebral health and regularity; and this health and regularity of action may be overthrown and finally destroyed by excesses of any and every kind, physical, mental, or moral. Reason is too sacred a trust to be trifled with, as the debauchee and the drunkard are accustomed to do.

BOOK II.—THE SENSIBILITIES.

PRELIMINARY DISCUSSION.

SECTION I.—ANALYSIS OF THE SENSIBILITIES.

¶ I. **Evolution of the Generic Idea.**—In accordance with our original analysis, we now pass to consider the second general division or form of mental activity, viz., the Sensibilities, including the emotional and passional elements in the soul of man. This is no strange or foreign region, known only to a few favored sons of men, but the common inheritance of humanity, the theatre of all our hopes and fears, our joys and sorrows, our happiness or misery. Men may not remember, imagine, or reason; but they cannot choose but feel, enjoy, suffer, love, and hate. In truth, in the sensibilities we enter upon the most universal, all-pervading element of soul-life.

¶ II. **Relations of the Sensibilities to the Intellect.**—These have already, perhaps, been sufficiently indicated, and need only, for the sake of distinctness, to be formally reannounced here. The sensibilities, in all their manifestations, postulate or presuppose antecedent intellections. This precedence may be, and often is, distinguishable only logically, and not chronologically, since the perception and the emotion may be, in any given instance, practically simultaneous.

But while intellection logically antecedes and conditions the action of the sensibilities, the fact must not be overlooked that the latter in turn, both immediately and mediately through the will, react upon and stimulate the intellect to intenser and more persistent action.

¶ III. **Importance of the Sensibilities.**—In the light of preceding discussions, it were idle to stop to argue the relative importance of the sensibilities as functions of the soul, or to enforce the necessity of carefully investigating their phenomena. These facts are so obtrusively evident as to be in fact axiomatic; but, as might naturally be expected, the difficulties of the study are in direct proportion to its intrinsic and relative importance; yet they are neither insuperable nor discouraging to the earnest student.

Sec. II.—Classification of the Sensibilities.

¶ I. **General Principles of Classification.**—The direct and positive nature of the processes of intellection suggested at once, if it did not necessitate, the general principles of classification actually adopted; but the relations of the sensibilities to each other are not so marked, and it is not so easy to determine principles of classification which will decisively and satisfactorily part the sensibilities into appropriate and natural groups. This difficulty is indicated, as we might rationally have anticipated it would be, by the variety of terms used in popular language to express the phenomena and affections of the sensitive nature. The thoughtful student here, as well as elsewhere, will find in this spontaneous consciousness of humanity, i. e., in popular language, a valuable guide to a true scientific classification.

The most general as well as the most obvious principle of classification of the sensibilities arises out of their relations to the will and the phenomena of volition, and is into: first, those that do not, and, second, those that do, act upon the will directly in the relation of motives to volition.

¶ II. **Evolution of the Emotions.**—Tested by the principle of division noted above, the first general class or order of the sensibilities that emerges in consciousness is that ordinarily represented by the generic term *Emotions*. As thus conceived, it includes all those states or affections of the sensibilities, whether simple or complex, which result merely in an affection of the sensitive nature, and do not immediately act upon the will in the relation of motives to choice; such as emotions of beauty, of sublimity, etc., etc.

¶ III. **Evolution of the Desires.**—The second general class of the sensibilities evolved by the application of this principle of division may be denominated, *generically*, Desires; and it formally includes under it all those states or affections of the soul which act, or tend to act, upon the will in the relation of motives to volition. It is obvious that this use of the term *desire* is, in the true sense, generic, and is broader than its popular use warrants; but the principle of division here adopted seems to be the only philosophic one; while the term desire, as the name of the central class of those states or affections of the soul which act upon the will in the relation of motives to volition, seemed best fitted to the uses of a generic name for the whole class of any word at our disposal.

The whole department of the sensibilities may therefore, from this stand-point, be exhaustively considered under the two general heads, or divisions, viz.:

Division I. The Emotions.

Division II. The Desires.

THE SENSIBILITIES: DIVISION FIRST.

THE EMOTIONS.

Preliminary Discussion.

Section I.—Nature of the Emotions.

¶ I. **Their Essential Characteristics.**—The emotions are known only in the light of the personal consciousness. As original elements of soul-life, they are indefinable save to the consciousness; and any definition of them can serve no other purpose than to point the individual consciousness to the particular state or affection of the soul intended in the concrete instance. Their special characteristics, as compared with the desires, are:

1. *Intensity of action* for the time being; and—

2. *Instability of duration* or activity.

In these two respects they are decisively discriminated from the desires, whose characteristic element is *persistence.*

¶ II. **Their Relations to the Intellect.**—These have already been indicated, and may be reduced to the single category of *logical dependence;* we here emphasize the adjective *logical*, since at times, practically, emotions are indistinguishable, *chronologically*, from perceptions, and yet in all cases there must be a perception of beauty, sublimity, etc., etc., before the corresponding emotion can be awakened.

¶ III. **Final Cause of the Emotions.**—This may be logically evolved under two general heads, viz.:

1. *Human pleasure, or happiness;* and—

2. *Human development, or perfection.*

These are related to each other as a proximate end is related to a means to a higher end, which, in this instance, from the Christian standpoint might be considered as the fulfilment at once of man's destiny and of the Divine Will.

SEC. II.—CLASSIFICATION OF THE EMOTIONS.

¶ I. **General Principle of Classification.**—The obvious principle, according to which the emotions must be parted into classes, is involved in their several relations:

1. To the physical organism and its complex states and affections; and—

2. To the rational, or, rather, spiritual nature of man. It only remains, therefore, to apply this principle, in order to evolve at once the *various species of the genus Emotions.*

¶ II. **Evolution of the Physical Emotions.—The Feelings.**—Applying, therefore, this general law or principle of division to our complex sensitive states, there emerges at once, in consciousness, a class of states or affections which we are accustomed to call the Feelings. Their distinctive characteristic is, that they are dependent, directly and immediately, upon the states or affections of the physical organism, and always accompany some affection of one or more of the special or general senses; and hence they have been, by some writers, classed under the head of special products of sensation. Such, for example, are the feelings of *heat* and *cold*, of *comfort* and *discomfort*, of *languor* and *weariness*, etc., etc. But in this case, as in the allied phenomena of sensation, we must discriminate accurately between the actual physical state and the resulting psychical affection, which we rightly denominate, in view of its double relations, a feeling, and class with the emotions.

¶ III. **Evolution of the Physio-Psychical Emotions.**—These, like the preceding class, are based in part, directly and immediately, upon states or affections of the physical organism; but, unlike them, they involve at the same time a rational or spiritual element, which is often the exciting or provoking cause of the peculiar physical state or affection. They connect themselves specifically with the physiological phenomena of temperament, and are largely dependent upon these peculiarities of the individual organism. Under this general class we recognize, among others, such states as *cheerfulness* and *melancholy*, *interest* and *ennui*, and *anxiety* and *indifference*. The remark is as appropriate here as any where, and is necessary, that no exhaustive enumeration of either the emotions or desires is either necessary or desirable. Generic completeness satisfies the necessities of the problem.

¶ IV. **Evolution of the Psychical Emotions.**—These constitute the true generic type of the whole class, and are essentially states or affections of the soul, based upon *rational* or *spiritual*, and *not* upon *physical* or *organic* conditions. Under this class are included, among others, our emotions of *surprise*, *wonder*, *beauty*, *sublimity*, etc., etc., which are all based, according to our previous definition, upon our rational or spiritual perceptions, and not upon the states or affections of the physical organism.

¶ V. **The Term Emotion here used in a Generic Sense.**—It may not be improper here, for the sake of distinctness, to note the fact discretely, that the term emotion is used in this treatise in a broad *generic*, and not in its ordinary *specific*, sense. This is, perhaps, unfortunate, but there seemed to be no alternative, as no more significant word was available, and the principle of classification adopted necessitated the grouping together under *one genus* of the *feelings proper* and the *emotions proper*, as well as the intermediate *physio-psychical affections.*

THE EMOTIONS—CLASS FIRST.

PHYSICAL: THE FEELINGS.

Preliminary Discussion.

¶ I. **The Nature of the Feelings.**—Like other primitive states, the feelings are definable only in and to the human consciousness. They are the simple mental expressions or exponents of our actual physical states or affections. The relation between the two is analogous to that between the actual impression made upon an organ of sense and the subjective sensation resulting from it. In this case, as in that, the mode of the relation between the physical and psychical elements is unknown.

¶ II. **Classification of the Feelings.**—The feelings, generically considered, may be divided into two classes, corresponding to the positive and negative states or conditions of the physical organism, as follows:

1. *Negative states* of the organism, as weariness, languor, discomfort, etc., etc.
2. *Positive states* of the organism, as vitality, pain, pleasure, heat, etc., etc.

Section I.—Negative States of the Organism.

¶ I. **Physical Weakness.**—Physical weakness is at once a physical fact and a conscious feeling, and enters, at times, as a fatal factor into the complex problem of human life. The fact of physical weakness, singly and apart from its mental and moral relations, is of comparatively little import; but when its paralyzing influence enters into the feelings, and reacts upon the vital energies of the soul, it is to the man as the breath of the deadly Bohun Upas of Java, the signet of death. The true man rises superior to such influences, and vitalizes failing physical energies by the omnipotence of a resolute will, while the coward droops and dies, simply because he has not mental fortitude sufficient to overcome morbid physical weakness.

¶ II. **Physical Weariness.**—This, like the preceding, is the resultant of certain antecedent conditions more or less clearly defined to the consciousness of the individual, such as exhausting physical or mental labor. It may extend to the whole organism, or it may localize itself in some special organ or member of the body; but is identical in principle and relations in either case. Like its congener noted above, it is strongly influenced or controlled by the power of a resolute will, and is in turn capable of reacting powerfully on a weak or irresolute nature.

¶ III. **Physical Discomfort.**—Kindred to those feelings already noted, but yet differing from them, is that indefinable state recognized as a feeling of discomfort. In such cases, men do not say, "I am weak, or weary, or in pain," but "I am *uncomfortable*," and, in many cases, are utterly unable to localize the feeling itself, or to determine its cause or causes. They recognize the feeling as real, and refer it to their physical organisms, however little, sometimes, they are able to comprehend its causes or its cure. These three forms of negative states or feelings may fairly be taken as specimens of the class; to enumerate them all would be useless, if practicable.

¶ IV. **Final Cause of these Feelings.**—The final cause of these states is, obviously, to impose a check upon the desires and volitions of men, and to prevent undue exertion and permanent injury to the delicate physical organism. Each of the states noted is the expression of a demand of Nature for rest and repose, which ordinarily it is unsafe to ignore or refuse.

SEC. II.—POSITIVE AFFECTIONS OF THE ORGANISM.

¶ I. **Physical Strength, or Conscious Vitality.**—There is no one of the feelings common to men more intrinsically pleasant or grateful to the soul than the sense of conscious vitality—strength, power—which throbs in the heart and animates the life of the young man as he goes forth to do and dare for his country, for humanity, and for God. It is no mere negative state, like weakness or weariness, but an intense consciousness of inborn vitality and strength, which, reacting upon the soul, quickens its perceptions, intensifies its emotions, stimulates desire, and vitalizes and energizes volition.

¶ II. **Pain and Pleasure.**—Few feelings are more familiar to man than pain and pleasure. The first, pain, we locate in this or that organ or member of the body, yet the real perception of the pain itself is an affection of the soul. With pleasure, there is not the same tendency to specific localization, though in some cases such a tendency is unquestionably present, but ordinarily the psychical element predominates. But in both the presence of the physical element is marked and decisive. The mutual relations of the two to each other are peculiar and interesting. In the human organism the possibility of pleasure is measured by the counter-liability to pain; and, while the latter is less agreeable than the former, it is, as the guardian of the physical organism against injury, scarcely if at all less valuable to man.

SEC. III.—RELATIONS AND FINAL CAUSE OF THE FEELINGS.

¶ I. **How distinguished from True Emotions.**—The feelings are distinguished from the true emotions by the facts:

1. That they involve physical sensations, or, more correctly perhaps, affections of the physical organism, as their central element and condition precedent.

2. That they are not, like the emotions, based upon a true intellection, i. e., they are *sensible* rather than *rational* affections.

¶ II. **Reasons for classing them with the Emotions.** — 1. Like the emotions, they belong, legitimately, to the side of the sensibilities, and involve, like them, the idea, or rather the experience, of the agreeable and disagreeable.

2. Like the emotions, they tend to generate desires, corresponding to their own essential natures, conditions, and relations. Thus the sense of weariness generates the desire for rest, a sense of pain the desire for relief, and so of the rest.

¶ III. **Final Cause of the Feelings.**—The feelings are obviously designed to maintain a constant sympathy and coöperation between the physical and spiritual elements in the complex organism, and thus to prevent the tireless, energetic, ambitious soul from prematurely wearing out and destroying the body. All experience proves that even cultivated minds cannot safely be trusted with the care of the body, unguarded by these ever-faithful monitors.

THE EMOTIONS: CLASS SECOND.

THE PHYSIO-PSYCHICAL.

Section I.—Nature and Characteristics of Physio-Psychical Emotions.

¶ I. **Their Nature.**—The physio-psychical emotions, on the one hand, partake of the nature of the feelings; and, on the other, of the attributes of the emotions proper:

1. Like the feelings, they are directly dependent (as will appear in the sequel) upon the states or conditions of the body.

2. They are, to an extent that the feelings are not, affections of the soul.

3. Unlike the emotions proper, they are but slightly dependent upon prior intellections, though they may, and often do, react strongly upon the intellect.

¶ II. **Their Characteristics.**—These are marked and peculiar, and fully vindicate the propriety of grouping them in a class by themselves, viz.:

1. They are less intense than the emotions proper, which at times attain to such a degree of power as to entirely absorb the consciousness, and exclude every thing else. The physio-psychical emotions, on the contrary, do not seem to be capable of this intensity of action or expression, in their normal state, under any circumstances.

2. They are more permanent and lasting in their characters than the true emotions. The very intensity of the true emotions renders them necessarily short-lived; these affections, on the contrary, are characterized by persistence, and by a tendency to become habitual, of which cheerfulness and melancholy are conspicuous illustrations.

Sec. II.—Forms or Modes of the Physio-psychical Emotions.

¶ I. **Cheerfulness and Melancholy.**—These two affections may fairly be taken as true types of the whole class of physio-psychical emotions. They represent states or habits of mind rather than simple transient emotions; and—

1. *Their nature.*—This is familiarly know in consciousness, and is a marked and important element of mental development, and, in fact, of mental power. We instinctively refer to this element in all our estimates of human character, recognizing this or that *temperament* as cheerful or melancholy; and we just as instinctively recognize the fact that the influence of these temperaments is contagious in the social circle.

2. *Their causes or conditions.*—The fact has been already noted that these affections or states of the soul depend largely upon the physical organism and its conditions, or, as we familiarly say, upon the temperament. So strong, indeed, has been this conviction in the past, that some physiologists have fixed upon the spleen as the physical organ or seat of melancholy. The fact is well ascertained that both states exist, independently of any proper intellectual causes. Men are cheerful in the midst of abundant causes for melancholy, and melancholy despite the most rational causes for cheerfulness.

3. *Their relations.*—Cheerfulness and melancholy have already been noted as decided elements of social and moral power. As temperaments, they react strongly upon all the elements of soul-life, and limit and determine, to a considerable extent, their characters and development. They react still more powerfully at times upon the relations of the individual to his fellow-men, and modify and sometimes determine the sphere of his influence over them. Ordinarily, a cheerful man attracts, and a melancholy man repels others.

The fact has been noted that these states are but slightly and indirectly under the control of the intellect and the will, yet man is able to modify and control them, both directly and indirectly, by his power over the conditions of his own physical life. Melancholy, especially, is predisposed to become chronic and abnormal, and to result in confirmed hypochondriasis, which in turn sometimes ultimates in complete insanity.

The peculiar form of melancholy called the poetic may be deemed worthy of a passing notice, though it may fairly be questioned whether its relations to poetic genius are not rather accidental than essential; the fact, however, cannot be denied that some of our greatest poets have been infected with it.

¶ II. **Interest and Ennui.**—Analogous to, and yet differing from, cheerfulness and melancholy, we recognize the correlated mental states denominated *interest* and *ennui*, which, in some persons, are as marked characteristics as their congeners. In fact, they are not only analogous, but also, ordinarily, coexisting states. The cheerful man is commonly eager, watchful, interested in every thing that concerns himself or his fellow-men, thinking nothing to be foreign to him that pertains to humanity; the melancholy man, on the contrary, is usually sluggish and uninterested in any thing—in a word, is *ennuyé*. This phenomenon is readily accounted for by the fact that, the complementary states compared, both depend largely upon analogous, if not in some cases upon identical, conditions of the physical organism. We note:

1. *The conditions or causes of interest and ennui.*—These are obviously twofold, viz.:

(*a*) *Physical*, i. e., pertaining chiefly to what is familiarly known as *temperament*. Every thoughtful student has noted the comparative ease with which he is able to apply his mind to a given subject in certain states or conditions of his physical organism, and the almost utter impossibility of shaking off the listlessness and *ennui* that have seized upon him under the influence of opposite conditions.

(*b*) *Intellectual and moral*, i. e., causes depending upon personal character and its influences, as well as upon the rational motives to action, present to the intelligence, and, through it, acting upon the soul. Here the problem of the synthesis of the physical and rational elements in these physio-psychical states becomes exceedingly complex, and merits an investigation that cannot be given to it here; it must suffice to call attention to its intrinsic difficulties and importance.

2. *Their psychological relations.*—Interest and *ennui* react upon the whole physical and mental natures of man, as well as upon all his social and moral relations. The first fits him for every relation and duty of life, the second unfits him for every thing save listless inanition. Normally the one should be the regular, the other the exceptional, state of the soul, and is normal only as a provocative to necessary rest and sleep. Its final cause, as an element of man's complex nature, undoubtedly is to prevent too unceasing activity, by taking away its stimulus. Morbid or chronic *ennui* is perhaps the most miserable subjective state known to man on earth.

¶ III. **Anxiety and Indifference.**—Varying from, and yet analogous to, interest and *ennui*, are the correlated states known as anxiety and indifference. We consider:

1. *Their nature.*—Anxiety and indifference as affections of the soul are so familiar as to need no definition. Their analogy to *interest* and *ennui* is marked and decisive; and yet they may be definitely discriminated by the fact that the latter are general states of the soul, extending, to all the objects that concern it, with almost equal impartiality, while

anxiety and indifference fasten upon and are vitalized by some special object which awakens the one or provokes the other.

2. *Their relations.*—Anxiety and indifference as mental affections are dependent largely upon the nervous organization of the individual. Men instinctively recognize this, and say of the anxious man, "He is nervous;" of the indifferent man, "His pulse is quiet;" in either case recognizing the direct relation between the *mental affection* and the *physical state.* No psychological fact is better ascertained than that *anxiety*, no matter how deep and lasting the interest felt, cannot coexist with certain types of physical and nervous organization, or, in other words, with certain temperaments.

THE EMOTIONS: CLASS THIRD.

PSYCHICAL OR RATIONAL EMOTIONS.

Preliminary Discussion.

THEIR NATURE, CHARACTERISTICS, AND CLASSIFICATION.

¶ I. **Their Nature.**—1. *They are purely rational,* i. e., they are not, like the feelings or the mixed emotions, conditioned in whole or in part upon the states or affections of the physical organism.

2. They predicate in all cases a prior perception or intellection. They rest, therefore, in their ultimate analysis, upon our percepts of the actual, our concepts of the ideal, and our beliefs in the true.

¶ II. **Their Characteristics.**—Here the true characteristics of the emotions proper distinctively manifest themselves, viz.:

1. Intensity, depth, or energy of action; and—

2. Instability of duration. The duration of an emotion is, as a general rule, in inverse proportion to the energy of its manifestations. Intense feelings are usually short-lived, while moderate emotions are usually more persistent.

¶ III. **Their Principle of Classification.**—This, obviously, is determined by the objects which call them into being, or in view of which they are evolved. It follows, therefore, of necessity, that the number of possible distinct emotions is practically indeterminate. All that is either practicable or desirable is the evolution of those characteristic representative groups which practically constitute in their synthesis the emotional life of man.

SECTION I.—EMOTIONS OF SURPRISE, WONDER, AND ADMIRATION.

¶ I. **Their Natures and Conditions.**—1. *Emotions of surprise.*—These are familiar, and are the simple resultant of the perception by the soul of something unusual, unexpected, or strange, either in its nature or its conditions. As true psychical emotions, they postulate, as their logical condition precedent, a rational percept, concept, or belief, which may in any given case pertain to self, to not-self, or to the relations connecting them. The emotion may arise either in view of a familiar object in strange relations, or of a strange object in familiar relations. The sight of an elephant on the streets of an American city excites emotions of surprise, but would excite none at all in a Hindoo city; while there, in turn, an American elk or buffalo would excite surprise in the highest degree.

2. *Emotions of wonder.*—If surprise be heightened and intensified by the introduction of a paradoxical element, it then becomes, distinctively, *wonder.* To recur to a previous illustration, it would excite surprise to see an elephant walking unattended on our streets; but the surprise would be changed to wonder if we should chance to discover that he was accompanied by a royal Bengal tiger.

3. *Emotions of admiration.*—In the last example, our wonder would yield to admiration should we learn that some wise and skilful man had discovered a certain method of subduing the ferocity of, and taming, the most blood-thirsty animals, and of rendering them as tractable as ordinary domestic animals. Emotions of admiration are not, however, limited to

objects of surprise or wonder—there are many things which excite these emotions that awaken no admiration; and, on the other hand, men admire many things which excite neither surprise nor wonder. It may, however, be questioned whether, in its highest and intensest form, it does not always include them as elements.

¶ II. **Their Final Cause and Relations.**—The relations of these emotions to human development and happiness are apparent, and, in fact, obtrusive. They stimulate curiosity, awaken desire, and react powerfully upon all the processes of intellect, as well as minister to us a pleasure or happiness peculiarly their own. They are most vivid, most active, and most energetic in youth, declining with advancing years, and sinking almost to zero in the second childhood of age—"when the keepers of the house tremble, and the strong men bow themselves, and the grinders cease because they are few, and those that look out of the windows be darkened."

SEC. II.—EMOTIONS OF THE LUDICROUS, OF DISGUST, AND OF CONTEMPT.

¶ I. **Their Nature and Conditions.**—Lying in the same mental plane with surprise, wonder, and admiration, are the emotions of the *ludicrous*, of *disgust*, and of *contempt*. Their objects may or may not be identical; an object may be at first an object of surprise or wonder, and may afterward become an object of emotions of the ludicrous, or even of disgust or contempt.

1. *Emotions of the ludicrous.*—These involve, to some extent, elements of surprise; but invariably superadd to them an element of incongruity, either in the object conceived, or in its relations to the surrounding objects which, for the time being, condition its existence. The power of thus grouping images and objects in incongruous relations is called wit or humor. Practically, the term wit is applied to brief, sharp collocations or groups of words and thoughts; while humor is applied to more lengthy and sustained passages, descrip-

tions, or caricatures. Two characteristic forms of wit have been discriminated, namely:

(*a*) Degrading elevated things by presenting them in new and incongruous relations; and—

(*b*) Elevating insignificant things, and attributing to them an absurd importance which neither their essential characters nor relations will warrant.

2. *Emotions of disgust.*—The addition of a single element to the ludicrous transforms it into the disgusting. Precisely what this added element must be, in any given case, is perhaps difficult to determine; yet there are few who have not turned away in disgust from a witticism which, in the beginning, had excited laughter, but which the one word too much, added with the simple intention of heightening its effect, had rendered disgusting. It is not, of course, affirmed that the emotions of the ludicrous and of disgust are identical. They are not, but the fact remains that they are intimately related.

3. *Emotions of contempt.*—The step from disgust to contempt is immediate and direct. We laugh at a *weak, vain man;* we turn away in disgust from a *haughty fool;* but we look with contempt upon *a self-important villain* who boasts of his own shame and weakness. The lines of demarcation between these several emotions are narrow, and difficult to define in words, but are clearly marked to the consciousness of the thoughtful student of human nature.

¶ **II. Their Final Cause and Relations.**—The final cause of these emotions must be adjudged to be moral, chiefly. Emotions of the ludicrous afford at times occasions of innocent mirth, but this result is a secondary one; their primary use is obviously that of a moral restraint upon the individual to preserve him—

(*a*) From the undignified, the incongruous, and the little; and—

(*b*) From the low, the mean, the vile, and the contemptible.

The laughter, the disgust, and the contempt of society, are often stronger safeguards against wrong action than higher and nobler impulses. God has not only thrown around man's pathway in life every rational inducement to right action, but He has hedged it in with barriers against shame, and wrong, and sin.

Sec. III.—Emotions of Shame, of Sorrow, and of Pity.

¶ I. **Their Natures and Conditions.**—1. *Emotions of shame.*—These are the counterparts, legitimately, in the one party, of emotions of disgust and contempt in the other. They presuppose something incongruous, improper, wrong, or sinful *in ourselves*, that brings a blush to the cheek, and shame to the soul. There are few, alas! who need to be told what such emotions are. It is well, indeed, that men should be susceptible, in a high degree, to a sense of shame, but sad, indeed, that they should ever realize its power.

2. *Emotions of sorrow.*—These are of two classes, representing entirely distinct principles and responding to diverse conditions, viz.:

(*a*) Sorrow, of the nature of repentance, for our own personal acts of impropriety, shame, or sin; and—

(*b*) Sorrow, in the sense of grief, for evils endured, losses sustained, or friends snatched from us by the hand of death, or for any one of the myriad forms of suffering to which man is liable in this life.

The essential distinction between the two is, that the first is the direct and legitimate result of our own personal demerit or wrong, and is based upon antecedent emotions of shame; the second is the result of a loss of that which was precious to us in itself or in its relations, but has been lost through no fault or demerit on our part, and our sorrow is the simple expression of the apprehended reality and greatness of our loss. It is obvious, as a practical fact, that the two, in any concrete instance, may coincide, and our loss be the result of our own misconduct, and thus involve shame as well as sorrow.

3. *Emotions of pity.*—These are the exact counterparts of the preceding, and are, ordinarily, awakened in the soul in

view of the sorrows of others. They may also arise in view of the sin and shame of another. The two forms differ in this: the former presupposes a certain sympathy with or kindred feeling for the sorrowing person, involved in the emotion of pity, which is not implied in the latter. Thus the Master wept at the grave of Lazarus, not merely that He pitied, but that He sympathized with, the weeping sisters; but He wept over Jerusalem, doomed to destruction for its pride and its crimes, tears of *compassion*, but *not* of *sympathy* with its pride and its sins.

¶ II. **Their Final Cause and Relations.**—Emotions of shame and sorrow, in their first and correlated forms, are obviously designed to exert a true regenerating moral influence upon the guilty soul, awakening it to a just sense of its own unworthiness, and stimulating it to struggle upward to a new and higher life. Shame and sorrow can make no atonement for sin, but they can and do exert a purifying and regenerating influence upon the guilty soul that yields itself to their healthful influences.

The emotions of sorrow, in their second form, and of pity, belong to a purer and higher sphere of soul-life. They do not, of necessity, imply personal guilt; but they do appeal to, strengthen and intensify some of the gentlest, sweetest impulses of humanity. *Sorrow* for the loss of loved ones taken from us by the destroyer, and *pity* for the sorrows, the agonies, and the shame of our fellow-men, may rend our very souls, and yet the very depth and intensity of our helpless soul-agony may lift us up to lean on the strong arm of Him who is touched with a feeling of our infirmities. The cup of sorrow may be, nay, surely is, very bitter to the soul; but it is none the less God's message of love, designed to win our affections from earth, that we may anchor them more surely within the veil.

Sec. IV.—Emotions of Fear, of Horror, and of Despair.

¶ I. **Their Nature and Characteristics.**—1. *Emotions of fear.*—Life has its shadows as well as its sunshine, and there are none that have not at some time experienced emotions of fear. None need therefore to be told what they are or whence they arise. They are simply the soul's recognition of the presence of an apparently impending evil, the expression of its own conscious weakness, and sometimes of its conscious guilt, coupled with the recognition of possible adverse power antagonistic, for the time being, and superior to its own. Its essential elements are therefore:

(*a*) Conscious personal weakness.

(*b*) Sometimes conscious personal guilt, or demerit; and—

(*c*) Anticipated or threatened danger or liability to evil.

It is proper, though scarcely necessary, to add that fear on the one hand, and its opposite, courage, on the other, are strongly affected by *temperament* and *physical* conditions.

2. *Emotions of horror.*—Fear, when it attains to a certain degree of intensity, is liable to take on a new type, including new elements, and to become *horror*. In this new evolution, it seems to be generically a compound of dread (the essential element of fear), and of disgust or loathing. The filiation, at any rate, between this and some of the antecedent emotions noted, is marked and decisive. Save its ultimate congener, *despair*, there is perhaps no feeling known to man more dark and more distressing than this, and especially when it is (as it often is) the resultant of deep-seated remorse for black and damning personal guilt.

3. *Emotions of despair.*—In despair we attain to the culminating point of this class, or group, to the depth beyond which there is no lower deep; to the point at which, not only Faith and Hope, for the time, abandon the hapless victim, but the Will also abdicates its regal throne and crown, and yields up the soul to the anarchy of Despair. Men talk of this terrible emotion familiarly, as if it were a household thing, but few indeed realize the fearful meaning of the words they use.

¶ II. **Their Final Cause and Relations.**—Of fear and horror, the final cause is evident; they are only sentinels, sensitive, watchful, and energetic, placed in the soul of man to guard it against the approach of *danger*, *wrong*, and *sin*; and it is well that men should heed their warnings well and wisely, but not that they should weakly yield themselves up to base perversions of these normal principles, and slink away like cowards, because, perchance, the post of duty may be the post of danger. Despair, it is obvious, is but a resultant form of a synthesis of fear and horror, and in its primary forms sometimes lends courage to the soul, steadiness to the eye, firmness to the foot, and strength to the arm, and so wrings victory from the jaws of defeat. In its ultimate form it can only be regarded as God's seal of condemnation upon the hopelessly-depraved soul.

SEC. V.—EMOTIONS OF BEAUTY, OF SUBLIMITY, AND OF REVERENCE.

¶ I. **Their Nature and Conditions.**—1. *Emotions of beauty.*—The soul of man was not designed to live in *the shadow*, but in *the sunlight*, and God has accordingly endowed it with the most delicate sensibilities, enabling it, not only to appreciate the *actual* beauty of the *physical* world around us, but also the *ideal beauty* of the *spiritual* world within us and above us. The relations of our emotions of beauty to our intellectual faculties have, perhaps, been sufficiently declared, with the addition of the single remark that they are conditioned, logically, upon—

(*a*) Our actual perceptions of the real; and—

(*b*) Our concepts of the ideal, whether material or spiritual.

2. *Emotions of sublimity.*—The relations of emotions of sublimity to those of beauty are the precise analogues of the relations of the corresponding concepts. The one softens, refines, humanizes; the other expands, elevates, energizes—in a word, lifts the soul out of itself and raises it to a loftier plane of vision and to a purer atmosphere. He only half lives who does not seek to realize daily, in his own soul, all the heavenly purity and sweetness of the one, all the divine energy and power of the other. The beautiful alone, though it tends

to soften and purify, may, in fact, enervate; the sublime alone, though it may elevate and energize, may dehumanize. It is only in the perfect synthesis and utter harmony of the two that the soul attains to its loftiest emotions.

3. *Emotions of reverence or adoration.*—In these we have, at once, the culmination and perfect synthesis of the emotions of beauty and sublimity conceived specially from the intellectual and moral stand-point. Emotions of reverence or adoration, however, postulate as their object, not only a synthesis of the beautiful and the sublime, but of the true and the good also. It follows therefore, of necessity, that while these emotions of reverence go forth to our parents and to the noble, the wise, the great, and the good of earth, they attain to their highest development only in adoration of God, the Creator and Supreme Ruler of the universe, in whom alone *ideal beauty*, *ideal power*, *ideal truth*, and *ideal goodness*, centre and culminate. Man in his best and loftiest estate is never so worthy, never so noble, and never so great, as when he bows in adoration before God, in whose image he was originally created.

¶ II. **Their Final Cause and Relations.**—The final cause of these pure and elevating emotions is so obvious, nay even obtrusive, that it seems idle to state it formally. It is obviously twofold, viz.:

(*a*) Human happiness, as a proximate end, or purpose; and—

(*b*) Human perfection, as a necessary factor in the evolution of God's beneficent plans in the creation of the universe.

It is almost superfluous to add that our emotions of beauty, sublimity, and reverence, react upon, purify, and intensify every better element of our complex nature, and ever tend to assimilate us personally and socially to that ideal *beauty*, *power*, *truth*, and *goodness* which we adore. He spoke wisely who said: "Tell me the God you *really* worship, and I will tell you what you are."

SEC. VI.—EMOTIONS OF MORAL APPROVAL AND DISAPPROVAL.

¶ I. **Nature of the Moral Emotions.**—Above and beyond the various classes of emotions already noted, we recognize another, of markedly different character, based upon the concept of *the right* as a criterion of judgment, and postulating, as conditions precedent of its legitimate exercise, the *moral responsibility* and *free agency* of man. The essential and distinguishing characteristic of this class of emotions, discriminating them from all others, is, that they exist only in view of or in reference to moral agents and actions exclusively; emotions of wonder, surprise, admiration, beauty, etc., etc., arise in view of inanimate objects, or of simple animal life; but emotions of moral approval and disapproval cannot, and are, therefore, a class *sui generis*. Two facts, moreover, should be distinctly noted, namely:

(*a*) They are primitive elements of consciousness, simple and irreducible.

(*b*) They are universal elements of consciousness, limited to no particular race, age, or country. Different individuals, families, races, and nations, differ in their moral codes, in what they actually approve and disapprove morally, but no single individual, family, or race, can be found, or has ever been known, that recognized *no* standard of morality; nor any that regards all actions, taken indiscriminately, as equally right and praiseworthy. As psychologists, we have to do only with the actual existence of moral emotions as integral elements of soul-life; the question of the diversity of moral standards belongs to the science of ethics.

¶ II. **Objects of the Moral Emotions.**—These have already been indicated, and limited exclusively to the actions of moral agents, i. e., of men. No such emotions can, by any possibility, arise in view of the actions of even the more intelligent animals, no matter how much of surprise, wonder, or admiration, they may and often do excite. Limiting the investigation, therefore, to the actions of men exclusively, an important distinction at once emerges, giving rise to two distinct forms of the moral emotions, viz.:

1. Moral self-approval or disapproval, in which the personal acts of the moral agent are the objects of the emotion. As thus viewed, it is an integral element in every true act of conscience.

2. Moral emotions in view of the *voluntary* acts of our fellow-men. The emphatic distinction between the two forms rests upon this decisive fact that, in judging our own actions, we are cognizant of all the circumstances and conditions under which the act was performed, and, so far forth, are in a condition to render an impartial, or, at least, an intelligent, verdict. In judging the actions of our fellow-men we do not and cannot know all the circumstances and conditions under which any given act was performed, and consequently cannot, in all cases, however impartial we may be, render exact justice, and can never be sure that our emotions of moral approval or disapproval are either just or adequate. It is hardly necessary to add that the second form of the emotions noted are in no sense elements of conscience; *that* is exclusively a *personal* faculty.

¶ III.—**Relations of the Moral Emotions to the Moral Intuitions.**—The moral intuitions, i. e., the concepts of the true and the right, together with the possible forms of the analytic reason under which they are evolved, as well as the categorical imperative of conscience, have already been given in detail. It only remains to determine their relations to the moral emotions. These relations have already been indicated as those of *logical* antecedence. Chronologically, it is often practically impossible, in the concrete instance, to discriminate between the moral perception and its accompanying moral emotion; but nevertheless we are logically compelled to base the moral emotion upon the moral perception. Their simultaneity is apparent only, and not real; and is only one of the many illusions resulting from the fact that our intellectual processes are so inconceivably rapid that the mind itself is unable to follow and discriminate the successive steps of the oftentimes really complex process.

¶ IV. **Influence of Education, Habit, etc., upon the Moral Emotions.**—The dependence of our moral emotions upon our moral intuitions indicates decisively the power of education over them for good or evil. In this respect the sensitive responds to the intellectual nature with an energy and power that are ordinarily in direct proportion to the clearness and distinctness of our moral perceptions. If these be blunted, confused, or led astray, by wrong education, our moral emotions must to a like extent be perverted. One marked peculiarity of the moral emotions, in their relations to the law of habit, must be distinctly noted here, namely: their freshness, vividness, and intensity, are *not*, like the other emotions, blunted by frequency of repetition, but, on the contrary, every fresh exercise of these seems but to heighten their susceptibility, and prepare them to respond to more and still more delicate moral impressions and distinctions, so that their delicacy and perfection are almost wholly voluntary elements, for which the individual himself is morally responsible.

THE SENSIBILITIES: DIVISION SECOND.

THE DESIRES.

Preliminary Discussion.

Section I.—Analysis of the Desires.

¶ I. **Nature of Desire.**—Desire as a primitive affection of the soul is comprehensible only by a consciousness capable of the phenomena in question. It may be defined to be a *mental appetency*, i. e., a going forth of the mind beyond itself, in order to the gratification of some of its numerous wants. Two items must be noted here, viz.:

1. The characteristic element of desire. This is obviously its tendency toward or demand for some object of gratification coördinated to the *physical*, *spiritual*, or *mixed* nature of self, or the ego; and—

2. Its relations to the emotions. The desires and emotions are intimately related to each other, but yet are sharply and easily discriminated from each other. The desires go forth *as appetencies* to an external object, and are stable and persistent until their object is reduced to actual possession; the emotions, on the contrary, while they originate in view of some appropriate object, have no appetency for or tendency toward their object; and are, moreover, unstable and transitory.

¶ II. **Objects of Desire.**—The objects of human desire correspond to the complex nature, material and spiritual, of self, or the ego; and accommodate themselves to those relations, whether purely *physical*, as *the appetites ; physio-psychical*, as *the propensities ;* or *psychical*, as *the affections.* Their special characters and relative ranks will appear in the sequel.

¶ III. **Final Cause of Desire.**—The desires are the motive powers of the soul; its incentives to action, and its stimuli to labor. They thus supplement the reason, and strengthen it in its contest with the natural indolence and inertia of men. The inspired preacher, Eccles. xii. 5, gives expression to the culmination of human weakness as the time when "desire shall fail," and with it all the powers and activities, because all the motives, of manhood. It is almost needless to add that desire tends specifically:

1. To human happiness, by rendering possible present gratification; and—

2. To human development, by stimulating to legitimate normal activity.

Sec. II.—Relations of the Desires to other Mental States.

¶ I. **Relations of Desires to Emotions.**—These have already been indicated, incidentally, as those of sequence, both logical and chronological. Formally, every true desire is based upon a corresponding antecedent emotion. To this law, however, there are some apparent exceptions, as in the case of hunger and thirst, i. e., of our appetites for food and drink;

but this exception disappears in view of our classification of the feelings under the generic head of emotions, and the secondary fact that hunger and thirst must be grouped with the feelings as well as with the desires.

¶ II. **Relations of Desires to Intellection.**—The desires, based as they are immediately upon the emotions, postulate, necessarily, corresponding prior acts of intellection. Here, however, a decisive discrimination must be made between:

1. *Instinctive desires*, which *in the infant* antecede intellection, and at times, even *in the adult*, act independently of it; and—

2. *Rational desires*, which exist only in virtue of prior intellections, which, by awakening emotions of pleasure, excite rational desire for the pleasing object.

The distinction between instinctive and rational desires is important, if not fundamental, as marking one of the transition points from the animal to the human being. When the infant is in fact but a more beautiful and more helpless animal, and reason is at its minimum, instinct is developed; and, just in proportion as reason is developed and assumes its rightful sovereignty, does instinct fade away and disappear; and when true Christian culture attains to its ideal development, reason instantaneously supersedes instinct, and thus practically excludes it from the life. The relations of instinct to moral accountability are marked and decisive, as will appear more clearly in the sequel. Some of the problems it originates are curiously interesting, but cannot be discussed here.

¶ III. **Relations of the Desires to the Will.**—It is premature, at this point, to enter into any general discussion of the relations of the desires to the will, other than to indicate the fundamental fact, formally, which has already been announced incidentally, that under the general term *desires* are included all those elements which, in their relations to will and its volitions, are included under the generic class of motives to action. It is, however, necessary here to announce the fact decisively that the term *desire*, like its congener *emotion*, is here used in a broad *generic*, and not in a restricted *specific* sense.

SEC. III.—CLASSIFICATION OF THE DESIRES.

¶ I. **Principle of Classification adopted.**—The principle of classification of the desires here adopted corresponds to that of the emotions, and logically depends upon the complex nature of the personality; and involves their division into *physical*, *physio-psychical*, and *psychical.*

¶ II. **Evolution of Physical Desires.**—Corresponding to the physical nature of man and its corresponding class of emotions, i. e., the feelings, we recognize a class of desires, such as hunger, thirst, and sexual passion, which have been classed together under the general name of *The Appetites.*

¶ III. **Evolution of the Physio-Psychical Desires.**—Corresponding to the physio-psychical emotions and the complex physical and spiritual natures of man, there emerges a second class of desires, *the physio-psychical*, which partake of both a sensible and rational nature. Of these, self-love and sociality may be taken as the basal or typical forms. They have, in popular usage, been grouped together under the general name of *The Propensities.*

¶ IV. **Evolution of the Psychical Desires.**—Corresponding to the emotions proper, and the purely rational or spiritual nature of man, there emerges a third class of desires, viz., *the psychical*, of which the affections and the moral impulses are the normal types. These challenge for themselves, both in virtue of their intrinsic characters and of their relations, the highest places in the hierarchy of the sensibilities.

THE DESIRES: CLASS FIRST.

PHYSICAL: THE APPETITES.

SECTION I.—GENERAL ANALYSIS OF THE APPETITES.

¶ I. **Nature and Characteristics of the Appetites.**—The appetites are the mental expressions of the purely physical appetencies of the body as an organism. Their essential characteristics are:

1. That they are purely physical in their origin and conditions.

2. That they are occasional, and not continuous, in their manifestations.

3. That they involve, for the time being, that is, during their manifestation or season of activity, a sense of physical uneasiness or discomfort; and—

4. That their gratification results in a corresponding degree of pleasure, proportioned ordinarily to the intensity of the appetite.

¶ II. **Their Final Cause and Relations.**—The appetites postulate as their final cause:

1. Primarily, the preservation and continuous reproduction of human life, i. e., in other words, the development of the race; and—

2. Secondarily, human gratification or happiness in its lower subsidiary forms.

Recurring to a previous distinction noted, it is obvious that, in the outset of life, in infancy, their action is purely *instinctive*, and is not conditioned upon any prior act of intellection. In later life, they respond to both *instinctive* and *voluntary* or *rational* influences; and may in fact be called into activity by the power of an excited imagination without the usual antecedent physical conditions.

Sec. II.—Forms of the Appetites.

The more important appetites have been already enumerated, under the general heads of hunger, thirst, and sexual desire. Subsidiary to these may be classed the desires for rest, for sleep, etc., etc., corresponding to the physical emotions or feelings. Besides this primary enumeration of specific forms, there is a secondary distinction whose practical importance is so great as to demand discrete enunciation, namely:

1. *Natural or spontaneous appetites*, which manifest themselves originally, under the power of instinct and—

2. *Acquired appetites*, which are artificial in their nature.

¶ I. **The Natural Appetites.**—These all cluster in and

pertain to the physical organism, and manifest themselves sooner or later under the power of instinct, independently of intellection and volition. They are essential conditions of the health, the development, and the perpetuation of the human race. At first thought it might have seemed both safe and wise for God to have intrusted the interest of man's physical nature, and the perpetuation of his species, to his intelligence and sense of duty. But experience proves that reason and the moral sense alone cannot be trusted with interests so momentous. Not only do these elements, reënforced by parental affection, fail at times to secure proper care and attention to the helpless infant, but they fail quite as often in securing, on the part of the individual, proper care for the preservation and development of his own health and strength. All experience, in this respect, confirms the wisdom of the Creator in fastening upon the physical system, and embedding in the human sensibilities, desires and appetencies which, apart from all rational considerations, impel man, instinctively, to preserve his own life, and to perpetuate his species, and thus fulfil, in part at least, his God-given mission upon earth.

¶ II. **Acquired Appetites.**—The existence of secondary or acquired appetites, or rather of secondary forms of appetite, has already been noted. These are scarcely, if at all, less potential in their actual influence upon human welfare and destiny than the primary; they must, therefore, now be considered discretely:

1. *Their nature and conditions.*—Acquired appetites are, in all cases, based directly or remotely upon the natural, of which they are either *normal* or *abnormal* developments; and they may be acquired either accidentally or voluntarily. Although they may be wholly acquired and artificial, they are yet in many cases transmissible by natural generation, and may thus be perpetuated indefinitely. With acquired and even with hereditary appetites for stimulating food and intoxicating drugs and liquors, we are all, alas! but too familiar. We do not need to be told, in reference to alcoholic

drinks and opium, how terrible and how destructive is the power of an acquired appetite for such destructive stimuli, overpowering as it does conscience, reason, self-love, and every other better and higher impulse which interposes, for the time being, between the wretched victim and his fearful appetite. One marked peculiarity of these acquired appetites is, that their strength, persistence, and power, are usually in *direct* proportion to their *unnaturalness*, if not to their *foulness*. Perhaps not one man in a hundred who uses alcohol, opium, or tobacco, really liked it in the outset; yet there is no single article of food that the slave to tobacco, for example, would not sooner surrender forever than forego his foul indulgence.

2. *Their tendencies.*—In the light of the preceding discussions, it is hardly necessary to add that the tendency of *such acquired appetites* is evil, and only evil, and that continually. There is no single redeeming quality connected with them, directly or indirectly. Even the least destructive of them involves a fatal moral element which should insure their universal and utter rejection, namely: the conscious moral degradation resulting from the conviction that the habit has become too strong to be resisted or abandoned, save at a cost that the unhappy victim feels that he has not the moral power to pay, even to secure his coveted liberty. Of the slavery of the drunkard to his cups it is saddening, and alas! idle, to speak; its miseries are written in letters of tears and blood, but men heed them not.

Sec. III.—Moral Relations of the Appetites.

In the region of the desires, the moral element is almost omnipresent, and demands constant and candid recognition. Three classes of cases require investigation, viz.:

¶ I. **Instinctive Appetites.**—These, so far and so long as they are purely and wholly *instinctive*, possess no moral character whatever, precisely for the same reason that the actions of an animal, guided by instinct, possess no moral character; for, under the postulated conditions, man is simply and purely an animal. A difficult problem, however, emerges, at once, when the question is raised, At what point does true *instinctive* action cease, and proper *rational*, that is, *moral*, action begin? Theoretically, the solution of this problem is indeterminate; practically, in the concrete instance, it can usually be determined in the individual himself, by the conscious intervention of the categorical imperative of conscience.

¶ II. **Voluntary Appetites.**—These, necessarily, are amenable to the fullest extent to the control of moral principle, and should be regulated strictly by its requirements. In the concrete instance, the gratification of an appetite may be right in itself, and yet, under actually existing circumstances, may involve conditions and results which render it illicit and immoral. No man is at liberty morally, at any time, to take appetite alone as a guide and follow its impulses; he is bound to subordinate desire to intelligence and conscience.

¶ III. **Morbid Appetites.**—Under this general head must be included:

1. *Hereditary appetites.*—The fact has already been noted that acquired appetites may become hereditary; and this is still more common in reference to *abnormal* appetites originating in peculiarities of physical organization. The mere fact of the hereditary nature of an appetite cannot change its moral character, nor yet its moral relations, so long as its gratification is, in the *true* sense, voluntary. If, however, its power be so great as to absolutely overmaster reason and volition, it constitutes a case of natural insanity without moral responsibility. A man is not, in any sense, morally responsible for the existence of an hereditary appetite, but cannot escape responsibility if he voluntarily indulge it.

2. *Acquired appetites.*—Here the moral responsibility of the individual is perfect, inasmuch as the acquisition was a *voluntary*, though *not perhaps an intentional*, act. Many men acquire appetites which they never intended to fasten upon themselves; but, dallying with temptation, they are morally responsible for the actual results, no matter how unexpected

or disastrous. In other words, irresistible appetite is, at no time, a plea for drunkenness.

3. *Diseased appetites.*—Here the conditions change: what are here termed *diseased appetites* must be defined to be appetites resulting from causes really, or presumably at least, beyond the control of the victim at any period of their origination or existence. For such he is assuredly not morally responsible, and can only be held accountable for such actual control over them as is really practicable under the actual conditions of the special concrete instance. If, however, the origin of the diseased appetite was the result of his own wrong action, he is responsible alike for its origin and its continuance; he cannot plead his own original wrong act as a justification of his continuance in sin.

THE DESIRES: CLASS SECOND.

PHYSIO-PSYCHICAL: THE PROPENSITIES.

Preliminary Discussion.

¶ I. **Distinctive Nature of the Propensities.**—The general nature and relations of the propensities have been already indicated. They are closely allied to the appetites, in that, like them, they have intimate points of contact with, and interdependence upon, the physical organism. They are still more closely allied to the true psychical desires by the community of rational elements that characterize them. A decisive line of demarcation however, as will appear in the sequel, separates them into two groups: in the one, the basal element is *self;* in the other, it is in a modified sense *not-self*—i. e., it is the *human* element connecting *self to man as a species.* In other words, these two groups of propensities are based upon the fact that man is at once a *selfish* and a *social* being, using both adjectives in their better generic sense. Like all other forms of true desire, the propensities postulate the appetency of self, or the personality, for some object, end, or aim, pertaining either to self or not-self, and thus, somewhat curiously, they appear to involve the *possessory* principle as a common element entering into all of them.

¶ II. **Relative Rank of the Propensities.**—The position of the propensities as elements, lying in the double plane of the *physical* and *psychical*, indicates their true rank and relative importance. They are superior to the appetites, and inferior to the affections and the moral impulses.

¶ III. **Order of Evolution and Dependence of the Several Propensities.**—In the outset, it is obvious that the propensions naturally arrange themselves into two groups, which may be denominated, respectively, the selfish and the social.

1. *Evolution of self-love as the basal element of the selfish propensions.*—The first and most obtrusive of these affections of the soul which emerges into consciousness, is self-love. It includes the ideas of *self*-preservation, *personal* development, and *personal* happiness. But these ultimate ends of self-love involve, necessarily, certain coördinate desires indispensable to their perfect gratification, namely, the adjunct propensions of *curiosity*, *acquisitiveness*, and *ambition*, which cannot, like self-preservation, be resolved into mere elements of self-love, but which are yet so dependent upon it, as a central element, that they must logically be grouped with it.

2. *Evolution of sociality as the basal element of the social propensions.*—The social tendencies or appetencies of man, both *instinctive* and *rational*, are not less marked and obtrusive than the selfish. They are, moreover, their exact counterparts in rank and practical influence. Like self-love, sociality is the basal element or centre of certain adjunct propensions, viz., *imitativeness*, *approbativeness*, *emulation*, and *veracity*, which may be denominated *social* propensions.

CHAPTER I.—THE SELFISH PROPENSIONS.

Section I.—Self-love.

¶ I. **Nature of Self-Love.**—The fact has already been noted that rational self-love postulates three elements in order to its completeness, viz.:

1. The principle of self-preservation, which impels man, instinctively and always, to seek to preserve life and limb, body and mind, unharmed, however worthless either may seem to be.

2. The principle of self-assertion, or self-development, which demands, as a right, free scope for the fullest and most complete evolution of every element of manhood. And—

3. The principle of self-gratification, which demands, as a right, freedom to enjoy life, and all that life legitimately imports to the individual man.

¶ II. **Its Moral Character.**—Self-love has been alternately decried as immitigably base, and elevated to the summit of the moral hierarchy of the sensibilities—errors alike dangerous and baseless. It is neither necessarily evil, nor yet a safe guide or standard of moral action. Properly subordinated to the reason and conscience, it has a legitimate and vitally-important relation to the evolution of a perfect manhood. God in His infallible wisdom has determined its true rank, in the second great commandment, in the words—"Thou shalt love thy neighbor as (*thou lovest*) thyself."

Self-love, like other forms of desire, has both an *instinctive* and a *voluntary* activity. So far as it is purely and wholly instinctive, i. e., *until reason has had time to intervene*, it possesses no moral character whatsoever, for all moral action presupposes volition. So far as it is *voluntary*, its moral character is determined by its proper subordination to other and higher elements and impulses of the soul. In its proper sphere, it is right and praiseworthy; when depressed below or exalted above that, it tends to evil.

In consequence of the varying theories, prepossessions, and customs of men, there is an ambiguity about the words self-love, selfish, and selfishness, which almost wholly unfits them for the use of the psychologist; but there are none others to take their places. Self-love is ordinarily used in the better sense, and selfish and selfishness in a bad sense; and yet, at times, we are compelled to use *selfish* as a single adjective representing self-love in its better sense.

¶ III. **The Psychological Relations of Self-Love.**—These are so far-reaching and important, that, although they have been incidentally declared already, logical completeness demands that they should be formally reannounced:

1. It is involved either explicitly or implicitly in all our appetites and propensions which necessarily include a selfish element, using the term in its better sense. Every appetite and propension involves the idea of personal enjoyment, as an element more or less marked of its own existence.

2. It reacts upon and intensifies the higher forms of desire, i. e., the affections and moral impulses. Here the concealed possessory element, before indicated, crops out in the expressions, "my husband," "my wife," "my children," "my friends," "my God," etc.

3. It is legitimately subordinate to conscience, and should be, ordinarily, to the affections. The danger, in a majority of instances, is, not that self-love shall be too weak, but that it shall either be too strong or not properly guarded and guided by intelligence. God has recognized it as a legitimate moral appeal, by holding out to us future rewards and punishments as incentives to virtuous action.

Sec. II.—Curiosity, Acquisitiveness, and Ambition.

¶ I. **Curiosity, or the Desire of Knowledge.**—1. *Nature and conditions of the propension.*—The term curiosity has a double or ambiguous use, which must be noted here.

First. It is used to express a vain and idle desire to pry into every thing that chances to attract the attention, independently alike of the proprieties of time and place, and of the real value of the information sought; and—

Second. True curiosity, or a natural desire for knowledge as such, which is a primitive element of the human sensibilities, as universal as it is important. It is strongest and most persistent in youth, when, perhaps, it is least rational, but when the acquisition of knowledge is, at once, most easy, most pleasant, and most desirable. In mature manhood, it is conditioned or stimulated chiefly by the practical value, present or prospective, of the knowledge sought, and by the laws of habit. In old age, it diminishes, and often lapses back into an unmeaning, childish curiosity.

2. *Its final cause and relations.*—These are obtrusively evident, in the light of our practical experience of the value of knowledge, in all the relations of life, both as a means of happiness and of personal profit. Like the other desires, it has both an *instinctive* and a *voluntary* evolution. The first has obviously no moral character, the second responds to the ordinary laws of moral accountability. The fact must here be noted that this desire, like the appetites, has a special tendency to *morbid* action, proportionate perhaps to its great relative importance in the hierarchy of the sensibilities, conditioning as it does the development of the reason or intelligence.

¶ II. **Acquisitiveness, or the Desire of Possession.**—1. *Its nature and conditions.*—The possessory principle is among the earliest developed and the most persistent known to man, yet some authors have attempted to resolve it into a special form or manifestation of the desire of power. It is almost needless to say that this reduction, instead of simplifying our concepts, confuses them, and at the same time contradicts the very phenomena which it attempts to explain. Possessory pronouns are as universal as language, and are among the first which the child learns to use. The idea of *value* is obviously imbedded in the concept of possession, but must in this connection be dissevered from every thing else than the mere ability to gratify *this one desire.* The child claims property, for example, in objects whose sole value to him is that they are property, and to a morbid extension of this principle, rather than to any thing else, must be ascribed the miser's insane lust of gold, which is to him the one absolute expression of this all-absorbing passion.

2. *Its final cause and moral relations.*—The final cause of the possessory principle, as an element of humanity, appears at once when we consider man as a social being, and investigate its relations to the normal evolution of society,

which all experience proves to be practically impossible without due recognition and enforcement of the rights of property. A naked man without tools, implements, or adjuncts of any kind, is the most helpless of animals; but tools, implements, and adjuncts, postulate the idea of property and the possessory principle.

In its strictly instinctive action, it involves no moral responsibility; but the moment reason intervenes, or has time to intervene, moral accountability attaches to the agent, and he is adjudged innocent or guilty according to the intrinsic character and actual relations of the special act performed. The morbid tendency of acquisitiveness to degenerate into avarice in its lowest and vilest form, is proportional to the intrinsic power and value of the natural appetency, and is therefore very great, and, alas! very common. In the evolutions of humanity, great capacities for good cannot be dissevered from correspondingly great possibilities of evil.

¶ III. **Ambition, or the Desire of Power.**—1. *Its nature and conditions.*—Nearly allied to the possessory principle is ambition, or the desire of power. Its original manifestations in the child are, however, radically different: the one displays itself distinctively, in grasping after and treasuring up objects; the other, by the putting forth of muscular energy; the one leads the boy to fill his pocket with real or fancied treasures, the other arms his hands with sticks, stones, or other more deadly weapons, and prompts him to use them alike upon animate and inanimate objects. In the boy, as in the man, the two desires are often at war with each other, and ambition and avarice struggle for supremacy in the soul.

2. *Its final cause and relations.*—These are the exact counterparts of those of acquisitiveness, and need but little special discussion. Its instinctive action possesses no moral character; its voluntary evolution is amenable to the same moral conditions as the other selfish propensions. Of its great strength and unflagging persistence, in special instances, it were idle to speak, so long as the names of Alexander, Cæsar, and Napoleon, are familiar words. Like acquisitive-

ness, it has a direct relation to the problems of social organization, although it is decisively a selfish propension.

CHAPTER II.—THE SOCIAL PROPENSIONS.

SECTION I.—SOCIALITY, OR THE DESIRE OF SOCIETY.

¶ I. **Nature of the Social Propension.**—1. *Its conditions.*—The social propension is evidently conditioned alike upon the intrinsic nature of man and the necessary conditions of his being. It is, obviously, impossible for us to conceive of human life under the conditions of absolute eremitism, or asceticism; a single generation would legitimately close its useless, hapless, miserable history. It must be adjudged, therefore, that the social propension is a *primitive*, as it is undoubtedly a *universal*, tendency or appetency of humanity.

2. *Its strength.*—This is naturally proportional to its universality and intrinsic importance, and may be illustrated again, as it has been a thousand times before, by examples drawn from the animal races, from the records of prisons, and in fact from the whole history of humanity; but it were idle to do so. No man need go beyond the sphere of his own personal consciousness and experience to find abundant and varied illustrations of its strength and universality, both as an instinctive impulse and as a rational desire. We recognize intuitively an abnormal element in the life and character of the ascetic or the misanthrope.

¶ II. **Final Cause and Relations of the Social Propension.**—To state this problem intelligibly is to solve it, for it is to declare it to be the true basal element of all social and civil organization, from the simple arrangements of the primitive family to the most complex system of national government. Without it, neither the family, the tribe, nor the nation, could exist, nor, under its present actual conditions, could the race itself be perpetuated. The idea that society could be organized and maintained simply from a rational consideration of its intrinsic value to man, may be discounted at once, from the single consideration that man could never know or imagine the benefits of society in advance of some experience of them, and hence, apart from the social propension, there could be no impulse to an *original* social organization in which such experience might be gained.

Its relations to self-love have, perhaps, been sufficiently declared in the affirmation of the correlation and coördination of these elements as the basal principles of all the propensions which naturally group themselves around them; while these sustain to each other a complementary, rather than an antagonistic relation.

In its first or instinctive movement, sociality obviously possesses no moral character; as a voluntary principle it is amenable, to the fullest extent, to the authority of conscience, and is, legitimately, subordinated to it; while its moral relations to self-love have been divinely determined, as has been already noted, to be those of exact equality of rank and authority.

SEC. II.—IMITATIVENESS, APPROBATIVENESS, EMULATION, AND VERACITY.

¶ I. **Imitativeness: the Desire to do like Others.**—Perhaps there are few propensions earlier developed or more persistent and important than this.

1. *Its nature and characteristics.*—These are so familiar, both in our personal experience and in our observations of others, that to name them is to describe them to the thoughtful student. So obtrusive are they, in fact, in their manifestations, that they have been seized upon as characteristic marks of humanity; and man has been defined to be, "a creature of imitation." The child begins his unconscious or semi-conscious education by imitating, as best he can, the motions, the actions, the words of all with whom he comes in contact; and this process ceases only with his conscious life. The child imitates the boy, the boy apes the man, the man copies his fellow-man, until, perhaps, there is no kingdom upon earth so autocratic as that of the fickle goddess *fashion*, whose painted sceptre sways the world to-day.

2. *Final cause and relations of imitativeness.*—This propension obviously bases itself in the social principle and in the economy of society; is one of the great educating and organizing principles by which man, as an individual, is fitted for, and held in, his proper sphere of action. It is, in fact, one of the strongest bonds of human society, and is the origin of much of that conservatism which has been so much lauded as the balance-wheel of progress. Men, like a flock of sheep, are prone to follow their leaders, and to prefer the ways of their fathers to new ideas which they do not fully comprehend, and which have not the power of numbers and of example to back them.

In its *instinctive* action, imitativeness possesses no moral character. In its *voluntary* manifestations, it is amenable to the same moral principles as the other desires. As in the case of all other natural appetencies, men are prone to exaggerate its power, and plead its strength in abatement of judgment against their moral delinquencies. The plea, "I only do as others do," has been repeated and refuted so often that it seems idle to recur to it here, and yet, perhaps, no other single plea for wrong and sin is so universal or so potent for evil. Nevertheless, it neither deserves nor needs formal refutation, for no one pleads it honestly, and a dishonest moral plea it is idle to refute in the court of conscience, which must be sorely depraved before such pleas become possible.

¶ II. **Approbativeness, or the Desire of Esteem.**—1. *Its nature and characteristics.*—Closely allied to imitativeness is approbativeness. We not only like to imitate others, but we desire, not less earnestly, to win their approbation and esteem; and this appetency is prone to excessive and abnormal action, gaining in intensity, power, and persistence, with each new gratification of it. Insatiable as the maw of death, it still cries, "Give! give!" to its unhappy victim. No other propension, perhaps, is more liable to excessive action than this, and none leads to greater weakness, wrongs, or sins. Yet, in its legitimate sphere, it is an element of power, and was, undoubtedly, given a place in the hierarchy of the sensibilities for wise and beneficent ends. Indeed, the truth must be accepted as axiomatic, that great capacities for good in human life involve great possibilities of evil. God has wisely provided many avenues of approach to the sensitive nature of man, each potent for good, and fraught with blessings, if wisely improved; but no less potent for evil, if given over to the dominion of unrestrained selfishness. It is almost needless to add the discrete statement, that the desire of esteem is a primitive and universal element of man's sensitive nature, and is, in no sense, a resultant of education, or the outgrowth of circumstances.

2. *Final cause and relations of this propension.*—These have already been, in part at least, incidentally declared; and yet, perhaps, a fuller statement is necessary. The desire of esteem, as the counterpart of imitativeness, tends to like ends, and serves directly as a motive power or influence whereby society may react upon, influence, and mould, the characters of its individual members, and thus make them subservient to its organic ends and uses. It serves also a secondary purpose as a subsidiary bond of union between man and his fellow-man, as well as a counterpoise to the influence of self-love in the soul, which has a constant tendency to degenerate into absolute selfishness, one of the most hateful of passions. Its influence, in this direction, is indisputable, and is, unquestionably, on the side of man's better nature in this contest.

In the hands of the wise parent or teacher, the love of approbation in the soul of the child is an element of power for good; but there are, alas! but few who comprehend its nature and relations.

It must, however, always be remembered that the desire of esteem is not a safe ultimate rule of action. It might conceivably be so in a world of perfect beings, who never err in judgment and never yield to unholy impulses. Its true position is that of an impulse subsidiary to conscience, but legitimate in its own proper sphere. On the other hand, there are few indications of a depraved soul more decisive than an utter disregard of the good or evil opinions of others concerning us. That young man is not far from ruin who can deliberately say, "I do not care what good men think of me."

¶ III. **Emulation, or the Desire of Superiority.**—1. *Its nature and origin.*—There has been much discussion in reference to the nature and origin of this propension—some writers denying its legitimacy altogether, others ascribing to it a *derivative* origin and a secondary rank, making it nothing more than a conglomerate element based upon imitativeness, ambition, and approbativeness. The correctness of either hypothesis is not, however, apparent; the line of argument relied upon to prove the illegitimacy of emulation as a motive to action is based upon its *perverted*, and not upon its *normal*, action; and is equally destructive when applied to imitativeness, ambition, and approbativeness. The hypothesis which derives it from the last-named desires, overlooks the facts of its early development and its universality, as well as the correlated fact that it is clearly manifested as a natural impulse, not only in trained but in untrained animals. The writer never saw trials of speed among men or trained animals that interested him so much as a series of races he witnessed, one pleasant summer's day, among a herd of young colts, on a beautiful prairie-meadow, that emulated each other in race after race over the beautiful turf.

2. *Its final cause and relations.*—If its true character as an *original* propension be admitted, its final cause appears at once. It serves as a normal stimulus to activity among equals engaged in like pursuits, and pursuing like ends. It thus manifests itself as a true normal adjunct of the social principle, potent for good, yet liable to perversion. It may degenerate into envy, jealousy, or hatred, but it only shares this liability to evil with all the other social propensions.

In its instinctive form, it possesses no moral character; in its voluntary evolution, it is praiseworthy or blameworthy in proportion as it accepts or rejects the authority of an enlightened conscience. As a healthful stimulus to action, when rightly directed and controlled, it is an element of consummate power and incalculable value. Happy is that parent or teacher who knows how to wield its magic power wisely and faithfully!

¶ IV. **Veracity, or Love of Truth.**—1. *Its nature and characteristics.*—At first thought the propriety of ranking veracity among the social propensions may not be evident; but when the fact is considered that it is a necessary attribute of man's nature, as a *social* and not as a *solitary* being, the doubt will disappear. As a natural appetency of the soul, it fastens upon truth, or the true, as its object and ideal, and makes *that* the standard in all its dealings and communications with its fellow-men. *Veracity* is, therefore, the subjective attribute, *truth* the corresponding objective element, of desire. In virtue of man's finite and fallible nature, subjective and objective truth, or, more familiarly, veracity and truth, do not always coincide. A statement may be *subjectively* (intentionally) *true* and *objectively* (actually) *false*; or, *vice versa*, a statement may be *subjectively false* and *objectively true.*

2. *Its final cause and relations.*—Veracity obviously lies at the foundation of all true social organization. So long as men are truthful, however ignorant or mistaken, there is rational ground for hope for the permanency of the social fabric reared upon the foundations of their faith; but when veracity is lost, and faith in man is only a dream, there is no longer room for hope.

Veracity, as an element of human character, reacts upon, strengthens, and intensifies, every better and nobler impulse; and, however much it may in turn be stimulated and intensified by exercise or otherwise, there is no danger of its taking on an abnormal or morbid type. Truth is a stimulant to the soul so pure, so exalted, so godlike, that it can never result in evil, although love of truth may become a passion. Of its value to man it were idle to speak; it is a jewel so priceless, that the wealth of a world cannot compensate for its loss, or restore its tarnished beauty when sullied by falsehood.

Supplementary Topics.

Hope and Fear.

¶ I. **Peculiarity of these Forms of the Sensibility.**—1. *They have no single object, sui generis, like the other propensions.*—They attach themselves, on the contrary, to any special form or object of desire or aversion, and give to it a tinge, a coloring, and a power, peculiarly their own. Other propensions have a marked individuality, distinguishing them from each other; these have almost as marked a generality, allying them to all the rest.

2. *They represent concomitant, and not independent, states of the soul.*—The thought involved here is this: If I hope for some object of desire, the hope fastens upon some one of the *special desires*, or *propensions*, and adds a new element to it; but, apart from such propension, hope could have no object, and consequently no existence.

3. *They are intimately dependent upon physical relations and conditions.*—This fact is distinctly recognized and marked in popular language and modes of expression. Thus men say of this man, "He is of a *hopeful* temperament;" of that man, "He is of a melancholy temperament." The facts and relations underlying these popular forms of expression are real. Hope and fear are largely dependent upon temperament and nervous organization; but they are none the less mental states, and forms of the sensibility.

¶ II. **Hope.**—1. *Analysis of its elements.*—Hope has been defined correctly to be a compound of *a desire*, and *an expectation* that that desire will be realized. This definition fully accords with and justifies the previous statement, that hope has no special or peculiar objects, but that it fastens indifferently upon the object of any one of the special propensions, and makes that the basis of its own evolution, or development. The expectation which hope conjoins to desire may be rational or irrational, well or ill founded, based upon sufficient cause, or be the mere reflex of inordinate desire; but, whatever may be its origin, in any special instance, it is the characteristic element of hope.

2. *Analysis of its relations.*—Hopefulness is an element of power in the evolution of mind. It reacts strongly and decisively upon the intellect, the sensibilities, and the will, in all their relations to each other, and to the complex problems of life. No man ever lost true power by the predominance of a hopeful temperament; and none was ever happier, stronger, or wiser, in consequence of a predominating element of despondency. It is true that, in a particular instance, a man may be unduly or unwisely hopeful, and may rashly intermit the effort necessary to insure success; but despondency will neither nerve his arm nor stimulate his failing energies. In its moral character, hope responds to the ordinary law of the desires, and is marked by no peculiarities requiring discrete investigation.

¶ III. **Fear.**—1. *Analysis of its nature and conditions.*—Fear is, in some respects, the counterpart or contrary of hope. It involves the expectation of evil, both negative and positive. In its simple negative form, it may be defined by the term "not-hope" (i. e., despondence) of attaining our chosen objects or desires. In this sense, it is the expression simply of our sense of impending failure in our plans and purposes. In the positive sense, it imports much more than this; and, figuratively, may be defined to be the shadow of impending evil; or, in plain language, it is the expectation or dread of threatened danger or evil to body, soul, life, health, property, or reputation, etc. As hope animates and stimulates in its normal action, and enervates in its abnormal, so also fear energizes and stimulates to action, in order to avoid the dreaded evil, so long as the passion is kept within reasonable limits; but, when it degenerates into despair, it unmans and utterly demoralizes, and hastens the evils against which it was designed to guard.

2. *Analysis of its relations.*—These have already, per-

haps, been sufficiently declared. Fear, like hope, is primarily designed as a stimulus to human efforts, in order to the conservation of personal interests. Both passions within their normal limits stimulate to activity; when abnormally excited, they tend to enervate and destroy. Both, perhaps, have an instinctive and a voluntary evolution, though this distinction is less clearly marked in them than in the other propensions; they are amenable, therefore, to corresponding moral relations and conditions.

THE DESIRES: CLASS THIRD.

PSYCHICAL: THE AFFECTIONS AND MORAL IMPULSES.

Preliminary Discussion.

¶ I. **Why the Affections and Moral Impulses are classed with the Desires.**—1. *They express appetencies of the soul, and not mere emotions.*—This is so obvious that it scarcely needs to be argued. They centre, generically, in the impulse or affection termed love, which, like a true desire, goes forth to its object, as a real appetency, and not as a mere emotion which begins, exists, and ends, in the soul itself. Love invariably carries with it a desire for the welfare or happiness of the loved one; hence the propriety of the generic term benevolent, applied to one great division of these affections. In the congeneric class of malevolent affections, based upon *not-love*, i. e., upon *resentment*, there is the corresponding element of malevolence, or ill-wishing, constituting them likewise true desires. The moral impulses are less distinctly desires, but yet the analogies of thought demand their classification with them.

2. *Like true desires, they act upon the will in the relation of motives to volition.*—This is a fact so obvious, in the light of conciousness, that argument is idle; and on this point, chiefly, rests the claim of the moral impulses proper to a place in this department of the sensibilities—the analogies between them and the true typical desires being obviously

fewer and more remote than between the desires proper and the affections; but there seemed, nevertheless, an obvious simplicity and propriety in adopting a single principle of classification, in the sphere of the sensibilities, which would reduce all these multiform phenomena to the unity of *two*, and *but two*, genera, viz., the emotions which do *not*, and the desires which do, act upon the will, in the relation of motives to volition.

¶ II. **Reasons for discriminating the Moral Impulses from the Affections.**—1. *They differ in their objects.*—The affections, as such, predicate a *personal* object upon which they rest, and to which they tend constantly, as to an object of desire; the moral impulses do not, unless the abstract conception of *the right* be taken as such an object, and it be conceived, at the same time, as embodied in the personality of Jehovah. To such an analysis, or reduction, there is, perhaps, in principle, no valid objection; and it harmonizes perfectly with the well-known fact that the moral impulses are never so energetic and so efficient as when they are vitalized by the love of God in the soul.

2. *Their central or vitalizing elements are diverse.*—In the one, it is love, or its contrary, resentment; in the other, it is the impulse or feeling of moral obligation. Whether the secondary analysis, suggested above, would legitimately remove this disparity or dissimilarity, is worthy of consideration: but in any case, as a primary fact of consciousness, the distinction is real. The unity suggested, if it exist at all, is the resultant of an ultimate analysis, and is not a primary fact.

DIVISION I.—THE AFFECTIONS.

Preliminary Discussion.

SECTION I.—PSYCHOLOGICAL BASIS OF THE AFFECTIONS.

¶ I. **They are grounded in the Propension of Sociality.**—This proposition is little less than a mathematical corollary from the preceding discussions. The affections go forth and fasten upon the individuals with whom, and to whom, the man is united in virtue of his social propensions, and add new and stronger links to the chain that binds him to them.

¶ II. **They are based upon Intellections mediated by the Emotions and conditioned by Self-Love.**—1. *They are based upon intellections.*—Our natural affections, such as the love of parents, of children, etc., obviously postulate *perceived* and *comprehended* relations as the ground of their existence. A long-separated father and son, for example, might meet and part, again and again, *not recognizing* each other, without the slightest emotion, who would be moved to tears at the perception of the relationship between them.

2. *They are mediated by the emotions.*—The feelings that would swell the hearts of father and son, in the case supposed above, are true mediating elements of the affections, vitalizing and intensifying them, while they themselves result spontaneously from the intellectual perception of the fact of their mutual relationship.

3. *They are conditioned or limited by self-love.*—The soul of man is a complex of complementary and coördinate impulses, each having an abnormal tendency to excessive and exclusive action. Our affections, partaking of this character in a very high degree, find a legitimate counterpoise in self-love and a guide in the moral impulses.

¶ III. **Their Common Vitalizing Element, Love.**—The term love it were idle to attempt to define. It is known in consciousness, or not at all, and the word itself is potent to call the subjective elements which it imports, into the thought. It is necessary, however, for us to analyze:

1. *Its possible forms or degrees as a generic conception.*—The first and most obvious distinction arising out of the concept is its evolution, under the canon of contradiction, into the contrasted categories of *love* and *not-love*, i. e., of love, and its contrary, *resentment.* Each of these terms, in turn, is capable of a relative existence, as expressing varying degrees of the essential feeling, ranging from the common zero-point of absolute indifference to absolute love or absolute hatred severally.

2. *Its conditionating elements.*—Love, considered as a generic term (including its contrary, resentment), is conditioned:

(*a*) *Upon character.*—Intrinsic excellence or its opposite naturally excites love or generates resentment. Mankind are so constituted that excellence tends to excite admiration and love; while its contrary, the mean, the worthless, the vile, repels and excites, or tends to excite, disgust, contempt, resentment, hatred.

(*b*) *Upon relations.*—Aside from intrinsic character, love, and its contrary, resentment, ground themselves severally in the relations subsisting between the parties. These, in social life, may be brought under two generic classes, viz.:

First. Relations of consanguinity, which, in turn, may be subdivided into relations of blood, as of father and son; and of affinity, as of husband and wife; and—

Second. Relations of interdependence. These include all the various bonds of friendship, of interest, etc., etc., which correlate men to each other in actual life, under all its diverse conditions.

In the two concepts of intrinsic character, and actual or potential relations, we have an exhaustive summary of the conditions of love and resentment, severally and collectively considered. It is obviously unnecessary to spend time to analyze the reasons why character, on the one hand, or relations of consanguinity and interdependence on the other, tend to excite love or provoke hatred. However plausible the provisional reasons might seem, which such an investigation would evolve, they must all ultimate in the conclusion that such is the law of our being; or, in other words, that constituted as men actually are, physically and mentally, it could not be otherwise.

Sec. II.—Classification of the Affections.

¶ I. **General Principles of Classification.**—The affections obviously group themselves, primarily, into two general classes corresponding to the two contrary generic forms of their vitalizing element, viz., love and not-love, or resentment, giving rise respectively to the two classes:

1. Of the malevolent affections, based upon *not*-love, or resentment; and—

2. Of the benevolent affections, based upon love.

Secondarily, the affections are classified with reference to the special objects of the several malevolent or benevolent affections.

¶ II. **Evolution of the Malevolent Affections.**—These are familiar to the consciousness, and present themselves under two generic forms, viz.:

1. *Negative, based on simple not-love, or indifference;* and—

2. *Positive, or resentment proper.*—This implies actual hostility, and culminates in hatred, or absolute malevolence.

¶ III. **Evolution of the Benevolent Affections.**—Here the concept love must necessarily be taken in its positive sense, as the *indifference* ground has been assigned to the sphere of the malevolent affections. This classification, it may be remarked, is justified by the fact that, in the spheres in which the affections operate, there is no proper place for, or justification of, *indifference* on the part of one intelligent being toward another. The necessary relations existing between man and his fellow-man morally presuppose, and in fact demand, some more *positive* state of the affections than absolute indifference. In other words, for *sufficient* reasons, a man may be justified in indulging in feelings of natural resentment against his fellow-man, but he cannot be justified in yielding to feelings of absolute indifference. Such a state is hateful alike to God and to man, and admits of no palliation; it is, in fact, the worst form of malevolence.

CHAPTER I.—THE MALEVOLENT AFFECTIONS.

Preliminary Discussion.

¶ I. **Malevolence.**—This has already been presented under its two generic forms, viz., negative, or *indifference*, and positive, or *resentment.* The latter is obviously susceptible of great diversities of form and strength, varying, as it may, from the mere resultant of a transient emotion of anger to settled hatred. The former, i. e., indifference, representing the zero-point between love and hatred, obviously does not admit of degrees, but must, in all cases, be taken absolutely, and is the expression of an abnormal and abhorrent moral state of the affections. God has said of such a one, "I would thou wert either *hot* or *cold.*"

1. *Simple resentment*, as a positive affection of the soul, postulates some cause or causes of its being in virtue of which it assumes to justify its moral right to a place in the legitimate evolution of humanity. A worse insult can scarcely be offered to an intelligent, sensitive gentleman, than the bare intimation that "he is angry without cause." This phenomenon obviously implies a universal consciousness:

First. That resentment involves in itself an element of evil; and—

Second. That its existence in the soul, without adequate cause, is consequently immoral and degrading.

Accordingly, it will be found that the personal consciousness testifies to every individual, that men, habitually, find it necessary *to nurse their wrath* in order to keep it alive; and also to review carefully, from time to time, the numerous and grievous provocations they have received, in order to justify to themselves the malevolent feelings in which they indulge, and which otherwise would be felt to be degrading. To the same cause must be attributed the singular fact that men who are reticent in the extreme, in other matters personal to themselves, love to rehearse their quarrels, thus manifesting an unacknowledged consciousness that, unless thus fully justified by ample reasons stated, their resentment and anger will lower them in the estimation of their fellow-men.

Resentment must, therefore, be adjudged, if not an abnormal, at least an exceptional, state of the unperverted consciousness. It is always an unpleasant frame of mind, however completely it may be justified, or even necessitated, in any concrete instance. In cannot, however, be assumed, legitimately, as has been done sometimes, that it has no proper place in the evolution of the human sensibilities. It is to them what the whirlwind and the storm are to Nature, or pain and suffering are to the physical organism, namely, a necessary concomitant or condition of elements indispensable to man's perfection and happiness. Accordingly, we find the Holy Scriptures ascribe anger or resentment to God Himself, and in Him, as in man, it is the necessary correlated or concomitant condition of intelligent love or moral approbation.

2. *Hatred.*—It is necessary, at this point, to note some special forms or modifications of resentment which possess marked individuality, and thus challenge discrete notice. Hatred may be defined to be the ultimate form of the passion, where it becomes a permanent and settled principle of action. It may exist in varying degrees of intensity and activity, depending upon the temperament of the man, its own special causes, and other circumstances, which it is needless to discuss.

3. *Envy and jealousy* are simply degenerate and abnormal forms of resentment, and are purely and wholly evil, alike in nature and tendency. Envy, normally considered, is the expression of the causeless malevolence in which men sometimes indulge toward their superiors in rank, in social position, in wealth, or in other accidents of humanity.

Jealousy obtains only between equals; and, in its typical form, originates in the sexual relations and affections. It springs up in some souls upon the slightest causes, and often without cause, and ultimates in envy, and perhaps settled hatred of, the supposed more fortunate rival. It is almost idle to repeat that neither envy nor jealousy has one single better quality to redeem it from utter infamy.

Finally, the moral character of resentment must be determined, like that of the other desires, by analysis of the actual facts of the concrete case. Strictly instinctive resentment, of course, possesses no moral character whatever. Voluntary or rational resentment must be approved or condemned in view, first, of its causes; second, of its conditions; and, third, of its extent.

¶ II. **The Objects of Human Malevolence.**—Malevolence, as a rational element or affection, exists only with reference to sentient beings as objects. It is true that the child or the savage may indulge resentment against the stick, the stone, or the arrow, that wounds him, but intelligent resentment takes no such form, but, on the contrary, postulates in its victim sensibility to suffering, if not some degree of intelligence, as the condition precedent of its own existence. As thus defined, the objects of human resentment may be reduced to three classes, viz.:

1. *Animals*, whether conceived as non-intelligent or as partially intelligent.
2. *Men*, in all their varied characters and relations; and—
3. *God*, whether conceived *individually*, as a *personality;* or *generically*, as the *representative of all the unknown spiritual beings*, whose spheres of action may intersect or react upon that of humanity.

As a fact, men do recognize, with more or less of universality, a spiritual world filled with inhabitants, allied, in some way, to themselves. They almost uniformly, moreover, postulate, but cannot demonstrate, some actual relations between themselves and the inhabitants of that spiritual world, who are, consequently, only ideally objects of either love or resentment. The practical result is, that the moment the concept of God takes possession of the human soul (and we have seen that it cannot, logically, be exscinded or excluded), the Divine Being becomes, not only a positive object of malevolent or benevolent affection, but He becomes, moreover, the generic representative of the unknown spiritual world, with all its inhabitants. As referred to the Divine Being, there is no point of *indifference* possible; love and hatred are the poles of a true logical contradiction, which admits *no middle* term, *no zero-point* of absolute indifference.

SECTION I.—MALEVOLENCE TOWARD ANIMALS.

¶ I. **Relations of Man to the Animal Races.**—Reason and revelation alike declare man's sovereignty over the animal races, and recognize his right to use them for his own personal profit, in accordance with the decisions of an enlightened judgment and sensitive conscience; but he has, and can have, no right whatsoever to maltreat, injure, destroy, or otherwise indulge in malevolence toward them, without adequate cause. For sufficient reasons, he may, at any time, take their lives, and, *a fortiori*, exercise over them any minor degree of sovereignty; but he may, in no case, indulge in causeless malevolence toward any of them, however low in the scale of sensibility, or unconscious of suffering.

¶ II. **Moral Character of Resentment toward Animals.**—1. *Of indifference.*—Here, as everywhere, indifference, as a moral state, is wholly reprehensible. The relations of the animal races to man, as the creatures of God, are such as to demand at his hands, legitimately, proper respect and recognition of their welfare and their rights, which are as truly God-given as his own; and the very sovereignty over them with which God has endowed him, precludes indulgence, rightfully, of indifference toward them.

2. *Of resentment.*—This has already been declared to be allowable, within certain well-ascertained limits; beyond these, it is obviously entirely inadmissible. Of resentment, in the sense of mere anger, toward animals, there can be no true moral justification. That is an affection which legitimately postulates in its objects, not merely *rationality*, but *moral accountability* as well. Of cruelty to animals it were idle to speak; it is too base, too cowardly, and too infamous, to admit of suitable words to characterize it.

SEC. II.—MALEVOLENCE TOWARD MAN.

¶ I. **Nature and Conditions of Resentment toward Man.**—Resentment or malevolence toward men manifests itself, in practical life, in both the negative and positive forms; i. e., as indifference, and as positive resentment or hostility. Its causes and conditions, just and unjust, good and bad, are almost as endless and as various as are the possible relations of man to his fellows. They manifest themselves in all ranks, all circumstances, and all conditions of life, and under forms as various as these ever-varying conditions.

¶ II. **Moral Character of Resentment toward Men.**—Here, as elsewhere, we meet the problem of the negative and positive forms of this affection, under allied but not identical conditions. Instinctive resentment, like all similar manifestations of our desires, may be dismissed with the single remark that we are never responsible for the origination of an instinctive impulse of any kind, but we are accountable for its continued existence, just so soon as reason has time to intervene, whether or not it does actually intervene, in any concrete instance. The legitimate law of human development demands that we should accustom ourselves to supersede, *instantaneously*, the instinctive action of all our faculties, by the corresponding voluntary acts morally appropriate to the special occasion. It is only by so doing that we attain to the level of a true Christian manhood.

1. *Moral character of indifference.*—This may be decisively declared, at once and without exception, to be evil and only evil continually. Human misconduct may warrant positive resentment, but can never justify cold-hearted, selfish indifference; *that* has no legitimate status in the human soul under any possible conditions.

2. *Moral character of voluntary resentment.*—This is amenable to the requirements of the moral law to the fullest extent, and is an admissible moral element of human character on condition:

(*a*) That it is based upon adequate cause.

(*b*) That it is conformed to correct principles; and—

(*c*) That it is controlled by an enlightened conscience. Subordinated to these conditions, it is possible for us to be angry and sin not.

¶ III. **Final Cause of Malevolence.**—The term malevolence is here used strictly as the generic expression of the more specific feelings included under the term resentment. Its final cause as a normal element in human nature may be presented under two heads, viz.:

1. It is designed for the protection of self, or the personality, against sudden attack, or aggression; and—

2. It is designed as a permanent affection, to insure the promotion of the ends of justice, by securing the final punishment of the criminal, although he may, in the outset, elude the deserved penalty of his crime.

It is not obvious, under the actual conditions of human life, how either of these important ends could have been secured, had no element of resentment entered into the constitution of human nature. That it is liable to excessive or abnormal development is simply incident to it as an attribute of humanity.

Sec. III.—Malevolence toward God.

A priori, it would seem to be an incredible thing that any man can be so corrupt and so debased as to indulge in *malevolent* feelings toward God, yet the shameful fact exists. Resentment toward God can have neither reason nor apology, under any possible conditions; and its inception in the soul of man, as well as its perpetuation, in every stage of its evolution, is a shame and a crime. Nor is there room for choice here between *indifference* and *positive malevolence.* If the one is impious, the other is sacrilegious and blasphemous. God has expressed His loathing of the *indifferent soul* in the words: "I would thou wert cold or hot; so then because thou art lukewarm, and neither cold nor hot, I will spue thee out of my mouth."

CHAPTER II.—THE BENEVOLENT AFFECTIONS.

Preliminary Discussion.

Analysis of the Benevolent Affections.

¶ I. **Benevolence.**—The terms *benevolence* and *benevolent*, like *malevolence* and *malevolent*, are here used in a generic and philosophic sense, radically different from their ordinary use in daily life. This is an evil, but in the present state of language seems to be wholly unavoidable, there being no other less ambiguous terms available to the uses of the psychologist. The term benevolence is here used as the simple expression of good will, good wishes, or, in a word, of love in its generic sense, as contradistinguished from indifference or resentment. The vitalizing element of the benevolent affections has already been declared to be "*love*" in its true specific sense. Its nature and conditions are familiar to consciousness, and have already been pointed out; but an additional formal remark or two may not be inappropriate. Love as the basal principle of the benevolent affections is:

1. *A generic term*, including many varying forms and degrees of the affection; and—

2. *Is modified and conditioned by the specific objects upon which it fastens.*—There is no generic difference in the principle of love itself, intrinsically considered, however much its forms and degrees of intensity may vary in accommodating itself to its objects.

¶ II. **Classification of the Objects of Benevolence.**—Benevolence takes a wider range, legitimately, as a positive element of human character, than its contrary congener, malevolence; since it does not necessarily presuppose, in its object, any sensibility to its effects, or consciousness of its existence. It may, therefore, attach to *inanimate* as well as *animate* objects; to localities as well as to the beings inhabiting them. Its objects will, therefore, be considered under four generic heads, viz.:

1. Love of Home and Country.
2. Love of Animals.
3. Love to Men; and—
4. Love to God.

Section I.—Love of Home and Country.

¶ I. **Analysis of the Affection.**—The only form of love to inanimate objects which demands any special notice, is the love of home and country; i. e., the attachment that men instinctively feel to the home of their childhood and to their native land. It seems to be a universal principle in the soul of man, and to be almost wholly independent of local conditions and circumstances; or, if affected by them, to be strongest where, antecedently, it might have been anticipated that it would be weakest. For example, the inhabitants of bleak and barren mountains are, usually, more strongly attached to their native land than those who dwell on the fertile plains below. So also the Greenlander and the Esquimaux manifest an instinctive love for their native lands that would do no discredit to more favored nations. This general fact may be accounted for, in part, by the influence of habit, but is due chiefly, perhaps, to the fact that there is more individuality or intensity of life, if such expressions be admissible, in mountain and glacial life, than in countries whose natural scenery is less marked. To the dweller on the level fertile plain, one spot differs but little from another, and a change of locality scarcely breaks the habits and associations of daily life. A mountain-peak, on the contrary, has an individuality about it which attracts the soul, wins the affections, and makes it, as it were, a part of the life of the man.

¶ II. **Final Cause of this Affection.**—This is so obvious that it scarcely requires either statement or elucidation. A rambling, nomadic people are never a progressive people; and true civilization and culture do not begin until men find settled homes, and a country around which the sweeter, purer affections of the heart may cluster. Of the intensity and power of this affection under the generic form of Patriotism, the records of history are full, and it were idle to quote illustrations here.

Sec. II.—Benevolence to Animals.

¶ I. **Grounds of this Affection.**—Love, as we have already noted, is based either upon essential character or upon actual relations; or, still more frequently, upon both. These principles are distinctly marked in the case of man's affection for animals, which is actually and legitimately based upon:

1. *The intrinsic character of the animal.*—Thus men who feel an instinctive repulsion to animals, generally, sometimes single out some particular animal, as a horse or a dog, and become intensely attached to it, from the real or fancied discovery, in the favored animal, of some intrinsic excellence not discoverable in its species or in animals generally.

2. *The actual relations which the animal may sustain to us.*—These relations are, in general:

(*a*) *Those of nature;* i. e., those of a common dependence upon God, their Creator and ours; and—

(*b*) *Of dependence.*—The animal races have, by the decree of Jehovah, been subjugated to the *will* and the *welfare* of man; and that very dependence constitutes a claim upon our benevolence.

On the other hand, no man who truly honors God can despise or needlessly injure any creature of God; and, on the other, no man who realizes the inferiority of the animal races to and their dependence upon the human race, can, consistently with his own sense of *moral right* and *self-respect*, regard these dependent races other than with feelings of benevolence. Subsidiary to these, there are special cases of individual relationship, or rather association, between men and animals, generating strong mutual affection, which need only be named here to be comprehended.

¶ II. **Relations and Limitations of this Affection.**—The obligation of benevolence toward animals, as a practical fact, is limited only by man's own necessities. He may legitimately destroy ferocious or noxious animals whose existence imperils his own life, health, or material interests, or he may take the life of, or otherwise use, any animal for his own profit, but in any case he is bound to cultivate benevolent feelings toward them. He may not, rightfully, make their sufferings, as such, minister to his pleasure, as in bull-baiting and cock-fighting, and he who does so brutalizes his own nature, and does himself even a greater wrong than he does the wretched animals which he tortures. Cruelty to animals is unnatural, and is repulsive alike to reason and the moral sense of man, but is, alas! disgracefully common.

Sec. III.—Benevolence to Man.

This affection presents itself to us familiarly in consciousness, under two general forms, viz.: 1. Love of kindred; and, 2. Love of humanity.

¶ I. **Love of Kindred.**—1. *Its germinal principle.*—Love of kindred, with its ties of blood, is so familiar to our consciousness and so vital an element in our daily lives, that we rarely stop to analyze it, or seek to evolve its vital element. The affection of the parent for his child is so intense, so persistent, and so essential to the interests, not to say to the existence, of society, that we accept the fact as a thing of course, and do not pause to investigate its philosophy; we say it is natural, and are satisfied. We ignore the fact that ties of blood, as bonds of attachment between parent and offspring, have no such persistence among the animal races, but that, on the contrary, all recognition and affection between them ceases with the maturity of the offspring, and they are thenceforth strangers to each other. In the human race, however, a contrary law prevails, and parental and filial love usually continue during the lives of the parties. There is, moreover, with men, an extension of the principle, as manifested in love of kindred, not only in the direct, but in the collateral, lines of consanguinity. In reference to this peculiarity, but little more can be said than that we are so constituted, doubtless for wise and beneficent purposes.

The tie recognized is specifically that of blood, and its strength is proportioned to its nearness and directness.

2. *Its special forms.*—These correspond to the actual sexual relations of man, with its secondary or derivative filiations, and include:

(*a*) *Conjugal love.*—This is the basal element at once of the marriage relation and of the love of kindred. It is obviously an affection *sui generis*, involving principles peculiar to itself. Originating as it does, spontaneously, in the souls of the man and woman who, perhaps until the hour, were entire strangers to each other, it unites them in a bond stronger than life itself, and justifies by its intimacy, intensity, and endurance, the words of Adam concerning Eve: "This is now bone of my bone, and flesh of my flesh." Here there is no tie of blood, or natural kindred, and yet no tie of blood is stronger than this, or more essential to human development and happiness.

It should be remarked in this connection that the essential characteristics of conjugal love, viz., its intensity and exclusiveness, indicate strongly that *monogamy* is the normal relation between the sexes, and tends to the purity and happiness of the race. No man is content to share the love of his wife with another, and no true woman feels that less than the *exclusive* love of her husband is an adequate return for her own. Of the origin of this peculiar affection, philosophize as we may, we come at last to this conclusion—we are so constituted; and conjugal love is an original impulse of the human soul.

(*b*) *Parental and filial love.*—In this we have the complementary nexus, or bond, of the resultant parental and filial relation, so that in a modified sense the latter may be said to be itself a resultant of conjugal love. Parental and filial love differ from each other, necessarily, both in their natures and their relations. The former is obviously the more intense, persistent, and enduring, and is just as obviously stronger in the mother than the father. These differences accommodate themselves precisely to the necessities and the moral relations of mankind, which require just such a special guarantee for the perpetuity of the race, by providing for the infant in its helplessness. These peculiarities may perhaps be accounted for, by the actual relations subsisting between parents and children, on the supposition of the natural equality of their affection for each other; but in point of fact the difference is primitive, though it may be, and often is, intensified by circumstances. The final cause of these affections is unquestionably, *first*, the conservation, and, *second*, the happiness, of the human race.

(*c*) *The love of consanguinity.*—This may also, perhaps, be regarded as an original principle, grounding itself in the two forms of affection previously noted; but it is much less powerful than either, and is amenable in a greater degree to the influence of education and the power of habit. Among some races, as the Scotch Highlanders and the Bedouin Arabs, it is recognized as a real bond so long as the relationship is discoverable, however remote. Among nations generally it is scarcely recognized beyond the nearest collaterals. In the primitive forms of society, it was the organizing link of the patriarchy, and the germinal bond of the tribe or nation. In modern times, its influence as an element of social organization is much less marked and less important. Yet even now it is an element of social and moral power, as well as of human happiness.

¶ II. **Love of Humanity.**—Beyond the utmost limit of cognizable consanguinity, we still recognize a natural love in the human soul for man as man. This may be, and often is, smothered by selfishness, obscured by passion, or obliterated practically by sin, but it is none the less a normal primitive affection of the soul, complementary to, rather than based upon, or evolved from, the natural bonds of *unity of nature*, *unity of relations to God*, *and unity of interest*, which bind man to his fellow-man. The fact, however, is recognized that these relations, just in proportion as they are realized in consciousness and intelligently comprehended, react upon and strengthen the corresponding affection of man to man, as men; and it is one of the most pleasing developments of modern times, that the brotherhood of humanity is not only recognized as an intellectual perception, but as a vital faith and a living principle of action.

Sec. IV.—Love to God.

¶ I. **Nature of the Principle.**—Love, as an affection of the human soul, may be diverse in its conditions, its degrees of intensity, its persistence, and its objects; but it is essentially one and indivisible in its essence. As directed toward God, it approximates more or less perfectly toward its normal ideal form and its perfect development, since in God every element of love, whether it be conceived as based upon *intrinsic excellence*, or upon *relations* the most interesting and beneficent in their character and ends, culminates in an absolute ideal perfection. Love to God must be considered under two distinct points of view, which determine its character, viz.:

1. *As a generic form, or principle.*—Love to God differs from any other form of the affection in its breadth or necessary extension. Love of home, of a favorite animal, of a wife, of children, etc., are of an individual or personal character, and involve to a greater or less degree the idea of appropriating the loved object, and each form of the affection noted tends in a greater or less degree to become exclusive and to shut out all other affections. Love to God, on the contrary, while it absorbs the affection into itself with wonderful power, at the same time opens and expands the soul, and prepares it to embrace with unwonted intensity and power every other legitimate object of affection. The philosophy of this generic fact seems to be this: love, as directed toward God, grasps every possible element of truth, beauty, and goodness, i. e., every element that may generate, intensify, or sustain, the passion of love. But grasping these in their absolute perfections, as individualized in God, the soul is at once quickened and intensified, and its love for truth, beauty, and goodness, so stimulated that it fastens upon them,

wherever found, as its richest treasures. Love to God, therefore, necessitates and strengthens every lower normal affection. It should, perhaps, be added that this is a peculiar characteristic of love to God, which it shares with *no other affection* of the soul.

2. *As an exclusive principle.*—Paradoxical as the grouping may seem to be, love to God is at once *generic* and *exclusive.* For while, on the one hand, it includes, generates, and necessitates, all minor forms of normal affections, it will, on the other hand, brook no equality or rivalry with any. In this sense, it challenges for itself *the right to dwell alone* in the innermost sanctuary of the soul. The divine expression of these apparently paradoxical attributes of love to God, is found in Christ's authoritative exposition of the divine law, viz., "Thou shalt love the Lord thy God, with all thy heart, and with all thy soul, and with all thy mind, and with all thy strength;" and "Thou shalt love thy neighbor as thyself." In which we have exhibited at once the *generic* and the *exclusive* characters of the affection.

¶ II. **Basis or Grounds of Love to God.**—The general doctrines or conditions of love, as an affection of the soul, have already been discretely enunciated, namely, *intrinsic excellence* and *actual relations.* It only remains to note their application as elements of love to God; and here, it would seem, that words were idle and argument impertinent. Every conceivable rational element and condition of love, in its purest and most exalted type, centres, in all its fulness and completeness in the character of God, and in His relations to man. He is, on the one hand, the ideal of truth, of beauty, and of goodness—in a word, of all perfection; and, on the other, He is the fountain of being, of life, of happiness, and of hope, to man. Every conceivable element of intrinsic excellence converges in the infinite perfection of His character; and every tie of admiration and of gratitude appeals to the deepest fountains of affection in the human soul, and tends to draw us to God, our Creator, Preserver, and Redeemer, in a bond of love, sweeter than life and stronger than death.

¶ III. **Reflex Influences of Love to God.**—1. *Upon man's intellectual life.*—The concept of truth stimulates the intellect to seek after it as an object of desire, the love of truth energizes the soul and intensifies its efforts to grasp the coveted prize; but, when truth is individualized and becomes *a living personality*, the pure, earnest, truth-loving soul fastens its affections upon that personality, i. e., upon God, with a power that reacts upon the whole intellectual life of the man, intensifying the perceptions, elevating the conceptions, and strengthening the judgment—in a word, lifting the thoughts, above the clouds and above the shadows, into the glorious sunshine of divine truth.

2. *Upon the moral life of man.*—It is, however, only when we turn and consider love to God, in its influence upon the moral nature of man, that we attain to an approximately adequate conception of its vitalizing and energizing power. In the struggle between the *animal* and *rational* natures of man, between his *physical appetites* and *moral impulses*, the love of God is an auxiliary so potent, when thrown into the scale on the side of the rational and spiritual natures, as to insure victory in the otherwise doubtful contest. It is only in the wisdom and strength of a pure, exclusive, all-absorbing love to God, that the intellect of man achieves its loftiest efforts, that his purest and sweetest emotions are awakened, that the nobler, holier desires of his soul are aroused, and that his moral impulses are stimulated to assert and vindicate fully their sovereignty, consuming the dross of selfishness, expelling all base desire, and attaining to perfect rest in a vital union with God.

¶ IV. **Is Love to God an Original Principle.**—1. *Testimony of consciousness.*—Our inquiries here touch upon the point of contact between psychology and revelation, and call in, almost unavoidably, elements that belong rather to revealed religion than to positive science; yet, in the light of preceding discussions, the inquiry raised here cannot be legitimately evaded.

Our analysis of the intellectual processes revealed the

fact, decisively, that the concept of God is a necessary resultant of the laws of thought, and is one of the primitive faiths of humanity; that in this concept our loftiest ideals of truth, beauty, and goodness, meet and are individualized; that in the sphere of the emotions it alone is capable of awakening their intensest life; that it reacts powerfully upon our desires and stimulates conscience to its most energetic action, and infuses into its monitions a vital force which otherwise they could not possess. All this and more is true, and yet the problem, Do men naturally and intuitively love God? remains unanswered. All the elements seemingly necessary to the generation and evolution of genuine love seem to be present. The character and relations of God to man alike challenge love, but *there is no decisive evidence*, either in personal consciousness or experience, that men do *naturally love God* as they love home and country, the animals around them, their kindred, or their fellow-men. All these minor affections spring up normally in the human soul, and manifest themselves, with more or less of intensity and power, universally among men; but he were a venturesome, not to say a reckless psychologist, who would risk the assertion that love to God is at least as universal among men as the concept of God. It is, alas! not so; untold myriads of men know God only to hate Him. Every element, seemingly essential to the evolution of love in the human soul, is present; and yet men naturally do not love God. Such is decisively the testimony alike of reason, of consciousness, and of experience.

2. *Testimony of the Holy Scriptures.*—In passing, transiently, as we now do, from the sphere of science to that of revelation, we discover how exactly the latter coincides in its supernatural teachings with the former, and thus meets, in its Divine fulness, the actual necessities of man. In the first place, revelation explicitly declares it to be man's supreme duty to love God; in the second place, it charges with equal directness that, in fact, men do not love God, although every claim that could challenge their rational love has appealed to them again and again; in the third place, it postulates

the absolute necessity of Divine help, as the only possible condition on which men can be brought to love God, but this help it tenders freely to all who will in any wise accept it. Revelation and science are thus in accord with each other; and when men point, as they sometimes do, to a beautiful instance, here and there, of some lovely child growing up, under the wise care of God-fearing parents, in the knowledge and love of God, revelation responds at once to the precious psychological phenomenon with the still more precious promise: "I will circumcise thy heart, and the heart of thy seed, to love the Lord thy God." Men *ought, but do not, naturally love God*, albeit God has not only given them a loving nature, but also abundant positive cause to love Him above all things else.

DIVISION II.—THE MORAL IMPULSE, OR CONSCIENCE.

Preliminary Discussion.

¶ I. The Intellectual Basis of our Moral Impulses, or Conscience.—Our sensitive nature, as has been already noted, is conditioned upon our intellectual, and cannot operate apart from it; and this is preëminently true of the moral impulse, or conscience, which is wholly rational in its character and conditions, and predicates in its every act a prior intellection or perception of the right. This perception appears under two distinct forms, viz.:

1. An intuition of the right as an *a priori* concept of the soul, as well as a necessary alternative attribute of human action.

2. *An intuitive judgment*, "I ought to do right," denominated the categorical imperative of conscience. This peculiar judgment carries with it a conviction as clear, as positive, and as self-evident, as that which results from the axioms of mathematics.

In this primitive concept, with its corresponding judgment, we discover the true intellectual basis of conscience as the ultimate appellate motive principle of the soul. It should be remarked, in passing, and will appear more clearly in the sequel, that every specific act of conscience implies, in addition to these general intellectual elements, a concrete judgment that this or that proposed specific act is *right* or *wrong*, as the case may be, and this concrete judgment is purely an intellection based upon the ordinary processes of the reason, evolved under precisely the same conditions of truth or falsity as any other judgment whatsoever, and is hedged around with no peculiar guarantees against error, in view of the fact that an act of conscience must be based upon it. It is precisely here that the element of fallibility manifests itself in conscience conceived as a moral guide.

¶ II. **The Emotional Element in Conscience.**—Conscience as a complex faculty involves an emotional element of an intensity, rank, and power, corresponding to its intellectual basis. This is found in our familiar emotions of moral approval and disapproval, which we found to be at the summit of the hierarchy of the emotions, whose peculiar double movement was there noted, viz.:

1. *Their abstract movement*, in which they are spontaneously evolved in view of abstract action, considered as right or wrong, independently of the personality; and—

2. *Their personal movement*, in view of the voluntary right or wrong actions of the personality. In this case they are evolved under the higher and intenser forms of remorse and shame for *wrong* actions; and of emotions of purest, sweetest self-approval in view of *right* actions.

¶ III. **The Motive Power of Conscience.**—Did conscience rest in the moral judgment, however decisive, that "I ought to do this because it is right," and in the correlated moral emotions of approval and disapproval, however sweet and intense, it would be powerless to struggle against desire and passion, and to limit their influence upon the will. Neither the intellect nor the emotions have any direct or immediate influence in the evolution of volitions, or in producing voluntary action. Conscience, therefore, predicates, as a condition precedent of its existence, a place at the summit of the hierarchy of the desires; i. e., of the motive powers of the soul. It challenges in fact for itself, in virtue of its transcendent importance, the right to be the supreme motive power of the life.

Conscience, as a faculty of the soul, attains to its true rank and position only in this perfect synthesis of elements, which brings it in complete sympathy and contact with every department of soul-life, and thus enables it authoritatively to propound its mandate, "Do right, because it is right."

Section I.—Nature of the Moral Impulse

¶ I. **It is not a Simple Judgment.**—The question here is not of clearness of intellectual conviction; that may be practically absolute, and yet conscience may be powerless. The judgment "I ought to do this," or "I ought not to do that," unquestionably underlies and conditions every true moral impulse, or act of conscience, but it does not constitute that impulse, or act. No simple judgment, as such, can sustain the relation of a motive to the will, save on the condition that it generates a corresponding desire or impulse of the sensitive nature.

¶ II. **It is not a Simple Emotion.**—The emotions, like intellections, possess *no direct* motive power, though they may, and do, generate desires and impulses corresponding in nature to their own, which do sustain to the will the relation of motives to volition.

¶ III. **True Nature of the Moral Impulse.**—This must be adjudged to be, generically, of the nature of desire, that is, it is of the nature of a motive power, in its relations to volition. It has, moreover, the characteristic persistence of a true desire, and will not rest or cease till its demands are satisfied by appropriate moral action. Or, more discretely:

1. It resembles the true desires in two particulars, viz.:

(*a*) In that, like them, it acts upon the will in the relations of a motive to volition; and—

(*b*) That, like them, it is persistent until its demands are satisfied.

2. *It is unlike the desires*, in the fact that it perpetuates itself, long after the decisive moment when gratification is attained, or forever becomes impossible by the introduction of alternative and persistent emotions:

(*a*) *Of moral self-approval*, consequent upon *right* action; and—

(*b*) *Of moral disapproval*, i. e., of remorse, consequent upon wrong action. The pleasures of gratified desire are transitory, and serve rather to disquiet, by generating a fresh desire for the repetition of the pleasure, than permanently to satisfy the soul; but the smiles of an approving conscience bring a peace and joy that are enduring. For this peculiarity no other reason can be assigned than that God has so constituted us.

Sec. II.—Characteristics of our Moral Impulses.

¶ I. **They are simple and primitive.**—In this respect they respond to the essential characteristics of all our original faculties or powers. The moment a mental process is found to be resolvable into more simple elements, or factors, the mind seizes upon those new factors, and declares them to be the proper mental faculties, of which the former are but subsidiary complex forms. Psychologists, in their unwearied efforts to reduce the complex elements and processes of thought, feeling, and volition, to unity, are prone to forget the fact that science, in its very nature, postulates and deals with *second causes only*, and must, therefore, rest in them; and that any attempt to pass beyond them, in its own proper plane, can only result in confusion, and not in knowledge.

¶ II. **They are universal.**—No family, race, or nation, is known to-day, or finds a place in the records of history, in whom the moral impulse is, or was, wholly wanting. Men may, and do differ, *toto cœlo*, as to what is right or wrong, in this or that concrete instance, but they never differ in reference to the more general problem that right and wrong are real attributes of human action. This fact is attested alike by consciousness, by language, and by history.

¶ III. **They are authoritative.**—In this respect conscience is a faculty, *sui generis*, and wholly peculiar. A desire may be *intense*, *exacting*, *urgent;* but a moral impulse is *rational*, *imperative*, *authoritative*. It thus, instinctively, or intuitively, vindicates its right to the throne, the crown, and the sceptre, in the hierarchy of the sensibilities.

SEC. III.—ARE THE DECISIONS OF CONSCIENCE FINAL?

¶ I. **They are not infallible.**—This is a simple corollary from the necessary laws or conditions of their evolution, whether they are considered with reference to their intellectual or their sensitive elements or conditions. In the first case, it is obvious that the intellect of man does not and cannot attain to *absolute* truth, and consequently does not and cannot render an *infallible* decision in reference to any case of conscience submitted to its decision; for neither its processes nor its data are absolute. The reason of man, in this life, does not and cannot, therefore, possess any infallible guide to truth. The fact is not ignored here, that it does possess a divine revelation, but it possesses it only in *earthen* vessels, i. e., under the variable forms of human (not divine) language, as conceived and comprehended by human faculties, and hence (however perfect the revelation) the liability to error and mistake remains in the application of this perfect law to the concrete cases of conscience that arise in daily life. Nor would the infallibility of priests, pope, or Church, aid us here, were we assured of its reality, since it could not remove this subjective liability to error. In the second case, it is obvious that, if absolute intellectual verity could be postulated in any concrete instance, there could still be no sufficient guarantee that the sensitive nature would respond by emotions and moral impulses exactly conformed in all respects to the supposed infallible moral judgment. The whole paragraph may, in fact, be summed up in three discrete remarks, viz.:

1. Errors of conscience are, or may be, conditioned upon

errors of judgment, or reasoning, even when the latter are conditioned upon correct data or premises.

2. Errors of conscience may be conditioned upon false or imperfect data, where the processes of reasoning are logically correct; and—

3. Errors of conscience may be conditioned upon a failure of the moral emotion, or moral impulse, even when the intellectual elements are correct.

It is evident that the last-named form must be characterized as moral imbecility, when there is simple failure of the moral impulse; and as moral insanity, if the case be conceived possible that a man's conscience should impel him to do what he himself believed and knew to be wrong and sinful; but it may safely be doubted whether such a case ever actually existed. Practically, depravity of conscience involves: first, errors in the processes of judgment; second, false data of judgment; or, third, imbecility of moral impulse; or it may include any of these singly, or may combine them all.

¶ II. **The Decisions of Conscience are final.**—The reason of this conclusion is obvious, in the light of the preceding discussions. Conscience involves and includes the highest elements of both the intellectual and sensitive natures of man; and, failing these, there is nothing to which man can appeal as a moral guide and pilot over the ocean of life. Will it be said in reply, that, since conscience is fallible, man should take refuge in authority, the answer is decisive and final: first, that this fallible conscience must be absolutely trusted to select the proposed infallible guide; and, second, granting the fitness of the selection, the same fallible conscience must still be trusted to receive, comprehend, and enforce, the teachings of this infallible authority —so that in the end we come back to conscience as a final authority in morals. But this problem is so radical in its relations to humanity that it demands more extended discussion, and especially does it require a discrete investigation of the actual authorities which have been proposed to man as a substitute for conscience, namely:

1. *The authority of the state.*—This, it is obvious, is, after all, only the resultant or sum-total of the consciences of the individuals composing the state; or, more correctly, of the ruling minds in the state. We thus come back, at once, to the individual conscience as the ultimate appeal. But no man at the present day seriously proposes to make the state, in any proper sense, a universal conscience for all its citizens; this hypothesis may, therefore, be discounted without further notice.

2. *The authority of the Church.*—This is the theory of Rome, which postulates infallibility in the Church, without having been able as yet to determine satisfactorily where this infallibility rests; whether in the pope, in a general council, or in the unity of pope and council. In the outset the fact should be noted that this uncertainty, however convenient as a shield against attack, is after all fatal to the dogma, since infallibility is worthless so long as it is intangible and undefined. How, for example, can it help me, in a case of conscience, to know that there is an infallible guide *somewhere*, so long as I do not know, and cannnot discover, *who he is*, *where he is*, *nor how to find him?* I know that much now, for I know that God is absolutely infallible, but I find, like Job, that I cannot come at pleasure to His throne. Although the Ecumenical Council of the Vatican has decreed the infallibility of the pope (which they could only do on the hypothesis, which nobody believes, that both pope and council were separately infallible), we have practically gained nothing, for equally infallible popes and councils have, in the past, again and again, condemned and anathematized each other; and the question still remains insoluble, whether the pope is infallible simply as a pope, or as a man, or as both pope and man. Who, then, shall tell us, in any given case, whether the pope or the man speaks or acts, so that we may know whether the given act or decision is infallible which is offered in solution of our case of conscience? But if it could, in order to avoid this difficulty, be conceded, as clearly it cannot, even on the Roman hypothesis, that both *pope* and

man are infallible, still our poor consciences are not helped, for nobody pretends that each individual Roman bishop, or priest, is an infallible expounder of the infallible decree of the infallible pope, and so we are forced back at last upon our own poor fallible consciences, and must trust them, in the end, to decide upon the application of the infallible dogmas of pope and council to the special cases of conscience upon which our personal salvation must at last depend. Practically, an infallible pope, enthroned in the Vatican, is less accessible to the masses of mankind than Jehovah enthroned as King of kings, in the third heavens; for He, at least in Spirit, is present everywhere. The figment of an *infallible* church, could its reality be proved, could not be substituted in the soul of man for the paramount authority of conscience.

3. *The authority of revelation.*—A divinely inspired and satisfactorily authenticated revelation is the only remaining alternative. But this, inestimable and priceless as is the boon, does not and cannot supersede the authority of conscience in the soul, for the obvious reason that, like the state and like the Church, it must itself at last appeal to conscience, *first, to accept, and, secondly, to enforce its authority.* No one needs to be told, at the present day, how vain are all civil or criminal laws of the state which the moral sense of community does not sustain; nor yet how powerless are the decisions of pope and council when the consciences of men revolt against them, as in the days of Luther and Calvin. Rationally, from this ultimate right of private judgment there is no appeal and no escape. The sincere and devout Catholic is such only in virtue of the standing decision of his own conscience, that the authority of the Church is legitimately paramount. *Take that consent of conscience away, and his Catholicism is an empty name.*

The fact is, no truth whatever can be stated in human language so briefly, so decisively, so unequivocally, that the first three men to whom it is proposed shall be able to comprehend it, *in all respects, exactly alike ;* so that an infallible divine revelation is just as powerless to produce absolute uniformity of faith and conscience as an infallible church. It does not follow, however, that it is just *as mythical* or *as valueless*. Its value as furnishing reliable data to reason and conscience is priceless, but none the less conscience is, and must ever be, the ultimate court of appeal in the sphere of the human personality.

¶ III. **Moral Responsibility for Conscientious Action.**—Finally, but a single problem remains. Is a man morally responsible for a wrong action wrought in obedience to the behests of conscience? It is obvious that, in the discussion of this question, we must pass from the sphere of psychology to that of ethics; yet the question is so intimately related to our legitimate line of thought, that it seems to be necessary to recognize it here. The principles involved are few and simple, and easily comprehended. Every legitimate act of conscience postulates at least three related conditions, viz.:

1. *Unbiassed inclinations.*—Or, in other words, a sincere desire *both to know and to do the right.* He who approaches the examination of a case of conscience with a biassed mind, i. e., with strong prepossessions for, or against, a certain course of action, is but little likely to arrive at correct conclusions concerning it. If we throw the sword of Brennus into the scale, we shall not mete out exact justice in the court of conscience.

2. *Conscientious use of all the light possible.*—He who shuts his eyes to the light has no right to plead the darkness in bar of judgment against his errors and mistakes. The question is not, how much light the man has actually used, in any given instance, but how much was fairly within his reach, if he had conscientiously sought after it. No man can honestly decide *on worse evidence* than is possible to him in the given case.

3. *Logical precision of judgment.*—Candor and intelligence alone cannot insure correct results if logical precision in the evolution of our complex processes of reasoning be

wanting. Man ordinarily is justly held to be accountable for his logic, or want of logic, and may not plead his own careless use of his reasoning powers as an apology for his errors of conscience; but where an individual, fully recognizing his own moral responsibility, approaches a case of conscience in the spirit of the three conditions noted above, and yet errs at last in his decision, and, in obedience to his conscience, performs a wrong act, he must stand acquitted of all wrong or sin alike at the bar of conscience and of Jehovah.

BOOK III.—THE WILL.

PRELIMINARY ANALYSIS.

SECTION I.—NATURE OF THE PROBLEM.

IN order to any intelligent comprehension of the problems of the will, upon the investigation of which we must now enter, it is indispensable that we thoroughly comprehend the results already reached in the process of the evolution of mind, and that we comprehend adequately at once the difficulty and importance of the subject.

¶ I. **Analysis of Results reached.**—Our investigations thus far into the phenomena of our complex human personalities have revealed two general classes of facts, differing decisively from each other, and have indicated or foreshadowed a third, which now remains to be noted.

1. *The intellect and the phenomena of thought.*—These have already been discretely investigated; and their three general movements, or processes, with their resulting products, viz., *percepts*, *concepts*, and *beliefs*, have been clearly evolved in consciousness, and correlated to each other.

2. *The sensibilities and the phenomena of feeling.*—Here our investigations revealed the two general classes of *emotions* and *desires:* the first representing simple states or affections of the complex physical and psychical organism; the second, its appetencies, in virtue of which they react upon the will, as will be seen in the sequel, in the relation of motives to volitions.

3. *Will and the phenomena of volition.*—These were dis-

tinctly indicated in our preliminary analysis, and now remain for discrete examination, as the only remaining element in the trinal evolution of the human soul.

As compared with each other in general terms, intellect may be said to evolve the problems of life; the sensibilities, to furnish the motive power to action; and the will, as the autocratic sovereign, to determine decisively and authoritatively the action to be taken in view of the problems proposed. As thus conceived, the will is obviously identified strictly with *self*, or *the true ego*, and made the central element in the sphere of consciousness, a conclusion whose necessity and propriety will become increasingly evident as our investigation proceeds.

¶ II. **Importance of this Department of Mind.**—It is almost superfluous, in view of these facts, and others which will present themselves obtrusively to the thoughtful student, to pause to argue the necessity of an intelligent comprehension of volition and its laws, as the central and crowning element of soul-life. Apart from this, the phenomena of moral responsibility and accountability, the most important elements or attributes of humanity, are unsolved and insoluble mysteries. No fact is better ascertained in consciousness than that, apart from volition, there is, and can be, neither moral responsibility nor accountability.

¶ III. **Difficulty of the Investigation.**—This is, as usual, in direct proportion to the intrinsic importance of the subject, in its relations to human evolution. Its special difficulties appear to result from two general considerations, viz.:

1. The evolution of its processes and products is, from their nature, less obvious than those of the intellect or sensibilities. The soul, in the act of volition, is so thoroughly occupied and engrossed with the immediate problem that is pressing upon it for decision, that it is less capable of reacting upon and determining, in the light of personal consciousness, its own actual processes than in any other form of mental activity whatever. In addition to this, the fact must be

distinctly noted that the processes themselves are intrinsically more obscure than any others known to us in the evolution of soul-life, lying as they do in the very inner sanctuary of the soul.

2. The phenomena of volition are wholly *sui generis* and *peculiar*, having nothing analogous to them, even remotely, in the sphere of human experience. The necessary consequence is, that all attempts to illustrate them by analogies drawn from man's varied experience, not only fail to cast any light whatever upon their acknowledged mysteries, but actually tend to mislead, by introducing factitious elements into the problem, which vitiate the results reached, necessarily and hopelessly. This is especially true of all analogies drawn from the physical world, such as Edwards's famous balances, introduced in order to illustrate the power of motives over choice. He who would investigate the phenomena and laws of volition, intelligently, must fix in his thought, firmly and decisively, this fundamental principle, *that volition is a phenomenon of the soul, sui generis, unlike any thing else known to man, either in consciousness, or in the external world, and that it must be studied in itself, or not at all.*

Sec. II.—Methods of Investigation.

¶ I. Consciousness the Sole Instrument of Investigation.— It is obvious, in view of the facts already stated, that consciousness is the sole instrumentality through which it is possible, intelligently, to investigate the real phenomena of volition, since it alone can penetrate the inner sanctuaries of the soul, and bring into view the play of the hidden springs of action that dwell there. Here analogies drawn from the material world, not only utterly fail to cast any light upon the problems we seek to solve, but actually mislead us; for, in no one of its processes or movements is the soul so far removed from mechanism and its laws as it is in the phenomena of volition. The veriest materialist would be ashamed to attempt to illustrate the evolution of thought proper by the movements of a self-acting steam-engine; but, most strangely, otherwise consistent spiritualists have fallen into the strange blunder of attempting to solve the mysteries of volition by purely *material* analogies.

A priori theories here, however beautiful and clear, are utterly valueless. It is easy for us to theorize what the relations of motives to volition, on the one hand, and of volition to action, on the other, *ought to be;* but, after all, *that* is not what the psychologist either needs or desires to know. The question with him simply is, What are the actual phenomena and laws of volition *as we know them?*

Finally: with all due respect for theologians, on the one hand, and real reverence for the Holy Scriptures, on the other, the psychologist can accept neither the *a priori* theories of the former, nor yet their dogmatic declarations of the testimony of the latter, as decisive in reference to any element involved in the evolution of the phenomena of volition. So long, moreover, as he confines himself to his legitimate sphere of action, and sincerely seeks truth for its own sake, there is little danger of his coming in collision with God's Word, however frequently he may collide with theological dogmas professedly evolved from that Word.

The conclusion, therefore, is decisive, that consciousness is our only authoritative guide in the investigation of the phenomena and laws of volition, and *that its well-ascertained facts and necessary inferences must be accepted as final, however much they may collide with a priori theories or theological dogmas.*

¶ II. **Evolution of the Generic Phenomena of Will.**—Here a somewhat important distinction between the *immediate* and *mediate*, or the *primary* and *secondary*, phenomena of this department of mind emerges; a distinction resulting from a fact already indicated, that in the will we attain to the central element of soul-life, and the true representative of self, or the conscious personality:

1. *As the primary product or phenomenon of the will, we recognize volition*, with its concomitants, both antecedent and subsequent.

2. *As the secondary product or phenomenon of the will, we recognize moral agency*, with its concomitants, moral responsibility and moral accountability.

It is not, of course, intended here to exclude the intelligence and sensibilities of man from their proper relations to moral agency; nor can it be done, in face of the decisive relations predicated between the three departments of mind; but it is intended to assert that moral responsibility and accountability are only predicable of true voluntary action; and hence that they only emerge into consciousness as derivative phenomena of volition. They are, of course, subordinated to volition only in the sense that they postulate it as a condition precedent of their own existence.

The inherent relations between volition and moral agency noted here, will appear more clearly and decisively in the sequel, and are, in fact, of fundamental importance in their practical relations to psychology.

¶ III. **General Plan of Discussion.**—This has been already indicated in the declaration that consciousness is the only legitimate witness available to us in the study of the phenomena and laws of volition. We shall, therefore, endeavor to ascertain the actual facts of consciousness bearing upon the phenomena of volition, and seek in their scientific coördination and correlation for the laws governing their normal evolution, seeking at the same time, as far as possible, to verify our conclusions by the testimony of language, of history, and of observation, which are but the crystallized products of human consciousness.

CHAPTER I.—FUNDAMENTAL CONCEPTIONS: NECESSITY, LIBERTY, AND MORAL AGENCY.

Section I.—General Conceptions.

¶ I. **Evolution of Concepts.**—There are various generic concepts which emerge in consciousness whenever the soul reflects upon its own voluntary actions in their relations to not-self, or the universe, which must be discretely noted here, as prime factors in any intelligent discussion of the phenomena of volition, viz.:

1. *Operation and action.*—One of the most obtrusive ideas of our daily practical life is the distinction between *operation and action;* i. e., between a mechanical movement, as of a steam-engine, and the action of a man. This discrimination of the one from the other is necessary and universal, and is the expression of the consciousness of the human soul that there is, in the manifestations of its voluntary activity, an element or elements which require it to be discriminated absolutely from mere mechanical operations of every kind.

2. *Causation and volition.*—A second universal distinction, drawn by the popular consciousness, separates between *causation proper* and *volition proper.* The boy expresses it wholly and completely in his answer to two familiar classes of questions; as, for example, "Why did you fall from that tree and break your arm?" His answer would be, "I could not help it; the limb broke upon which I stood." Ask him now, "Why did you climb into the tree?" and the answer will not be, "I could not help it," but "I wanted to gather some fruit;" i. e., "*I chose to do it.*" He thus distinguishes *decisively* between *causation* and *volition;* and this distinction, thus spontaneously taken, is a universal and ineradicable conception of man as man.

3. *Necessity and liberty.*—These concepts, it is needless to say, are familiar to man as household things, and are peculiar to no particular race, age of the world, or degree of culture. The question is not raised here, whether either or both represent actual realities, but are they universally recognized as contradictory actual concepts of mankind? To this question there can be *but one answer:* either of them may be an illusion, in fact, but it is *a universal* illusion. Men universally conceive both liberty and necessity as *actual* attributes of beings.

¶ **II. Identification, severally, of the First and of the Second Terms of these Correlated Pairs of Concepts.**—A second preliminary step may now obviously be taken, namely: all the *antecedents* in these several pairs may be coördinated into one category, and all the *consequents* into another, without contrariety, and without doing violence to any one of them as conceived and affirmed by either the *personal* or the *popular* consciousness of men.

1. We may identify *operation*, *causation*, and *necessity*, as coördinate and congruous attributes of being, thus originating *the category of necessity;* and—2. We may identify *action*, *volition*, and *freedom*, as similarly coördinate and congruous, and thus originate *the category of liberty.*

It is not apparent how these complementary processes can be refused or contravened, in the light of either the *personal* or the *popular* consciousness of mankind. The fact, if fact it be, is easily verified by any earnest student, and, when thus verified, must be accepted, no matter what may be its bearings upon preconceived theories of volition. No theory of the will is worth any thing that will not abide, absolutely, a simple appeal to the *actual* consciousness of the individual and of the race.

Sec. II.—Affirmation of the Reality of the Category of Necessity.

¶ I. Causation and Necessity are the Actual Attributes of Operation.—The terms here used are familiar ones, and enter into the daily experience of common life, and their actual congruity is easily determined. We speak indifferently of the operations of Nature, of mechanism, and of our own minds, and in every case we recognize *causation* and *necessity* as attributes essential to the thought involved. Nature is uniformly conceived as under the dominion of law; machinery, as controlled by it; and, where the term *operation* is intelligently applied to the processes of mind, it is done in view of the fact that many of the *psychical*, as well as of the *physio-psychical* and *physical*, processes of man's complex soul-life are as really under the domination of causation, and consequently of necessity, as are the processes of the material universe. The fact, however, remains unimpaired, that, whenever the term *operation* is strictly applicable to any process, it is uniformly accompanied by the correlated attributes of *causation* and *necessity.*

¶ II. **Operation, as conditioned by Causation and Necessity, is attributed primarily to Matter.**—This truth has been incidentally stated in our previous discussions, and needs little more than formal restatement here. No one at all cognizant with the developments of modern science can doubt its propriety. The extension of the terms *operation*, *causation*, and *necessity*, to the psychical nature, may at first thought, by some persons, be deemed improper; but, as will appear more clearly in the sequel, our intellections, emotions, and desires, are operations of mind conditioned by causation and necessity, and are *not free* actions, in the proper sense of the term.

Men universally and spontaneously speak of the *operations* of Nature and of natural causes, but never of its *actions*, notwithstanding the popular tendency to personify or individualize Nature, and attribute to it human or rather divine intelligence and attributes. Men, instinctively, conceive of winds and tempests, of sunshine and shower, of melting snow and freezing waters, of revolving planets and falling leaves, as *operations always, as actions never.* These facts can be so readily verified that to offer proof were idle.

SEC. III.—AFFIRMATION OF THE REALITY OF THE CATEGORY OF LIBERTY.

¶ I. **Volition and Liberty are actually identified as the Necessary Attributes of Action.**—Action and agency are concepts as familiar as process and operation; and, as the latter are conditioned by causation and necessity, so the former predicate *volition* and *liberty* as their essential attributes. This partition and predication of attributes is at once primitive and universal among men. The child and the savage recognize it as spontaneously as the philosopher; the peasant as decisively as the scholar; and he who would theoretically deny it must do it in language based upon the hypothesis he denies.

¶ II. **Action or Agency, as thus conditioned by Volition and Liberty, is predicated, spontaneously, universally, and exclusively, of Man.**—It is not, of course, intended here to deny the existence of God, or of other voluntary intelligences; but only to draw the line sharply between the categories of necessity and liberty as we know them practically in this life. As thus conceived, men as spontaneously and universally affirm action or agency, as conditioned by volition and liberty, to be an attribute of man, as they do operation, conditioned by causation and necessity, to be an attribute of Nature. It would, *a priori*, seem incredible that any one could contravene truths so obvious; yet it has been done, not however from the stand-point of the *personal consciousness*, to which such objectors *never appeal* in support of their hypothesis, but from that of some *a priori* metaphysical or theological theory. Nor is this strange; the most obvious facts are those, precisely, which ardent theorists overlook. The grass and flowers which we habitually tread under foot are always those which we practically *never see;* and the testimony of consciousness to the earnest polemic is as worthless as the trodden grass. But, since the truth of our proposition has been challenged, the issue must be fairly tried; and here we appeal to consciousness as manifested:

1. *In the personal consciousness of the reader.*—This is a question of fact, which every man is competent to test for himself by raising the simple inquiry: "Do I, *spontaneously* and *universally*, conjoin, explicitly or implicitly, to the conception of action or agency, as an attribute of manhood, the concepts of volition and liberty, or do I not? Would I hold any man morally responsible for an act performed *in a dream, in a state of somnambulism or of insanity*, in which there was obviously *no true volition* or *liberty of action*, or would I not?" These are questions every reader must answer for himself, and his answer is the decisive testimony of his personal consciousness on this issue.

2. *In the forms of language.*—These are but crystallized expressions of the popular or common consciousness of mankind. Their testimony, it need hardly be said, is *uniformly and decisively* in favor of the principle here posited. Common language uniformly identifies operation, causation, and necessity, on the one hand, and action, volition, and liberty, on the other; and this fact is so obtrusive that it were idle to offer examples.

3. *In the phenomena of moral responsibility and moral accountability.*—Here the argument is twofold, including, first, the existence and principles of human government, which are unquestionably based upon the postulate that the actions of men *are not mere operations* conditioned *by causation* and *necessity*, but *true actions* conditioned *by volition* and *liberty;* and, second, the phenomena of conscience, or the moral sense of man, in whose courts he holds himself accountable, independently of the civil law, for his own actions as conditioned by *volition* and *liberty*, but in which he utterly refuses to criminate himself *for mental operations* which were consciously *caused* and *necessitated* by any power external to and independent of his own will.

In other words, the plea of *absolute duress*, where actually sustained, is final, in bar of judgment, either in the civil court or in the court of conscience; and the plea of duress is nothing more, and nothing else, than a plea *of foreign or external causation* and *necessity.* Conscience and the civil law alike treat the acts of lunatics or madmen, where there is no true volition or liberty, as they treat the whirlwind and the storm; that is, as evils to be guarded against, but not as crimes to be punished. Where liberty and volition are wanting, civil government is an impossibility, and moral responsibility and moral accountability are unmeaning words.

It seems to be idle to multiply words in proof of a principle so obvious as the one in question; and there are, in fact, few persons who would either care or venture to challenge its truth, if stated as an independent proposition; but there are many who do, in fact, implicitly challenge it, in the interest of their own pet theories of volition, as an integral element of soul-life. The truth, therefore, cannot be too clearly stated, or too strongly enforced, that in all questions pertaining to the will, as to other departments of mind, the testimony of consciousness *is final and decisive*, and from it there can be *no appeal whatever.* What that testimony is has been clearly stated; and so stated, moreover, that every conscientious student can verify it for himself.

CHAPTER II.—EVOLUTION OF THE FREE PERSONALITY.

Section I.—Laws of the Physical Personality.

If we now turn from the general conception of human action as conditioned by volition and liberty, in order to determine the secondary problem, whether liberty is a general attribute of manhood, inhering alike in man's material organism and his spiritual nature, or whether it fastens exclusively upon some single element of his complex being, new conditions emerge. In the outset, it is obvious that his body, as a physical organism, must respond to the necessary laws of matter, both mechanical and chemical, and that all its powers and forces are conditioned by them. The soul may range at will, on the wings of thought, through all space and all duration; but the body, earth-born and earth-bound, is anchored to earth by the irresistible power of gravitation: the soul may soar to heaven and feed, in thought, upon angels' food; but the body owns the supremacy of Nature's laws, and demands earthly food and drink to satisfy its hunger, and satiate its thirst, and its power may be measured in pounds and ounces, and is, in fact, exactly measured by the food, the air, the water, it consumes. This subjection of the physical organism to the laws of Nature, i. e., to causation and necessity, is so obvious that the intelligent anatomist and physiologist would laugh to scorn any one who would venture to question a truth so well established. Wherever else, then, liberty, as an element of humanity, may or may not inhere, it is assuredly not an attribute of the physical organism.

SEC. II.—LAWS OF THE SPIRITUAL PERSONALITY.

¶ I. **Liberty not an Attribute of the Intellect.**—If, now, the inquiry after liberty, as an attribute of manhood, be prosecuted in reference to the spiritual nature of man, it will be found that his intellectual processes, like his physical system, respond to the laws of causation and of necessity, and not to those of volition and liberty.

1. Our percepts are mediated by our sensations, which obviously respond to the physical laws governing the material body and its organs of sense; while the purely rational element of perception, namely, intuition, responds to the necessary laws, not of matter, but of thought. The assertion that man's perceptions are free can be true in no other possible sense than that he may open or close his eyes at pleasure; or, in other words, he may, like the snail, withdraw himself, and refuse all perception whatever; or, that he may, to a limited extent, choose the conditions under which he will perceive objects; but, when he opens his eyes upon the light, he can in no wise choose what he will or will not see of the objects actually present to his senses. In other words, perception is a *necessary*, and *not* a *voluntary*, process.

2. Our concepts are based upon our percepts, and are mediated, as has been already shown, by memory, with its laws of association, by imagination, and the processes of the synthetic judgment, no one of which is voluntary in its character, so that, both in their origin and their evolution, our concepts exclude the element of liberty in the true sense. The fact is neither ignored nor denied here that in conception, in the play of the imagination, in recollection proper, and in the processes of abstraction, generalization, and classification, the will may and does intervene frequently and effectively to modify, control, and change, the direction, nature, or order of evolution of any one or more of these

several elementary processes, so that our concepts may, in a certain proper sense, be said to be *voluntary;* but the fact remains that it can only do this by intelligently acting upon the memory, the imagination, or the synthetic judgment, in and through its own proper necessary laws, just as it can intervene to change the current or course of a stream of water. It is sometimes said that imagination is lawless, but this is true in no sense different from that in which it is said that the wind and weather are capricious. It only means, in either case, that the problems are so complex, and involve so many factors, that the law of their evolution, in the concrete instance, is practically undiscoverable, but we do not, therefore, infer that they are governed by no law whatever.

3. Our beliefs are necessitated by the data given in perception, as modified in conception, and evolved under the necessary, logical forms of the analytical judgment. The syllogism, which has been shown to be the ultimate type of all reasoning, is not a type of volition and liberty, but of causation and necessity the most absolute. A man does not say, "I believe the truth of a demonstration in geometry, because *I choose to do so, but because I must; I cannot disbelieve it if I would.*" The same thing is true of every logical syllogism whatever, if the truth of the premises be conceded or proved.

An important problem, however, emerges at this point, in view of the necessary character of all human beliefs, namely: In what sense, and how far, is a man responsible for his beliefs or faith?

Moral responsibility for faith necessarily implies a voluntary element in faith, to which it attaches, and apart from which it cannot exist. The possibility of such a voluntary element, and the mode of its operation, have already been sufficiently indicated, in general terms, but need more discrete enunciation in its relations to this specific problem. Every belief or faith involves two generic classes of elements, viz., first, data, premises, or materials; and, second, logical mental processes; that is to say, every syllogism (hence all reasoning) involves premises and a conclusion. The first of these factors, the premises, may be characterized as *contingent*, and hence subject to modification by the will, which may at pleasure exclude part of the actual data of judgment really possessed on the one hand, or may earnestly search for and include *all* the additional data possible on the other. The will may thus either compel the reason to act on consciously imperfect premises, and thus necessitate an incomplete or false conclusion, or it may compel it to include perfect and complete data, and, so far forth at least, compel a correct conclusion.

The second factor, namely, the logical processes of the reason, are subjected to necessary laws which determine their evolution, and are therefore but very slightly, if at all, under the control of the will. Nor is it needful, in order to make man morally responsible for his beliefs, that it should be. In its control over, and determination of, the premises upon which the reason must rest its inferences, the will is abundantly able, at any time, to cast the sword of Brennus into the wavering scale, and to determine the practical faiths that govern the soul. Man is not only morally bound to judge correctly, according to the *actual* light he possesses in any given case, but he is bound to grasp and use *the best light possible to him* under the actual conditions of the problem. Failing in any case to do this, he is morally responsible for any evil that results from his neglect. But if, on the contrary, he has diligently sought the best light possible to him in the given case, has guarded jealously the logical correctness of the process of reasoning, and has thus candidly sought after truth, and truth only, he cannot be condemned if, at last, his soul fastens upon an imperfect or even a false faith. Man is here, as everywhere, judged according to that which he hath, and not according to that which he hath not. Man is, therefore, morally accountable for his faith so far as its development is actually or potentially under the control of his will.

¶ II. **Liberty not an Attribute of the Sensibilities.**—In passing from the sphere of the intellect to that of the sensibilities, the conditions of the problems are not materially changed; the same law of causation and necessity still rules supreme:

1. Our emotions are based upon and called into being by corresponding intellections, and are, like them, both in their origin and in their evolution, mediated by the necessary laws of the sensibility. We cannot, at pleasure, feel, or refuse to feel, emotions of wonder, surprise, admiration, pity, etc. These forms of the sensibility take possession of us as a strong man armed, and we cannot choose but feel.

2. Our desires, in turn, are based upon our intellections and conditioned by our emotions, and consequently partake of the like characters of causation and necessity that inhere in their conditioning elements. The relations of the problem are so obvious that argument seems useless. Our desires are not, in any sense, voluntary elements, although their evolution may be indirectly modified and controlled by the will. This thought brings us back to the results of our previous analysis, viz., that desire, so far as it is instinctive, possesses no moral character; and that no man is responsible for the simple springing up of desire in the soul *until the will consents to, or acquiesces in, its continued existence.*

The general truth that causation and necessity, and not liberty, are the normal attributes of our sensibilities, is decisively vindicated by this fact, that no man feels himself to be morally responsible for the awakening, or the transient existence, of emotions or desires which he neither indulges nor cherishes, but seeks to exclude and banish from his soul.

¶ III. **Liberty is an Attribute of the Will.**—The exclusion successively of liberty as an attribute of the physical, the intellectual, and the sensitive natures, both affirms and emphasizes our previous identification of volition and liberty as congruous attributes of action, or, in other words, of the true personality. *The will* is, therefore, *the man*, in the truest and highest sense of the word, the representative of the spirituality, of the autocracy, and of the moral responsibility and moral accountability of humanity. In volition, conceived as a free act, we have, in fact, passed to the limit of conception, in opposing *the spiritual* to *the physical* element in man. Causation and necessity are the true representative types of *the material*—volition and liberty of *the spiritual.* The one category distinctly allies man to earth and the sphere of *secondary* causation; the other just as distinctly allies him to God and the sphere of *primary* causation—a fact exactly corresponding to the divine word which declares that "God created man in His own image," words to which, it would seem, no intelligible meaning can be attached, on any hypothesis that does not recognize in man such liberty of action as constitutes him a true primary cause in his own proper sphere of activity.

Sec. 3.—The Will the True Personality and a True Cause.

¶ **I. The Will the True Personality.**—Our analysis of the actual facts of consciousness has thus resulted in the identification of the will, the personality, and self, or the ego: and the fact is self-evident, in the light of consciousness, that we, intuitively, postulate moral responsibility and moral accountability as attributes of self, or the ego, conceived as a free, voluntary agent, or, to recur to a previous distinction, all true action as such is predicated of a *free* volition, and, where this does not exist, no moral accountability can exist. The expressions, "I did this," "I willed that," "I chose the other," are familiar to us as household things, and are the expressions of the conscious existence of self, or the ego, as a free, morally responsible personality; and in them, will is decisively marked as the central and characteristic element of true manhood, the seat of all moral responsibility, the object of moral approval or disapproval, and the true sovereign in the complete hierarchy of the faculties and powers of the self-conscious soul. Without its action and assent, as expressed in a true volition, a man may, in dreams, in somnambulism, or in insanity, act instinctively or automatically, but his manhood is lost, and with it all moral responsibility.

¶ II. **The Will, or the Ego, is a True Cause.**—The concept of cause, rationally considered, involves two distinct classes of causes, radically distinct from each other, yet equally necessary and familiar as actual concepts, viz.:

1. *First or primary causes;* i. e., those which are *solely* causes, and *in no sense*, and under no circumstances, effects; and—

2. *Secondary causes;* i. e., those which are alternately effects and causes in the chain of causation—effects, when considered in relation to the proximate cause which called them into being and gave them their vitality; causes, when conceived in relation to the effects or events resulting from the causal force inhering in them.

It is obvious that secondary causes are not true causes, but mere effects conditioning other effects still farther removed from the real or efficient cause. If, for example, I should shoot a man through the heart with a revolver, and the question be raised as to the cause of his death, the surgeon making the *post-mortem* examination would refer it to the bullet in the heart; the coroner's jury, however, would not rest satisfied with that, but would seek the weapon, the gun or pistol, from which it was discharged. Nor would they then be satisfied; this would represent to them only a *secondary* cause, i. e., an effect; and they would still pursue their inquiries into the cause of the death in question. Now, let it be proved that I fired the fatal shot, will that jury still be satisfied and rest their inquiries? No! another question must still be asked: "Were you the *voluntary* or *wilful*, or only the *accidental* and *innocent* cause, or rather occasion, of the man's death?" Upon this question would rest my character and my fate. That jury seeks, and rightfully seeks, the *true* cause of the death in question, and does not and cannot rest satisfied with *any link* in the chain save the *first*—with *any cause* of the death save the *first cause;* and it will not accept any cause as a *first cause* save a *free, intelligent personality.* Had it been shown, for example, that the sudden death had resulted from the bite of a venomous serpent, and not from the accidental pistol-shot, the jury, as a *coroner's* jury, would have been satisfied, but the human soul would not, but would still ask, as a little child once asked the writer, "Who made snakes to bite men?" and, when I replied "God made them," asked the second question: "Was not God *bad* to make snakes to bite men?" The child grasped, strongly and decisively, the concept of *a true first cause*, and ascribed to it, exclusively, the moral responsibility involved in the facts, as it conceived them.

It is obvious that all our conceptions of moral responsibility, all our forms of language, and all government, are based upon the conception and affirmation of the fact that man is a *true cause*, i. e., a *first* cause, in relation to his own volitions or actions. In our classification of causes, we discriminate radically between *first* or *real* causes, and *second* or *apparent* causes. In the first class, men intuitively and universally place *God* and *men*, recognizing them as intelligent, free, voluntary agents; and, in the second, they include all elements or beings, material or spiritual, which are conditioned by causation and necessity.

It is precisely in this conception of will, as a true personality and a true cause, i. e., a *first* or *primary* cause, that we attain to any rational conceptions of true moral responsibility, on the one hand, or any intelligent comprehension of the divinely-revealed truth that "God created man in His own image," on the other. We cannot conceive God in any other relation than that of a free, voluntary cause; nor can we, in any comprehensible sense, conceive man to bear the image of God, only as he is also conceived as a free, voluntary cause.

CHAPTER III.—ANALYSIS OF AN ACT OF WILL.

Preliminary Discussion.

EVOLUTION OF THE INTEGRAL ELEMENTS OF VOLITION.

Every act of volition, in the light of consciousness, involves or presupposes certain elements or conditions, which must now be distinctly evolved and discretely investigated. These are—

1. The concept of a possible action that may be performed, if I so choose, or will.

2. The concept of motives inducing or persuading me *to do*, or *not to do*, the proposed action.

3. The power of choice, i. e., the power to choose or refuse the proposed act in its relations to me as a free personality; and—

4. The power of executive volition, i. e., the power to put forth a volition to do, or not to do, the proposed act, under the conceived conditions.

In order to the typical completeness of human action, as such, there must be a *fifth* element, namely, the actual putting forth of physical energy in accordance with the proper executive volition; but this, however important in itself, and in its actual relations to humanity, is not an element of an act of volition, but a consequent to it, that may, or may not, accompany it, since sudden paralysis, death, or any one of a thousand other conceivable causes, may intervene between executive volition and physical action; and, *morally*, an act is complete in the executive volition.

Some authors have identified choice and executive volition, but they are clearly not identical, logically; and grave reasons will appear, in the sequel, for doubt whether, in fact, choice and executive volition uniformly coincide with each other.

SECTION I.—POSSIBLE ACTIONS CONSIDERED.

In considering possible actions as conditions precedent of will, rather than as elements of volition proper, there are certain facts that need to be decisively stated, and thus brought out clearly in the light of consciousness, as essential phenomena of volition, which may not safely be ignored or neglected.

¶ I. **Alternativity is a Condition Precedent of Possible Action.**—In other words, under no possible circumstances can the soul be constrained to put forth a volition where but one single act of volition is possible to it. This principle is decisively established by the fact that, under no possible conditions of human life, can the category of contradiction be excluded from the sphere of volition. The will can at least, like his holiness the pope, as an ultimate alternative, always enter a "*non possumus;*" in other words, it may always choose between the *proposed* volition and *no* volition. Possible volitions, therefore, are *absolutely alternative.* Ordinarily, alternativity of possible volition presupposes the category of contrariety, and not merely that of *contradiction*, i. e., the will may put forth any one of many possible volitions under the given conditions. It is obvious that this alternativity is a necessary resultant of the essential conditions of human nature, and not merely an accidental circumstance that might conceivably, at least, have been otherwise.

¶ II. **Alternativity of Possible Action a Condition Precedent of Liberty.**—It has passed into a proverb, that "where there is *no choice*, there is *no liberty*," and manifestly there can be no choice where there are no alternatives between which I may choose. It does not follow, nor is it implied, that, in order to true alternativity, or to true choice, we ourselves should be able to predetermine the alternatives between which the volition must decide. Possible actions to any individual self, or *ego*, at any given period of his existence, are evidently a compound resultant, or complex, of his own past volitions coördinated with all other forces, voluntary and involuntary, acting in relation to or with him. But none the less is it consciously true, in every concrete instance, that true voluntary action predicates, as a condition precedent, alternativity of possible action.

SEC. II.—MOTIVES CONSIDERED.

¶ I. **Nature and Classification of Motives.**—A motive may be defined to be that which sustains to the will such a relation as to constitute it an inducement to the putting forth of some definite volition. Our previous discussions have indicated the fact that the will, as the representative of self, or the personality, is approachable only through the intellect and sensibilities, and through them only in their natural order. Our sensibilities all presuppose, logically, antecedent intellections; and our volitions, antecedent emotions and desires. The classification of the sensibilities, in fact, proposed in this treatise, predicates of the *generic class* of the desires the exclusive power to act upon the will in the relation of motives to volition. From this stand-point, it is obvious that all true motives fall into two classes, viz.:

1. *Natural desires*, including, in this category, the appetites, propensities, and affections of the human soul, which are here, for obvious reasons, classed together; and—

2. *Moral impulses*, or the power of conscience, which must here, for reasons just as obvious, be sharply and decisively discriminated from the *natural* desires.

We are here, incidentally but decisively, enabled to answer a question often asked, viz., "Are circumstances, *in any sense*, motives to volition?" As circumstances simply, they are not; but in so far as they have power to awaken emotion, generate desire, or stimulate conscience, they become actual motives to action, or, more correctly, they generate motives. Again, circumstances which are not motives, and which cannot generate motives in the soul, may, in fact, condition the operation of motives; but they are not, therefore, in any proper sense, motives.

¶ II. **Necessary Plurality of Motives.**—Motives to volition are never, in fact, singular. This principle is necessitated by the previously-established fact of the necessary alternativity of possible actions and volitions. Apart from this, however, the fact is susceptible of independent proof, drawn from the essential nature of motives considered in themselves. No voluntary action is possible to man under *normal* conditions (acts of insanity, etc., are of course excluded) which does not involve some degree of moral responsibility in itself or in its relations, and which does not, therefore, predicate *moral* motives to do or not to do, as well as *natural desires.* Ordinarily, the motives to action in any concrete instance are not merely plural, but manifold. Argument in a case so obvious as this is idle; the testimony of consciousness here is unequivocal.

¶ III. **Plurality of Motives the Second Condition Precedent of Human Liberty.**—This second condition precedent of liberty of volition is not less obtrusively evident than alternativity of possible action. If there were but one possible motive, in any concrete instance, we should be shut in to the affirmation, on the one hand, of a *necessitated choice*, which is a contradiction in terms; or, on the other, to the operation *of a choice in opposition to all the possible motives inducing any choice whatsoever.* In fact, however, as has been already shown, such a condition of things does not and cannot exist; motives are not singular but multiple, not one but many. No man ever yet has been able to plead, truthfully, as an excuse for wrong action, that there was no sufficient motive under the actual condition of things for him to do right.

Sec. III.—Choice considered.

¶ I. **Nature of Choice.**—Choice, as an act of the human soul, must be recognized as one of the primitive facts of consciousness. It may, perhaps, be defined with sufficient accuracy to be the expression of the preference of the conscious soul for one object or course of action rather than another, under the conditions of the problem actually presented, in any concrete instance. Choice is strictly a phenomenon *sui generis*, having absolutely no proper analogon in Nature whatsoever.

1. *Physical analogies considered.*—Psychologists have not unfrequently attempted to explain and illustrate choice by physical analogies. The best representative of this class is unquestionably Edwards's famous pair of balances, delicately poised, and sensitive to the touch of the millionth part of a grain. But in the light of consciousness, this simile must be rejected, as not only *illusory* but *deceptive.* It is argued that, as the balances are *free* to yield to the preponderating weight, in this scale or that, so choice is free, in like manner, to yield to the preponderance of motives in favor of this or that proposed cause of action. With reference to the balances, at least, this is a deceptive and false mode of stating the facts: they are *not free* to yield, they *are compelled* to obey, or, still better, they *are necessitated* to obey, the law of gravitation; and this *is not liberty, but necessity* of the sternest and most absolute character. Liberty implies *alternativity*, but here is no alternativity; the chained prisoner, who cannot lift hand or foot, is in this sense just as free as are the balances, for he is free to lie and rot in his chains and dungeon, precisely as the balance is free to sink down under the preponderating weight. In fact, the balance, yielding to the power of gravity, *is the type of the most relentless, peremptory, and absolute causation known to man.* Yet this is gravely presented to us as the true *analogon* of choice in the human soul. No man conceives the sinking of the balance to be a *free* act, but all men do conceive *choice*, as present to the personal consciousness, to be *a free* act; and to this Mr. Edwards himself was no exception, since he introduced this strange analogy as an illustration of *the freedom* of human choice. But if this illustration be rejected, as in principle it must, it is idle to note any other. The material universe does not and cannot throw any light upon the mysterious phenomena of human choice, however persistently and intelligently it be interrogated.

2. *Rational analogies considered.*—These are not really more apposite than the former, and cast no real light upon the problem, if their legitimacy be conceded. The only one which the writer now recalls, that merits even a passing notice, is a comparison of the phenomena of choice to the balance of probabilities in the doctrine of chances, as conceived and computed mathematically. The analogy is again unreal; and, if its reality were conceded, it amounts only to the illustration of one psychological mystery by another. The conclusion is therefore inevitable, that choice as an element of volition is a phenomenon *sui generis*, that is and can be known only in consciousness. It is not amenable to any *a priori* process whatever, and cannot be illustrated by analogies drawn from either the natural or spiritual world. He, therefore, who would comprehend the nature of choice, must interrogate consciousness earnestly, impartially, and persistently; it is *the only competent witness in the case.*

¶ II. **Conditions of Choice.**—These have been in part declared, in our previous discussions of the essential conditions of an act of will, but must be presented discretely here, viz.:

1. *Alternativity of objects.*—There can be no choice where but a single object, motive, or course of action, is present to consciousness. To use a cant phrase, "Hobson's choice is no choice at all."

2. *Plurality of motives.*—Alternativity of objects necessitates plurality of motives, and this, in turn, is an essential condition precedent of choice, which is the expression of the preference of the soul for the one or the other set of contrary motives presented, as well as of its preference for the one or the other course of action between which it is called upon to decide.

3. *Independence of agency, action, or causation.*—To this postulate some may be inclined to demur; and yet it is not obvious how, from the simple stand-point of consciousness, this conclusion can be avoided. As psychologists, we are bound to discount, decisively, all *a priori* theories based upon theological premises, or other foreign elements; and fasten

exclusively upon the direct testimony of consciousness *as a finality* in the decision of this issue. But, if consciousness testifies directly and decisively to any fact whatever in this complex phenomenon, it testifies to the unrestrained freedom of the soul in its choices. It may be said, however, that consciousness testifies only to the positive facts and phenomena, and not to *possible* facts or conditions of the actual phenomena. But this is a fallacy; consciousness, if it testify at all, in reference to its own acts and affections, must testify to them under the actual conditions of their evolution, or manifestation; i. e., it must reveal or testify to a *free* act, *as free;* and to a *necessitated* act, *as necessitated.* Will it then be said that consciousness does not and cannot testify to *liberty* and *necessity*, as attributes of self, or the ego? The answer is decisive: This is not only *not* true, but it is, on the contrary, *absurdly false.* The man who chooses or acts under *positive duress* is *painfully conscious* of the obnoxious fact. Will it then be said that only the liberty and necessity of which the soul is *unconscious*, are those that inhere in its own complex nature, in the correlation of its parts to each other, and to the external world? The decisive answer is: Man *is conscious of necessity* in the operations of his intellect and sensibilities, and especially in his processes of reasoning (as will appear more clearly in the sequel). On what pretext, then, can it be asserted that he is *unconscious* of an actually existing and controlling necessity in his acts of choice, if indeed any such necessity exists? The truth is, the soul is conscious of freedom in its acts of choice, and its testimony is just as credible here as it can be anywhere; if discredited here, it must be discredited altogether.

¶ III. **Relations of Motives to Choice.**—The next problem that presents itself is the real relation of motives to choice; and this must be carefully analyzed, for it is one of the pivotal elements upon which turns the whole controversy.

1. *Motives are, in no sense, the causes of choice;* i. e., motives are not causes of which choice is the effect. Edwards's theory that motives are to choice as the weights are to the

balances, and that choice responds invariably to the preponderance of motives, is wholly untenable. It was incumbent upon the author of this hypothesis, in order to entitle it to respectful consideration, not to say to credence, to determine, proximately at least, the nexus that connects the motive and the choice, as the physicist connects the force of gravity with the sinking balance. He assumes, indeed, that the motives actually chosen are in the concrete instance the stronger, simply because volition inclined to them rather than to their opposites. In other words, he argues in a vicious circle: 1. They prevail, because they are the stronger; and 2. They must be the stronger, because they actually prevail. The true appeal here must be directly to consciousness, since the phenomena considered have no analogons in nature, and must, therefore, be known in themselves, or not known at all. But the testimony of consciousness is decisive, that the soul is an absolute *autocrat* in its dealings with motives, and that it can, and does at pleasure, throw the sword of Brennus into the scale, and decide in favor of the *weaker* rather than the *stronger* motive, in any conceivable sense in which those adjectives can be applied to motives. Nay, more, it does, in every man's experience, at times act from mere caprice, for which it finds itself unable to account even to itself, against all the confessedly more powerful motives that urge men to a given cause of action. It is mere casuistry to urge, in opposition to facts so familiar as these, the objection that the motives actually preferred must needs be stronger in the given case, because they actually prevail. This is simply *to beg* the question, and is a gross misconception, resulting from the application of deceptive physical analogies. This procedure is all the more absurd, in view of the fact that it is used to discredit the testimony of the only competent and impartial witness in the case. The fact must here be insisted upon, decisively, that the *only* and the *final* appeal must be to consciousness, and it may fairly be presented in this form: Am I conscious of any sort or measure of constraint or necessity in choice, such as I experience in the processes of reasoning, where the presence of the element of necessity is marked and obtrusive? If I am asked, for example, "Why did you act so and so?" I answer, "Because I chose so to do." If now the second question is asked, "Could you not have chosen otherwise?" I must answer, in the light of consciousness, "Yes!" If it be asked yet again, "Why did you not choose otherwise?" I should not answer, and *I never heard any one answer*, "I could not!" Now let the same questions be asked in reference to some logical conclusion from a true syllogism, and the answer will not be, "I believe thus and so because I choose," but, "I cannot help believing it in the face of the admitted premises." It is sometimes said that mind is not and cannot be conscious of liberty and necessity, as such, in its processes. But this is absurdly false. We are distinctly conscious of necessity in our logical inferences; conscious that we *must* believe this, that we *cannot* believe that, however much we may desire not to do the one, and to do the other; and this consciousness of necessity all men *do* and *must* accredit. But if consciousness be accredited when it testifies to the presence of necessity, in the processes of reasoning, on what possible pretext can it be discredited when it testifies to its own freedom in choice? Again, we are conscious that the correlation of the premises, in a true syllogism, necessitates the conclusion; but we are not conscious that the correlation of motives, in any given act of choice, either causes or necessitates the actual choice; but, on the contrary, we have an invincible, intuitive conviction that, every other circumstance remaining the same, we could have chosen otherwise—that our choice was voluntary, and not necessitated; *a causal*, and *not a caused, act.*

2. *Motives are the occasions rather than the conditions of choice.*—Motives, adjudged strictly in the light of consciousness, are *occasions* rather than *conditions* of choice; though to the use of the term condition there is no other objection than its liability to be confounded with causation, in consequence of the fact that, in certain relations, the two are used interchangeably. Motives are the occasions or condi-

tions of volition, in the sense that, in the total absence of motives of every sort, the will, obviously, would not act at all; just as, in the absence of all sensation, there could be no intuition; yet sensation is, as has been decisively proved, the *occasion*, and *not the cause*, of intuition. Two or three discrete observations are pertinent here:

(*a*) The relation of causation is so familiar, and so universal in the material world, that it is difficult to avoid its unconscious influence even in the sphere of consciousness, where its incongruity is obvious.

(*b*) The postulate of *the absolute universality* of causation is rationally absurd, as it ultimates in the affirmation of an infinite series of secondary causes, decisively excluding the possibility of a *first* or *uncaused* cause. It results, moreover, in fatalism of the most remorseless character, which excludes, not only *chance*, but *liberty* of any and of every kind; and asserts an absolute dominion over the thoughts, the feelings, and the volitions of man, reducing them all to simple *mechanical* operations, not differing in fact, or in principle, from the revolution of the planets in their orbits. On this hypothesis, man is free in precisely the same sense, and to the same extent, that a leaf borne by the wind, or a twig floating upon the waters, is free; for he too is free to drift onward on the tides of remorseless destiny.

(*c*) The necessary laws of human thought compel us to affirm a *first cause*, as well as to recognize *second causes*. This has been already illustrated in the supposed case of the investigations of a coroner's jury into the cause of the death of an individual found dead under suspicious circumstances. There it was shown that the bullet in the head was a sufficient physical cause of death; but it was only a *secondary* cause. A discharged pistol lying near at hand would sufficiently account for the bullet; but that, too, is only a secondary cause, and the jury is still unsatisfied; but wherefore? Simply because the mind demands a cause of the phenomena, of an altogether different character; it demands a *first* or *independent* cause, i. e., *a moral agent*. This fact becomes yet more evident if we vary the supposition slightly, and suppose that the surgical examination had revealed the cause of the death to have been a blow upon the head, and examination had proved the fatal implement to have been the limb of a tree falling from above. At once the investigation ceases, but wherefore? Here, again, are only *second* causes, the limb, the tree, the wind; and yet the jury is satisfied. The reason is, the investigation has now connected the death of the man with a chain of *secondary* causes, whose *only possible first* cause is God, and hence the verdict, in such cases, is ordinarily, "Died by the visitation of God." No fact of consciousness is clearer or more marked than this intuitive and universal affirmation of a radical distinction between *caused* and *causal* acts; between *effects* referred to the chain of *natural causation* and *acts* referred to *human agency.* But this distinction is not merely *illusory;* it is *absurd, if motives are the cause of choice, and choice the cause of volitions.*

3. *Simple incomprehensibility is no evidence of the falsity of any theory of the phenomena of mental action.*—The distinction between simple incomprehensibility and self-contradiction must here be decisively recognized. No single mental process whatever, in itself and in its relations, is indeed comprehensible, however much familiarity may hide its real mysteries. The phenomena of sensation are, in fact, just as incomprehensible as those of volition, or as the theory of a *free non-necessitated* choice, uncontrolled by motives in the relations of causation. Self-contradiction or absurdity is, on the contrary, a decisive test or proof of falsehood, and is an absolute bar to belief; as, for example, no man *can* believe that two things *exactly* equal to the same thing are *not* equal to each other.

¶ IV. **Resulting Conclusions.**—1. A necessitated choice is, in the light of consciousness, a true self-contradiction, and therefore is at once false and absurd. The contrary theory, that the will, in the act of choice, is a *first* and *not* a *second* cause, is an *agent* and *not* an *effect*, may be incomprehensible, but it is neither self-contradictory nor absurd.

2. *Moral responsibility or accountability for a necessitated choice*, that is, a choice generated by motives as causes, in the same sense that gravity is the cause of the fall of the apple, *is self-contradictory and absurd.* No man could feel himself to be morally responsible for his choices, if the consciousness of freedom were taken away, and he should become conscious of the same necessity in choosing that he experiences in the processes of reasoning. Yet men are consciously morally accountable for their actual choices.

Psychologists have confused themselves and others at this point, by interpolating intelligence in the place of liberty, as the essential condition precedent of moral accountability. It is true that intelligence is a condition precedent of choice, but that very fact postulates freedom also; otherwise, intelligence were but a delusion and a mockery. A man recently fell from a lofty building upon the head of a fellow-man, killing him instantly. Now, let it be supposed that, in the act of falling, he saw the man beneath, saw that he was falling directly upon his head, and perceived that the result must be the death of the party below; would that knowledge have added to, or varied in the slightest degree, his own moral responsibility in the premises? Here, by the conditions of the hypothesis noted above, we have intelligence conjoined to a *necessitated* choice (*since he could not choose but to fall upon the man*); but could there be any moral responsibility for the death of the victim, if the supposition be posited that the fall was the result of unforeseen and unavoidable circumstances? Surely not, for here there was *no liberty*, and intelligence cannot take its place. A *necessitated choice* is a contradiction in terms, and, if it could exist, could carry with it no moral responsibility whatever. Moral accountability, therefore, demands, as an essential condition precedent of its being, *intelligent free agency*, or, in other words, a choice not causatively controlled by motives; precisely such a choice, in fact, as every man's personal consciousness spontaneously affirms when impartially examined, unbiassed by *a priori* hypotheses.

Sec. IV.—Executive Volition considered.

¶ I. **Nature of Executive Volition.**—In executive volition we have the crowning element or movement of an act of will. By some it has been identified with choice, but incorrectly, since they are distinguishable both logically and chronologically. Logically, choice is the decision of the soul as to its preferences, under the actual conditions of the problem, for one or the other of two or more correlated causes of action, with their several motives, while executive volition is the formal putting forth of the actual volition to do or not to do. Chronologically, choice precedes executive volition and conditions it. In fact, the choice in the concrete instance may be made, and yet no executive volition actually follow. Executive volition may, therefore, be defined to be the ultimate and complete expression of the free personality, or true ego, as a *free*, i. e., as a *first* cause, in its relation to its own volitions.

¶ II. **Psychological Relations of Executive Volition.**—1. *Its relations to choice.*—These have already been declared, both logically and chronologically; and yet a further problem remains, which must be fairly met, viz.: Is choice the cause or only the occasion or condition of executive volition? Here, again, the fundamental principle must be kept squarely before the mind—that consciousness is the only competent witness in the case, since executive volition, like choice, has no analogon in nature, and must, consequently, be known in itself, or not known at all. But consciousness not only discriminates choice from executive volition, both logically and chronologically, but it decisively refers both to the conscious soul, as to a common cause, and, at the same time, it refuses to accept motives as the cause of choice, or choice as the cause of executive volition, and thus affirms the soul to be a true *free* or *first* cause. The necessitarian theory, on the contrary, just as obviously exscinds and excludes all possibility of a *true self*, *true ego*, or *true moral agent*, and reduces man to the same class or category as a self-acting steam-engine.

The truth is, a decisive line of demarcation must be

drawn between the objective and subjective elements in the evolution of the free personality of man. The possible alternative actions and courses of action open to any individual man, with their corresponding motives, *pro* and *con*, must be assigned to the sphere of the objective, and of secondary causation; while choice and executive volition must just as decisively be assigned to the sphere of the subjective, or free personality, as essential elements of moral agency and of *free* or *primary causation.* In other words, in any concrete instance, the possible courses of actions and the corresponding motives are the effects of all the correlated causes, primary and secondary, which have resulted in the *status quo* of the personality and its surroundings, while choice and executive volition are *free* acts of the personality, *uncaused*, save as self, or the ego, as an uncaused, i. e., as a free first cause, causes them. This relation of choice and executive volition to each other and to the conscious soul, it is freely admitted, is incomprehensible from the human stand-point; but in this respect it only vindicates its right to a place among the primitive facts of consciousness, which, whether separately or collectively considered, involve corresponding elements of mystery which are unexplained, and from the human stand-point are unexplainable.

2. *Its relations to physical action.*—The relations of volition proper to physical action have already been indicated, but must here be formally reannounced. It conditions all voluntary, and consequently all morally accountable, action. In fact, where there is no true volition, there is no true action or agency of any kind. The converse, however, is not true: there may be morally accountable volitions, that is, voluntary action, where the physical action corresponding to the volition does not or perhaps cannot follow. Many a man is a murderer in the court of conscience, or in the sight of God, who has never actually lifted his hand against the life of his fellow-man.

At this point, a singular confirmation of the theory of the *non-causal* relation between choice and executive volition emerges in consciousness; namely, moral accountability attaches to the *free choices* of the soul in cases in which neither an executive volition nor a physical act has followed, as in the case referred to by our Saviour, in which He declares that he who looks upon a woman to lust after her hath commited adultery with her already in his heart. Here the act is clearly one of voluntary choice, and obviously may occur in cases in which either executive volition or physical action would be morally impossible. This state of facts is intelligible on the hypothesis of a non-causal relation between choice and executive volition, but not otherwise.

It indicates also, incidentally but decisively, the conditions under which natural desires take on the form of lust, and involve personal guilt. This can only be on condition that they involve the choice or consent of the will as a free personality; in other words, *voluntary* desire alone is criminal.

Sec. V.—Summary of Results.

Our analysis of an act of will may be briefly summed as follows: volition is the ultimate act and assertion of self, or the ego, as a free personality, and as an intelligent primary cause. It postulates, explicitly, as its conscious conditions, *free* or non-necessitated choice, *plurality* of motives, and *alternativity* of possible actions or courses of action. This conscious self, or personality, challenges for itself, also in the light of consciousness, the character of a voluntary, free, or uncaused cause of its own volitions. It thus opposes itself decisively, in the character and conditions of its self-conscious being, to *not-self*, or the universe, which responds necessarily and universally to the law of physical causation, i. e., to the dominion of second causes.

In executive volition the doctrine of the will culminates, and it only remains for us to evolve the general laws and relations of these elements to each other and to the hierarchy of the soul.

CHAPTER IV.—THEORIES OF VOLITION.

Preliminary Discussion.

¶ I.—**Evolution of Generic Theories of Volition.**—If the canon of contradiction be applied logically to the concept of liberty as a possible attribute of will or volition, it gives rise to two generic theories of volition, viz.:

1. Theories of absolute fatalism, based upon the negative concept of the *not-free;* and—
2. Theories of freedom based upon the generic concept of liberty.

The category of fatalism, or the not-free, may be discounted at once as unworthy of any practical consideration whatever, in view of the fact that no intelligent psychologist of any school whatsoever, at the present day, sustains or defends any of these theories.

¶ II.—**Theories of Freedom classified.**—The advocates of what is termed, in *a vague indefinite sense*, freedom of the will, agree in little else than in the general term, but may be reduced generically to two great classes, viz.:

1. *Necessitarians*, who agree in postulating causal relations between two or more of the integrant elements involved in every act of the will; and—
2. *Libertarians*, who agree in denying any such causal relations in the evolution of the phenomena of volition.

SECTION I.—NECESSITARIAN THEORIES.

The common principle of all necessitarian theories, viz., the affirmation of causal relations between the various elements of an act of will, has already been explicitly declared. It only remains to examine some of the discrete representative forms under which they have appeared.

¶ I.—**First Necessitarian Theory.**—This may be briefly and distinctly characterized, perhaps, in the light of preceding discussions, under two general statements, which sufficiently distinguish its peculiarities:

1. It distinctly postulates causal relations between motives and choice. In other words, it affirms motives to be the cause of choice and of volitions (for the theory practically, but decisively, indentifies choice and volition) in the same sense that the weight placed in the scale is the cause of the sinking of the scale-beam. The relation between them is, therefore, one of *absolute necessity*, and must, consequently, be invariable. In fact, it recognizes but three elements in an act of will, viz., *possible actions*, *motives*, and *choice, or volition*, and it distinctly predicates necessity under the law of absolute causation of each element taken separately. It affirms that the possible actions, or courses of action, open to any man at any instant of his life, are the *necessary* resultants of an inexorable chain of causation running back to God; that the motives present to his mind were also in like manner predetermined, and that these motives, in turn, predetermine or necessitate choice or volition; but—

2. It postulates *freedom*, or *liberty*, as an attribute of will, on the ground *solely* that man is free to will as he chooses; or, in other words, as the balance is free to yield to the heaviest weight, so the will is free to yield to the power of the preponderating motive, and it bases moral responsibility and moral accountability upon this illusory freedom. We say *illusory* freedom; for, in this sense of the word liberty, the leaf or the apple that falls, the broken wood that drifts helplessly on the waves, the planet that circles through the heavens—in a word, all material existences whatsoever are free, and might with equal justice be held morally accountable for their actions. Nor is it at all to the purpose that the objection is interposed that man is intelligent and the universe is not. That intelligence, as was decisively shown in the case of the man falling from the building upon the head of his fellow-man, does not and cannot, in this chain of invariable causation, alter or change, in the slightest degree, the predetermined result; on the contrary, intelligence itself is but one of the inevitable links in the resistless chain of causation, and can no more change it than the inertia of the planets can

change their orbits or stop their revolutions. No man ever did or ever can hold himself responsible, morally, for a consciously necessitated act; and, so far as the moral relations are concerned, it is a matter of indifference whether the *physical act* is necessitated *without volition*, or the *volition* necessitated *without choice*, or *the choice and the volition* necessitated in and through *the motives*. In none of these cases is there any real liberty or true moral accountability. The freedom of the will postulated by this theory is, therefore, wholly illusory and deceptive.

¶ II.—**Second Necessitarian Theory.**—1. *Its essential postulates.*—This theory formally analyzes an act of will into the same general elements that are recognized in this treatise; but it *implicitly* introduces other elements not indicated in its formal analysis, chief among which is the power of *inclination*. It denies any *causal* relation between motives and choice, but postulates such relations between *inclination and choice*, and admits that our inclinations are necessitated by conditions over which the soul has, and can have, no power; in other words, our inclinations are *necessitated*, and *not free* or *voluntary*, states or affections of our being.

2. *Its theory of liberty.*—This, stated in the language of one of its earliest and ablest advocates, is: "My will is free when I can will to do just what I please," and he adds, first, that "mere *strength of inclination* can by no means impair the freedom of the will;" and, second, "it is evident, furthermore, that freedom has *nothing* to do with *the source of my inclinations*, any more than with their strength. It makes no difference what causes my preference, or whether any thing causes it." Again, "It is of no consequence *how I came by that inclination or disposition*." Again, "The view now taken leaves it open, and quite in the power of, Providence so to shape circumstances, guide events, and so to array and to bring to bear on the mind of man motives and inducements to any given cause of action *as virtually to control and determine his conduct* by controlling and de-

termining his inclinations, and so his choice; while, at the same time, the man is left perfectly free to put forth such volitions as he pleases, and to do as he likes. *There can be no higher liberty than this.*"

Now, with all due respect for this learned author, I submit that in this theory we have only our old friend Monsieur Tonson come again. That which he calls *inclination*, Edwards would have called *motives*, and correctly too, for they must be included decisively under the general head of *desires*, which are assuredly, *on any rational hypothesis*, *true motives.* The learned author himself, in fact, expressly includes our affections and desires under his pet term inclinations, and, if these be not motives to action, it is difficult to imagine what he would include under the name of motives. The reader of his book can hardly avoid the suspicion that he has never discretely evolved the relations of his so-called inclinations to his recognized (but undefined) motives. The truth is, his theory is identical *in principle*, if not in form, with the one previously noted. He postulates *implicitly*, if not *explicitly*, that choice is invariably as the inclination, and that volition is invariably as the choice, or, in other words, he distinctly affirms that choice necessitates volition, that inclination necessitates choice, and that inclination is itself only the effect of an antecedent chain of *necessary* causation. Is it asked: "Where, then, does liberty exist?" His answer is explicit: "*The will is free, because man is free to will as he chooses, no matter how he comes by his choice.*" This, it need hardly be added, is *not liberty, but necessity; not freedom, but destiny.* Here, as before, there is no break or hiatus in the chain of causation; volition is but an effect, in an unbroken chain, of secondary causation, at the head of which he formally places Providence, i. e., of course (for he is a Christian theist), God. He forgets, however, to apply his peculiar theory of *free* volition, as he should have done, to the Divine Being, and thus test its truth by such a magnifying process. If it is true at all, it must be *universally* true, and, therefore, true *of God* as well as *of man.* The Divine will, consequently, must respond, like the human, to this absolute law of causation and to the *Divine inclination;* and is, therefore, only a link in an endless chain of blind causation that antecedes alike *all intelligence* and *all volition.* But it is idle to follow such a thought further. God, conceived as acting under *necessitated* volitions, *is no God,* but *a myth* or *a chimera;* and thus the *reductio ad absurdum* is complete.

¶ III. **Third Necessitarian Theory.**—A third theory sometimes emerges in this connection that, perhaps, merits a passing notice. This predicates necessity of all of the four successive elements of an act of volition, considered either severally or collectively, recognizing no formal or actual element of liberty in any of them, but it nevertheless predicates liberty of the human will, on the ground that it is free to put forth a *nisus,* or effort, to realize in *physical action* its *predetermined volitions.* It does not, however, affirm that any physical act whatever necessarily results, since a stroke of paralysis or other physical impediment may neutralize the volition, and prevent the actual putting forth of any physical force whatsoever. It is a waste of time to discuss this theory here, for, apart from the fact that simply to state it, intelligibly, is to refute it, the fact is obtrusive that, whether true or false in fact, the freedom it postulates is in no conceivable sense freedom of the will.

The three theories noted above have been stated in generic or representative forms, as expressing substantially the views of the various schools of necessitarians rather than those of individuals. In their ultimate principle they are identical, since they all affirm that human volitions are necessitated acts, mere links in the chain of predetermined causation. The fact has not, perhaps, been as clearly evolved in this controversy as it should have been, that the will must decisively be classed either as a *caused* or as a *causal* power, i. e., either as a *first,* or *primary,* that is, again, as a *real* cause, or else as a *secondary cause* purely; i. e., as alternatively *effect* and *cause* in the chain of natural causation, in precisely the same sense that any given link in a chain cable is effect in its relations to the link that precedes it, and is cause in its relations to that which succeeds it.

The distinction here taken is radical, and far-reaching in its influence, involving all our conceptions of God as well as man. If motives be *the cause* and volition be *the effect* in man, the same relation must exist in God, and His Omnipotent Will is reduced at once to the rank of a *secondary* cause dependent upon antecedent causes, and *absolutely* necessitated by them; and thus all freedom disappears from thought, and we come back to the scheme of absolute fatalism, which the world rejects as unworthy of consideration, simply because it contradicts the human consciousness in its most decisive affirmations. The truth is, all forms of necessitarianism belong logically to the category of the *not-free*, i. e., to the category of *fate*, or *destiny*, and our original classification decisively demands amendment. There can be no other alternative: either will, as the representative of self, the ego, or true personality, is a *free, primary, or first cause*, and hence lies outside of the chain of *secondary* causation; or else it is merely *a link in that chain*, and is no more a cause than a lever is *a cause* of motion. The lever is powerless to act save as it is acted upon, and the will is just as powerless, on *any necessitarian hypothesis whatever.* The fact must here be distinctly kept in view, that all theories of the relations of motives, inclinations, etc., etc., to choice and volition are just as applicable to the *Divine* as to the *human* will. Any theory, consequently, which necessitates human volition, or, in other words, subjects the soul of man to the dominion of necessity, reduces the will of God, and consequently God Himself, at once to the rank of a mere link in an endless chain of *secondary* causation; and thus theism proper disappears, and pantheism is the hopeless result. The only possible escape from this dilemma would seem to be a rejection of our initial identification of the will, as such, with the true personality, self, or ego; but on what principle this could even be attempted is not apparent, since the very essence of true personality seems to inhere in its power of free or voluntary action. There would seem, therefore, to be no escape from an absolute pantheistic fatalism, save by the entire rejection of all schemes of a necessitated volition, and the assertion that will is a *causal* power, i. e., that it is the *uncaused* cause of its own volitions.

Sec. II.—Libertarian Theories.

It is scarcely necessary, in an elementary work like the present, to individualize the various libertarian theories which have emerged during the prolonged controversies in reference to the true doctrines of the will. However much they may vary in details, they all involve certain essential postulates, which practically identify them in principle and in their moral relations.

¶ **I.—Their Essential Postulates.**—1. *An original free personality the uncaused cause of all things*, i. e., *God.*—To Him they ascribe true freedom of the will, i. e., they affirm the entire absence or non-existence of all causation and all causal relations whatsoever, until His Divine will put forth causal power or energy in an act of volition. In other words, libertarians postulate a Divine volition as absolutely, *both logically* and *chronologically*, the *first act*, *movement*, or *link*, *in the chain of causation.* They will not accept or acknowledge any causal relation whatsoever between motives and choice, inclinations and choice, or choice and executive volition. Recognizing fully the facts of the Divine intelligence and sensibilities, and coördinating them with the Divine will, they identify the last, specifically, with the *free personal consciousness*, and affirm it to be the ultimate seat or source of power—*the beginning of*, and *not a link in*, the chain of secondary causation. In yet other words, they place God above, and out of, the chain of secondary causation; and do not recognize Him as shut up within it, and as controlled by it, as are the divinities of necessitarianism and of pantheism. Here the differences between the rival theories are decisive and obtrusive. God, as conceived by libertarians, is an *absolute cause*, and His volitions are, in no sense, necessitated by inclinations or motives. God, as conceived *logically*, in accordance with necessitarian hypotheses, acts in accordance with the decisions of His own will, it is true, but none the less upon decisions which He Himself *neither causes nor makes*, but which are caused or made by causative powers or energies acting upon the Divine will from without; in other words, the Divine will is a *secondary*, and *not* a *first*, *cause;* but the will and the personality must be identified strictly from the psychological stand-point: hence the Divine personality, on this hypothesis, is a *secondary*, and *not a*, or rather *the*, *first* cause.

Finally, God, as conceived by logical pantheism, is neither *free* nor *intelligent*, save as He attains to *freedom* and *intelligence* in this or that secondary personality; hence the Divine personality is not a *reality*, *but an illusion;* and God Himself is but a figment of the imagination, representing either—

First. The mathematical sum total of all existence; hence, possessing neither volition, intelligence, nor freedom; or—

Second. He is the conceptual or ideal representative of force; or, in other words, a kind of *lay figure* introduced into the problem of the self-evolution of force, merely to satisfy the illusions of the imagination.

This theory, as before noted, must be ranked under the head of absolute fatalism, or the not-free, as it offers no conceivable basis for any postulate of freedom whatever.

2. *Libertarians postulate the existence of secondary or created free personalities.*—This postulate is based, decisively and directly, upon the first, and presupposes it. It accepts, *literally*, the declaration of the Holy Scriptures, that "God created man in His own image," and this image, whatever else it may or may not include, must obviously include the concept of the *free personality* of Jehovah, which is that which peculiarly discriminates Him from the universe which He has called into being. We must here assume, both logically and rationally, that the human personality is

the *type* of which the Divine personality is the *antitype.* If volition is necessitated in the one, it must be necessitated in the other also; if it be controlled by inclination, circumstances, or motives, in the one, it must be in the other also. So, on the contrary, if the will is the free or uncaused cause of its own volitions in the one, it must also be in the other. The existence of secondary or created free personalities is a fundamental postulate of moral freedom and moral responsibility.

3. *Libertarians postulate volition as a causal, and not a caused, act.*—This is a simple corollary of the preceding principle, and is involved in the personal consciousness of liberty which all men enjoy. There is no other feeling, impulse, or consciousness of the soul, more universal or more familiar than this. You may bind the body, shackle the limbs, paralyze the tongue, blind the eyes, and seal up the ears of your fellow-man, but, none the less, his soul will assert its liberty. "My will," he cries, "is my own, that you *cannot bind.*" Ask a man why he weeps, he will answer, "I suffer, and I cannot help weeping." Ask him why he laughs, and he will answer, "I cannot help laughing;" and so of other forms of mental action. But now ask him why he *willed* to do thus and so, and he will *never* answer, nor *think* of answering, "I could not help *willing* it." It would be safe to say that *no sane* man *ever*, *honestly*, made such a statement; and this fact is to the last degree significant, as it is the decisive expression and testimony of human consciousness as to the unqualified freedom of the human will in putting forth its own causal volitions.

¶ II.—**Proofs of the Libertarian Theory.**—Libertarians appeal, in proof of the truth of their several theories—

1. *To the testimony of consciousness.*—This has already been given, again and again, under a variety of forms, in the course of our investigations. It is again introduced here, discretely, in order chiefly to introduce one significant fact, of the nature of unconscious testimony, on the part of necessitarians, to the truth of the libertarian theory and the falsity

of their own, viz.: while necessitarians uniformly appeal to consciousness in proof of the general (*unlocated* and *undefined*) freedom of the will, and man's consequent moral responsibility, they do not even pretend to support their special theories, by locating and defining that freedom by the direct testimony of the personal consciousness, which is the only competent witness in the case; but they sustain, or endeavor to sustain them, on other and independent grounds. This fact—and its truth is patent to every student familiar with the literature of the subject—is exceedingly significant. The attorney who offers secondary evidence in a court of justice, where direct and primary evidence is within his reach, discredits his own case and insures his own defeat. If men were conscious of any causal relation between motives and choice, or inclination and choice, or between either or both, and volition, that consciousness would be final and decisive proof of the truth of the corresponding necessitarian theory; that no such testimony is adduced, is decisive proof that none such exists. But to say that none such exists, is simply to affirm that self, or the ego, *is consciously free*, and *not subject to any causal influence whatsoever in the acts of choosing and willing.* Again, no sane man perhaps lives, who cannot recall instances, in his own personal experience, of *pure autocracy* of will, in which he found himself utterly unable to account, even to himself, for the volitions which he actually put forth—cases in which the volition responded neither to the motives actually presented, nor to the inclinations felt, but seemed to be solely the expression of the caprice of an autocratic will. It will be said, perhaps, that this is irrational and incomprehensible; *that* it may be, and yet, as a fact, it is undeniably true, and must be accounted for like any other fact of consciousness. The writer is confident that, in stating the fact that, personally, he is often surprised at his own actual volitions under the conscious conditions under which he puts them forth, he does not express a fact peculiar to himself, but one common to humanity; and one, moreover, which is decisive in its bearings upon the problem of the *autocracy* or *causality* of will in its relations to inclinations, motives, choice, and volition.

To the sophism that "we are not conscious of freedom in volition, or, as some incorrectly express it, of the power of *contrary choice*," two decisive replies are opposed, viz.:

First. That *causal necessity*, as a condition precedent of volition, is a *positive*, and *not* a *negative*, fact; and it is a fact, moreover, of which every man is fully conscious in the spheres of the intellect and of the sensibilities, and is expressed familiarly in words like these: "I cannot help thinking thus and so; and I cannot help feeling as I do." No man cavils at or discredits such statements, because he is conscious of like necessity in his own intellectual and sensitive states. But let a man put in the plea in court, "I could not help *willing* to murder that man," and judge, jury, and community, libertarians, and necessitarians, would laugh to scorn the plea, *unless the counsel* for the criminal *conjoined to it the additional plea of insanity.* But, wherefore this decisive discrimination between the intellect and sensibilities on the one side, and the will on the other? The answer must be simply and decisively: "Because men are conscious of compulsion—necessity—causation—in the spheres of the intellect and the sensibilities, and are equally conscious of freedom in choice and volition."

Second. Men are conscious, in fact, of potential as well as of actual power.—In reference to a thousand things in human experience, this is recognized familiarly as an unquestioned fact. Nay, more, it is familiarly recognized in reference to volition. If I, as an individual, neglect or refuse to do an imperative duty, I am assailed, by necessitarian and libertarian alike, with the condemnatory question, "Why did you not do your duty?" To this query it would be a final and decisive answer (*if only it were consciously true*), "I could not." Yet if I had had no consciousness of power to do it, i. e., to put forth a volition to do my duty, I would be fully justified in answering, "I could not." Had I been chained, hand and foot, that answer would have been *the only proper one.* Is it, then, any less true, less appropriate, or less proper, if God, in His providence, have so chained my will *that I cannot put forth the volition to do my duty*, or, in other words, that I cannot put forth any other volition than the one I actually do? Which slavery is the most complete and most degrading, that which chains the body and leaves *the soul free*, or that which enslaves both soul and body, *by enslaving the will* to the power of inclination or motives, which are in turn predetermined by causes that the soul did not originate and cannot modify? Will it be said that the last is least painful, because it is unconscious? I answer: It is *most degrading*, because it takes away the last remnant of conscious manhood.

This consciousness of freedom in volition, or of power to will otherwise than I actually do in any given case, is not only not a delusion, but it is an absolute condition precedent of the conscious sense of moral responsibility and moral accountability that lives in every *sane* human soul.

2. *The testimony of language.*—All the forms of human language, whether popular or scientific, accommodate themselves spontaneously to the libertarian theory of freedom of the will. But forms of language are obviously the expression, either—

(*a*) Of the natural elements, tendencies, or impulses of humanity; or—

(*b*) Of its actual positive beliefs, true or false.

If, therefore, any tendency in language or form of expression is found to be practically universal and independent of race, climate, and culture, it may fairly be taken as the expression of an original element or impulse of man as man; if, on the contrary, it is found to be local in time and place, it must be ascribed to the influence of accidental causes. But all the forms of universal language point decisively to freedom of the will as the popular faith of humanity; and he would be a daring, nay, more, a reckless philologist, who would venture to appeal to the testimony of human language in proof of a necessitated volition.

3. *The testimony of civil government.*—This has already been quoted decisively in favor of the general doctrine of human freedom, but may be quoted just as decisively in favor of the libertarian theory of volition. Every civil government, in its enforcement of criminal law against crime, as theft or murder, looks not merely to the outward physical act, but to the mental act also; and, if a plea of partial insanity can be plausibly sustained, will at once acquit the thief or manslayer of guilt, on the ground of his *moral inability not to do the act*, or *not to commit the crime.* The defence, in such cases, is distinctly that *of a necessitated choice, or volition;* and, where this plea is fairly sustained, it must be accepted in any righteous human court as an absolute plea in bar of judgment. Yet every necessitarian theory of the will postulates, *in every case of voluntary action whatsoever*, precisely the conditions necessary to justify and sustain the plea of *moral inability* in a criminal court. And yet necessitarians, in full view of these facts, most inconsistently affirm man's moral responsibility for his necessitated volitions.

4. *The testimony of the moral nature.*—This is but a counterpart, clear and decisive, of the testimony of civil government responding to the same principles and resulting in identical conclusions. All government, in fact, appeals to and is based upon man's consciousness of moral responsibility and moral accountability. But this consciousness of moral responsibility in the human soul has, and can have, no existence, in fact, apart from the corresponding consciousness of freedom of choice and of volition. Place a man under absolute duress, and, though you may wring his soul with anguish in view of the evil resulting from his enforced action, to which his will neither assented nor consented, you cannot carry home to his conscience the slightest sense of guilt for an act to which *he never assented*, although perchance you may have used his physical powers to accomplish your evil purposes.

Conscious freedom of volition or action is an absolute condition, precedent of conscious moral responsibility and moral accountability. The two do not and cannot exist apart from each other in the human soul. All necessitarians recognize this fact, and hence the attempt, in each of the three theories noted, to interpolate somewhere, in the chain of necessary causation, an element of freedom, in fact or in form, upon which this consciousness of moral responsibility may fasten. How futile these efforts have been, the preceding discussions have, perhaps, sufficiently indicated. The truth is, however, and it should be kept sharply in view, that logically there are but two possible theories, viz.: The will is either a free primary or first cause, the uncaused cause of its own volitions; or, it is but an effect, or link, in the chain of *secondary* causation—the reign of necessity is consequently absolute, and all freedom whatsoever is excluded. As between these contradictory extremes there is no possible mean; and the simple alternative theories open to us are—1. The autocracy of will as a free primary or first cause, i. e., the uncaused cause of its own volitions; or, 2. The doctrine of a necessitated volition, excluding all real liberty, and ultimating, logically, in an absolute fatalism that engulfs and overwhelms alike man, the universe, and God.

CONCLUSION.

In the doctrines of the will psychology culminates, and it only remains for the thoughtful student, who has intelligently attained to this centre of soul-life, to review from that stand-point all the processes of thought and feeling. It is one of the necessary evils that inhere in all human processes, that we must needs study, in detail, that which, properly, can only be comprehended in its complex unity; for the soul, in its physico-spiritual earth-life, is, after all, a unit, and its intellect, sensibilities, and will, are but the multiple manifestations of this unique unity, or individuality. It is not enough, therefore, that the student of psychology should comprehend the different faculties of the soul, their processes and products, severally; he must also grasp them clearly and decisively in their correlation and coördination with each other. He who would intelligently comprehend a locomotive-engine, must not only study all its parts, boiler, cylinder, piston, pump, connecting-rods, levers, etc., etc., in detail, until he has mastered the forms, the uses, and the final causes of each, but he must study them in their coördination and correlation to each other in the perfect engine, as it stands in its massive beauty upon the side-track. Nay, more, he must go further. The anatomy and the physiology of the engine will not suffice; he will fail, after all, to comprehend it, if he ceases his investigations at this point: he must study it as well, standing beside its engineer on the trembling, heaving footboard, as it speeds on its fiery track, a thing of life and power, animated by the spirits of steam and fire imprisoned within its vitals. Even so the student of psychology has but begun his work when he has exhausted the science of the anatomist and physiologist, in the study of the physical organism, and when with the true psychologist he has studied one by one the faculties of the human soul, until he comprehends, severally, their natures, their processes, and their products; he must also take his place beside *the will*, the autocratic sovereign and engineer of this mighty human engine, and with it go forth to life's stern battle-fields, and study the soul as it lives and thinks, feels and acts, under the deepest, strongest, and most intense influences that may evoke its wondrous energies.

In other words, the earnest student of psychology must comprehend that his science is to be studied, not so much in books as in the depths of consciousness, and not so much in schools as in the busy haunts of man. Practical men (self-called and self-styled) may laugh to scorn his earnest researches as idle dreams, but none the less is it true that psychology is the basal science in the hierarchy of the sciences, underlying and vitalizing all the rest, and he knows nothing as he should who does not know himself. Men may excuse themselves from the study of other sciences on the score of want of books, of apparatus, of necessary facilities, of opportunity, etc., etc., but human nature is an ever open book, whose pages are spread out alike before the prince and the peasant, the child and the philosopher, and is filled with the richest lessons of instruction, indispensable to men in all the ranks, relations, and conditions of life; and, if these pages shall stimulate the zeal and smooth the pathway of a single earnest student, they will not have been written in vain.

THE END.

LIST OF WORKS

PUBLISHED BY D. APPLETON & CO.,

549 & 551 Broadway, New York.

A Descriptive Catalogue, with full titles and prices, may be had gratuitously on application.

About's Roman Question.
Adams' Boys at Home.
—— Edgar Clifton.
Addison's Spectator. 6 vols.
Adler's German and English Dictionary.
—— Abridged do. do. do.
—— German Reader.
—— " Literature.
—— Ollendorff for Learning German.
—— Key to the Exercises.
—— Iphigenia in Tauris.
After Icebergs with a Painter.
Agnel's Book of Chess.
Aguilar's Home Influence.
—— Mother's Recompense.
—— Days of Bruce. 2 vols.
—— Home Scenes.
—— Woman's Friendship.
—— Women of Israel. 2 vols.
—— Vale of Cedars.
Ahn's French Method.
—— Spanish Grammar.
—— A Key to same.
—— German Method. 1 vol.
Or, separately—First Course. 1 vol.
Second " 1 vol.
Aids to Faith. A series of Essays, by Various Writers.
Aikin's British Poets. From Chaucer to the Present Time. 3 vols.
Album for Postage Stamps.
Albums of Foreign Galleries; in 7 folios.
Alden's Elements of Intellectual Philosophy.
Alison's Miscellaneous Essays.
Allen's Mechanics of Nature.
Alsop's Charms of Fancy.
Amelia's Poems.
American Poets (Gems from the).
American Eloquence. A Collection of Speeches and Addresses. 2 vols.
American System of Education:
1. Hand-Book of Anglo-Saxon Root-Words.
2. Hand-Book of Anglo-Saxon Derivatives.

American System of Education:
3. Hand-Book of Engrafted Words.
Anderson's Mercantile Correspondence.
Andrews' New French Instructor.
—— A Key to the above.
Annals of San Francisco.
Antisell on Coal Oils.
Anthon's Law Student.
Appletons' New American Cyclopædia of Useful Knowledge. 16 vols.
—— Annual Cyclopædia, and Register of Important Events for 1861, '62, '63, '64, '65.
—— Cyclopædia of Biography, Foreign and American.
—— Cyclopædia of Drawing.
The same in parts:
Topographical Drawing.
Perspective and Geometrical Drawing.
Shading and Shadows.
Drawing Instruments and their Uses.
Architectural Drawing and Design.
Mechanical Drawing and Design.
—— Dictionary of Mechanics and Engineering. 2 large vols.
—— Railway Guide.
—— American Illustrated Guide Book. 1 vol.
Do. do., separately:
1. Eastern and Middle States, and British Provinces. 1 vol.
2. Southern and Western States, and the Territories. 1 vol.
—— Companion Hand-Book of Travel.
Arabian Nights' Entertainments.
Arnold's (S. G.) History of the State of Rhode Island. 2 vols.
Arnold's (Dr.) History of Rome.
—— Modern History.
Arnold's Classical Series:
—— First Latin Book.
—— First and Second Latin Book and Grammar.
—— Latin Prose Composition.
—— Cornelius Nepos.
—— First Greek Book.
—— Greek Prose Composition Book, 1.

Arnold's Greek Prose Composition Book, 2.
—— Greek Reading Book.
Arthur's (T. S.) Tired of Housekeeping.
Arthur's (W.) Successful Merchant.
At Anchor; or, A Story of our Civil War.
Atlantic Library. 7 vols. in case.
Attaché in Madrid.
Aunt Fanny's Story Book.
—— Mitten Series. 6 vols. in case.
—— Night Cap Series. 6 vols. in case.

Badois' English Grammar for Frenchmen.
—— A Key to the above.
Baine's Manual of Composition and Rhetoric.
Bakewell's Great Facts
Baldwin's Flush Times.
—— Party Leaders.
Balmanno's Pen and Pencil.
Bank Law of the United States.
Barrett's Beauty for Ashes.
Bartlett's U. S. Explorations. 2 vols.
—— Cheap edition. 2 vols. in 1.
Barwell's Good in Every Thing.
Bassnett's Theory of Storms.
Baxley's West Coast of America and Hawaiian Islands.
Beach's Pelayo. An Epic.
Beall (John Y.), Trial of.
Beauties of Sacred Literature.
Beauties of Sacred Poetry.
Beaumont and Fletcher's Works. 2 vols.
Belem's Spanish Phrase Book.
Bello's Spanish Grammar (in Spanish).
Benedict's Run Through Europe.
Benton on the Dred Scott Case.
—— Thirty Years' View. 2 vols.
—— Debates of Congress. 16 vols.
Bertha Percy. By Margaret Field. 12mo.
Bertram's Harvest of the Sea. Economic and Natural History of Fishes.
Bessie and Jessie's Second Book.
Beza's Novum Testamentum.
Bibles in all styles of bindings and various prices.
Bible Stories, in Bible Language.
Black's General Atlas of the World.
Bloomfield's Farmer's Boy.
Blot's What to Eat, and How to Cook it.
Blue and Gold Poets. 6 vols. in case.
Boise's Greek Exercises.
—— First Three Books of Xenophon's Anabasis.
Bojesen's Greek and Roman Antiquities.
Book of Common Prayer. Various prices.
Boone's Life and Adventures.
Bourne's Catechism of the Steam Engine.
—— Hand-Book of the Steam Engine.
—— Treatise on the Steam Engine.
Boy's Book of Modern Travel.
—— Own Toy Maker.
Bradford's Peter the Great.
Bradley's (Mary E.) Douglass Farm.
Bradley's (Chas.) Sermons.
Brady's Christmas Dream.
Breakfast, Dinner, and Tea.
British Poets. From Chaucer to the Present Time. 8 large vols.
British Poets. Cabinet Edition. 15 vols.
Brooks' Ballads and Translations.
Brown, Jones, and Robinson's Tour.
Bryan's English Grammar for Germans.
Bryant & Stratton's Commercial Law.
Bryant's Poems, Illustrated.
—— Poems. 2 vols.
—— Thirty Poems.
—— Poems. Blue and Gold.
—— Letters from Spain.
Buchanan's Administration.
Buckle's Civilization in England. 2 vols.
—— Essays.
Bunyan's Divine Emblems.
Burdett's Chances and Changes.
—— Never Too Late.
Burgess' Photograph Manual. 12mo.
Burnett (James R.) on the Thirty-nine Articles.
Burnett (Peter H.), The Path which led a Protestant Lawyer to the Catholic Church.
Burnouf's Gramatica Latina.
Burns' (Jabez) Cyclopædia of Sermons.
Burns' (Robert) Poems.
Burton's Cyclopædia of Wit and Humor. 2 vols.
Butler's Martin Van Buren.
Butler's (F.) Spanish Teacher.
Butler's (S.) Hudibras.
Butler's (T. B.) Guide to the Weather.
Butler's (Wm. Allen) Two Millions.
Byron Gallery. The Gallery of Byron Beauties.
—— Poetical Works.
—— Life and Letters.
—— Works. Illustrated.

Cœleb's Laws and Practice of Whist.
Cæsar's Commentaries.
Caird's Prairie Farming.
Calhoun's Works and Speeches. 6 vols.
Campbell's (Thos.) Gertrude of Wyoming.
—— Poems.
Campbell (Judge) on Shakespeare.
Canot, Life of Captain.
Carlyle's (Thomas) Essays.
Carreno's Manual of Politeness.

Carreno's Compendio del Manual de Urbanidad.
Casseday's Poetic Lacon.
Cavendish's Laws of Whist.
Cervantes' Don Quixote, in Spanish.
—— Don Quixote, in English.
César L'Histoire de Jules. par S. M. I. Napoleon III. Vol. I., with Maps and Portrait. (French.)
Cheap Edition, without Maps and Portrait.
Maps and Portrait, for cheap edition, in envelopes.
Champlin's English Grammar.
—— Greek Grammar.
Chase on the Constitution and Canons.
Chaucer's Poems.
Chevalier on Gold.
Children's Holidays.
Child's First History.
Choquet's French Composition.
—— French Conversation.
Cicero de Officiis.
Chittenden's Report of the Peace Convention.
—— Select Orations.
Clarke's (D. S.) Scripture Promises.
Clarke's (Mrs. Cowden) Iron Cousin.
Clark's (H. J.) Mind in Nature.
Cleaveland and Backus' Villas and Cottages.
Cleveland's (H. W. S.) Hints to Riflemen.
Cloud Crystals. A Snow Flake Album.
Cobb's (J. B.) Miscellanies.
Coe's Spanish Drawing Cards. 10 parts.
Coe's Drawing Cards. 10 parts.
Colenso on the Pentateuch. 2 vols.
——— On the Romans.
Coleridge's Poems.
Collins' Amoor.
Collins' (T. W.) Humanics.
Collet's Dramatic French Reader.
Comings' Physiology.
——— Companion to Physiology.
Comment on Parle a Paris.
Congreve's Comedy.
Continental Library. 6 vols. in case.
Cooke's Life of Stonewall Jackson.
Cookery, by an American Lady.
Cooley's Cyclopædia of Receipts.
Cooper's Mount Vernon.
Copley's Early Friendship.
——— Poplar Grove.
Cornell's First Steps in Geography.
—— Primary Geography.
—— Intermediate Geography.
—— Grammar School Geography.
—— High School Geography and Atlas.
—— High School Geography.
—— " " Atlas.
—— Map Drawing. 12 maps in case.
—— Outline Maps, with Key. 13 maps in portfolio.
——— Or, the Key, separately.
Cornwall on Music.
Correlation and Conservation of Forces.
Cortez' Life and Adventures.
Cotter on the Mass and Rubrics.
Cottin's Elizabeth; or, the Exiles of Siberia.
Cousin Alice's Juveniles.
Cousin Carrie's Sun Rays.
——— Keep a Good Heart.
Cousin's Modern Philosophy. 2 vols.
——— On the True and Beautiful.
——— Only Romance.
Coutan's French Poetry.
Covell's English Grammar.
Cowles' Exchange Tables.
Cowper's Homer's Iliad.
——— Poems.
Cox's Eight Years in Congress, from 1857 to 1865.
Coxe's Christian Ballads.
Creasy on the English Constitution.
Crisis (The).
Crosby's (A.) Geometry.
Crosby's (H.) Œdipus Tyrannus.
Crosby's (W. H.) Quintus Curtius Rufus.
Crowe's Linny Lockwood.
Curry's Volunteer Book.
Cust's Invalid's Book.
Cyclopædia of Commercial and Business Anecdotes. 2 vols.

D'Abrantes' Memoires of Napoleon. 2 vols.
Dairyman's (The) Daughter.
Dana's Household Poetry.
Darwin's Origin of Species.
Dante's Poems.
Dasent's Popular Tales from the Norse.
Davenport's Christian Unity and its Recovery.
Dawson's Archaia.
De Belem's Spanish Phrase-Book.
De Fivas' Elementary French Reader.
—— Classic French Reader.
De Foe's Robinson Crusoe.
De Girardin's Marguerite.
——— Stories of an Old Maid.
De Hart on Courts Martial.
De L'Ardeche's History of Napoleon.
De Peyrac's Comment on Parle.
De Staël's Corinne, ou L'Italie.
De Veitelle's Mercantile Dictionary.
De Vere's Spanish Grammar.
Dew's Historical Digest.
Dickens's (Charles) Works. Original Illustrations. 24 vols.
Dies Irae and Stabat Mater, bound together.
Dies Irae, alone, and Stabat Mater, alone.
Dix's (John A.) Winter in Madeira.
—— Speeches and Addresses. 2 vols.

Dix's (Rev. M.) Lost Unity of the Christian World.
Dr. Oldham at Greystones, and his Talk there.
Doane's Works. 4 vols.
Downing's Rural Architecture.
Dryden's Poems.
Dunlap's Spirit History of Man.
Dusseldorf Gallery, Gems from the.
Dwight on the Study of Art.
Ebony Idol (The).
Ede's Management of Steel.
Edith Vaughan's Victory.
Egloffstein's Geology and Physical Geography of Mexico.
Eichhorn's German Grammar.
Elliot's Fine Work on Birds. 7 parts, or in 1 vol.
Ellsworth's Text-Book of Penmanship.
Ely's Journal.
Enfield's Indian Corn; its Value, Culture, and Uses.
Estvan's War Pictures.
Evans' History of the Shakers.
Evelyn's Life of Mrs. Godolphin.
Everett's Mount Vernon Papers.

Fables, Original and Selected.
Farrar's History of Free Thought.
Faustus.
Fay's Poems.
Fénélon's Telemaque.
——— The same, in 2 vols.
——— Telemachus.
Field's Bertha Percy.
Field's (M.) City Architecture.
Figuier's World before the Deluge.
Fireside Library. 8 vols. in case.
First Thoughts.
Fiji and the Fijians.
Flint's Physiology of Man.
Florian's William Tell.
Flower Pictures.
Fontana's Italian Grammar.
Foote's Africa and the American Flag.
Foresti's Italian Extracts.
Four Gospels (The).
Franklin's Man's Cry and God's Gracious Answer.
Frieze's Tenth and Twelfth Books of Quintilian.
Fullerton's (Lady G.) Too Strange Not to be True.
Funny Story Book.

Garland's Life of Randolph.
Gaskell's Life of Brontë. 2 vols.
The same, cheaper edition, in 1 vol.
George Ready.
Gerard's French Readings.
Gertrude's Philip Randolph.
Gesenius' Hebrew Grammar.
Ghostly Colloquies.
Gibbes' Documentary History. 3 vols.
Gibbons' Banks of New York.
Gilfillan's Literary Portraits.
Gillespie on Land Surveying.
Girardin on Dramatic Literature.
Goadby's Text-Book of Physiology.
Goethe's Iphigenia in Tauris.
Goldsmith's Essays.
——— Vicar of Wakefield.
Gosse's Evenings with the Microscope.
Goulburn's. Office of the Holy Communion.
——— Idle Word.
——— Manual of Confirmation.
——— Sermons.
——— Study of the Holy Scriptures.
——— Thoughts on Personal Religion.
Gould's (E. S.) Comedy.
Gould's (W. M.) Zephyrs.
Graham's English Synonymes.
Grandmamma Easy's Toy Books.
Grandmother's Library. 6 vols. in case.
Grand's Spanish Arithmetic.
Grant's Report on the Armies of the United States 1864–'65.
Grauet's Portuguese Grammar.
Grayson's Theory of Christianity.
Greek Testament.
Greene's (F. H.) Primary Botany.
—— Class-Book of Botany.
Greene's (G. W.) Companion to Ollendorff.
—— First Lessons in French.
—— First Lessons in Italian.
—— Middle Ages.
Gregory's Mathematics.
Griffin on the Gospel.
Griffith's Poems.
Griswold's Republican Court.
——— Sacred Poets.
Guizot's (Madame) Tales.
Guizot's (M.) Civilization in Europe. 4 vols.
—— School edition. 1 vol.
—— New Edition, on tinted paper. 4 vols.
Gurowski's America and Europe.
——— Russia as it is.

Hadley's Greek Grammar.
Hahn's Greek Testament.
Hall's (B. H.) Eastern Vermont.
Hall's (C. H.) Notes on the Gospels. 2 vols.
Hall's (E. H.) Guide to the Great West.
Halleck's Poems.
—— Poems. Pocket size, blue and gold.
—— Young America.
Halleck's (H. W.) Military Science.
Hamilton's (Sir Wm.) Philosophy.
Hamilton's (A.) Writings. 6 vols.

www.ingramcontent.com/pod-product-compliance
Lightning Source LLC
LaVergne TN
LVHW010148110826
845151LV00002B/457

* 9 7 8 1 4 2 5 5 3 7 0 5 0 *